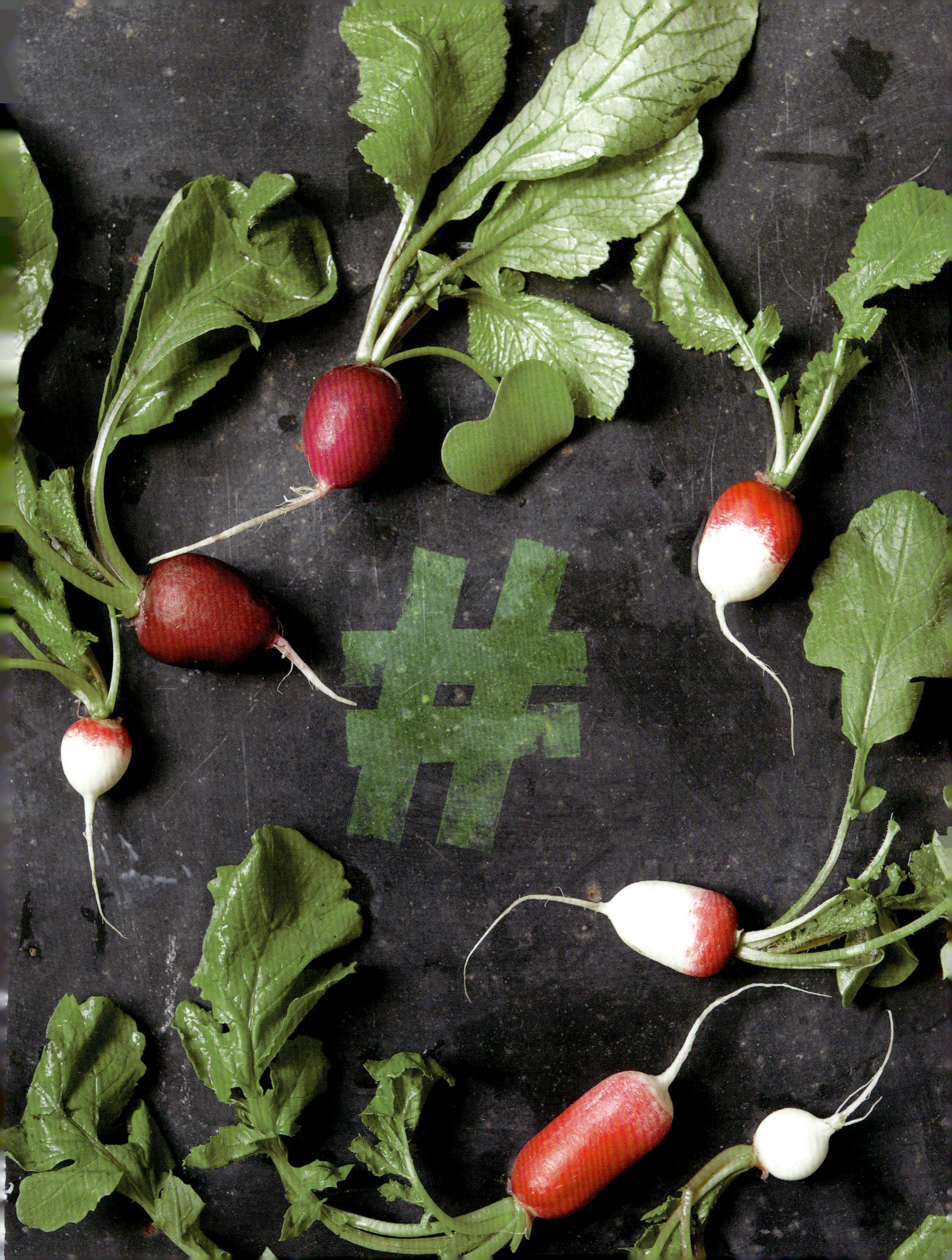

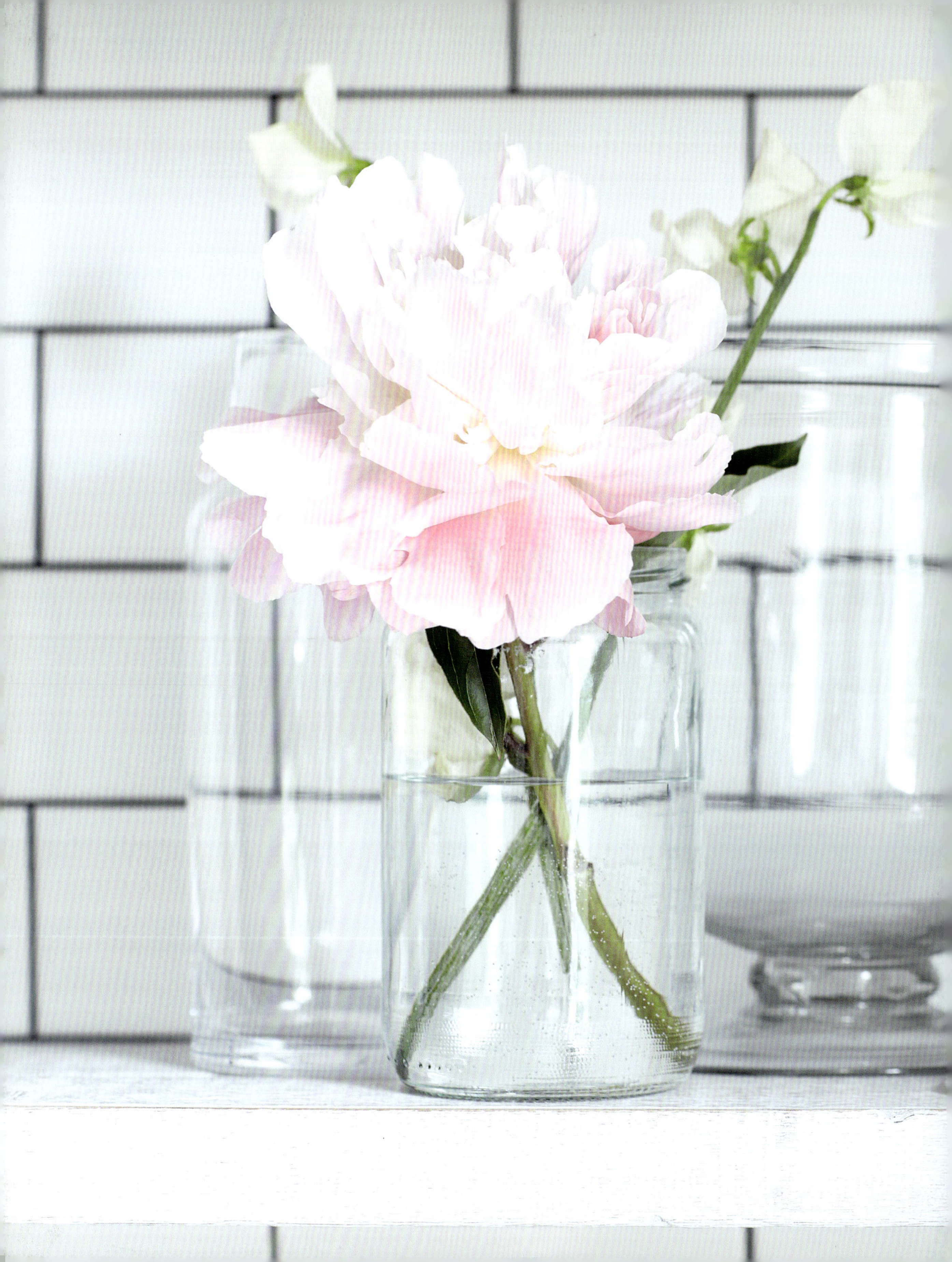

Natasha Corrett

alkaline cleanse

STERLING EPICURE

New York

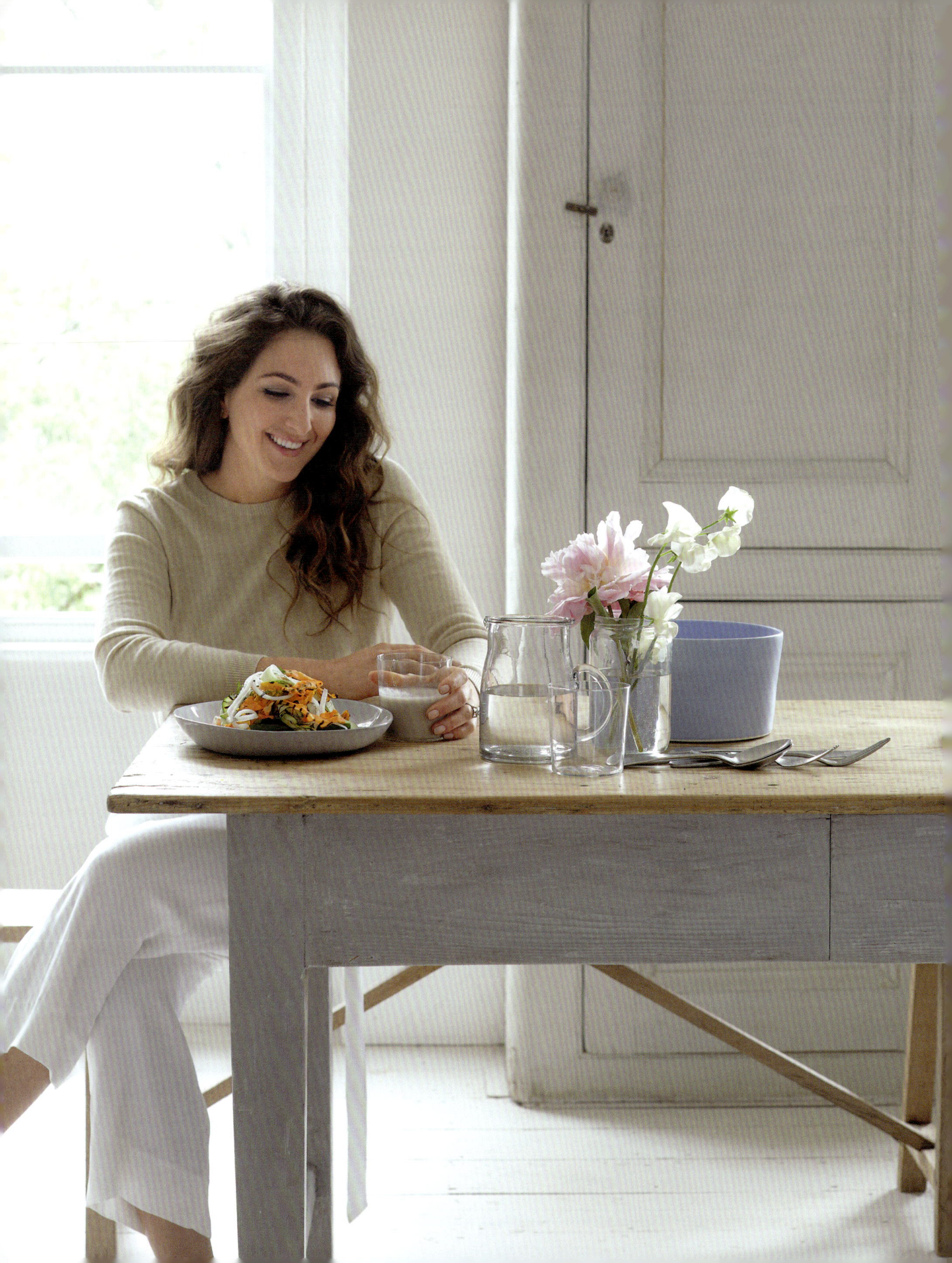

contents

#recipe index

Your at-a-glance guide to all the recipes in the book!

Salads

Sweet treats

Savory bites

Breads and baked goods

Juices, smoothies, and teas

#introduction

Nothing will benefit human health and increase the chances of survival of life on earth as much as the evolution to a vegetarian diet. Albert Einstein

I truly believe that things happen for a reason. One summer five years ago, I had been working so hard – cooking and delivering vegetarian lunches to people's offices – and my dodgy back gave way the day before my birthday. I could hardly walk. It was a Friday afternoon and I couldn't get an appointment anywhere; then, my mother told me to go and see her Ayurvedic doctor for some acupuncture, as it would help release the muscle spasm. During the session, as he was inserting needles into my back, the doctor told me that I was far too acidic and that I needed to do an alkaline cleanse. He said that my body had become incredibly acidic from years and years of yo-yo dieting, even though I thought I was super-healthy being vegetarian and knocking back a green smoothie with spirulina every morning. It seemed, too, that my body was in a toxic state from the stress and overwork I had put it through – such a state, in fact, that he said there was no way it could absorb the goodness and nutrients I was feeding myself.

Eating with your body in mind

So I set upon a 21-day alkaline cleanse. After the first week I started sleeping better; I had more energy, my skin started to clear up and the puffiness went. After the three weeks was over, I found I'd lost weight, my nails and hair started to grow stronger and I felt so full of energy. I realized that this alkaline cleanse was not a diet or detox but an amazing way of eating that I could easily incorporate into my day-to-day life. I continued with the alkaline eating and after three months I found out that my polycystic ovaries had gone and my digestion had recovered. I was so inspired by this way of living that I decided I must do more to spread the word. So I completely re-branded my food delivery company and Honestly Healthy was born.

When I wrote my first two books with nutritionist Vicki Edgson – *Eating the Alkaline Way* and *Honestly Healthy for Life* – we wanted to explain how easy it is to eat the alkaline way every day. We explained that the way we put the alkaline food tables together was by looking at how the pH of each ingredient reacts when it has been digested – what is called the "ash effect." These tables help you to learn which foods are alkaline and which aren't, as it's not an instinctive choice. There are certain ingredients that are quite surprising when you see their pH after digestion. Lemons, for instance, are supremely acidic when tested on litmus paper, but when digested, they are extremely alkaline. On the other hand, cow's milk registers as alkaline when tested on litmus paper, but when digested is terribly acidic.

In simple terms, acidity in the body causes "dis-ease," which later can show itself as everyday discomforts, such as bloating, exhaustion, acne, dry skin, and acid reflux, to much more serious illnesses, such as cancer, diabetes, heart disease and obesity. Dr. Robert Young, an American biologist, who pioneered alkaline eating, discovered that eating a plant-based diet free from processed foods can help to cure terminal diseases in the body. Unfortunately, his work, like that of many other holistic organisations, such as the Gerson Institute in California, is not recognized by the medical industry, perhaps because giant pharmaceutical organizations wouldn't be able to make money out of doctors prescribing vegetables.

My philosophy is to focus on prevention, not cure. By living a healthy balanced life you will hopefully never be at the extreme stage of having to cure yourself.

Cleansing the Honestly Healthy way

Cleansing with the seasons is an excellent and organic way to support your body. Spring and summer are great times to try the #slimdown as it is predominantly raw foods, so it feels easier to make and digest this type of food when the weather is getting warmer. The #feelgood cleanse is a wonderful choice for the cooler months, as it's a very nurturing cleanse full of warming soups. Our energy changes with the seasons and those times, according to holistic medical practitioners, are when it's best to cleanse the body and start afresh. Some people go as far as trying to catch a cold during the season changes so that they can completely clean out their systems. I am not sure I would go that far, but I love giving my body an overhaul a few times a year, and with the changing seasons is a natural time to do this.

In our first two books, we explained that following the 70:30 rule is an easy and healthy way to live – 70% of the time you eat alkaline foods and 30% you are free to eat what you want. By having a balance like this, it means that you're never relying on willpower (which is unsustainable) and that if you want to go out for a meal, then you can. Enjoy it, but know that your next meal with be back on the alkaline way.

A lot of people ask me "Can I still eat meat and follow the alkaline way?" The answer is that meat is highly acid-forming in your body, but if you want to include it as part of your 30%, you can; just be sure that all the meat you buy is organically and sustainably reared. It's better to buy good-quality meat and eat it less often than chow down every day on meat that's pumped up with hormones.

Each of the four cleanses in this book are designed to fit in with your lifestyle. So, depending how you are feeling and what type of cleanse you are looking for, be it a weekend cleanse, a pre-event slimdown or a cleanse that supports you during a week of heavy exercise, we have all bases covered.

#feelgood

A two- or three-day liquid cleanse, comprising smoothies, juices, teas, and soups – all designed to give your body a rest from digesting and to help draw out the toxins naturally.

#slimdown

This six-day cleanse will give you a gentle kick-start to shift any extra pounds before a party, holiday, or special event. In this cleanse you'll be eating raw salads with soups and smoothies, which will boost your immune system to no end.

#highenergy

This six-day cleanse is designed for people who are exercising a lot, who want to find out how to get more vegetarian protein into their daily diet and cleanse their body at the same time.

#lifechanging

This 30-day cleanse is a stepping stone to a new, healthier you. Once you've achieved the first 30 days, there will be no turning back – you will make definite lifestyle changes for the better as you'll feel so energized and full of life.

At the start of each cleanse you will be given in-depth information on what you are allowed and not allowed during that time. However, if you "break" the cleanse for any reason, please don't beat yourself up about it; it's not an all-or-nothing program. Just make sure that the next thing you put in your mouth is good and nurturing, rather than waiting to start again till the next day or Monday! What works for one person might not work for you, and it's more important to do as much as you feel you can without tipping over the edge into obsession. Having come out the other side of years of yo-yo dieting, I realize that my behavior was obsessive and that in itself is an eating

Top tips for any cleanse

Be prepared – get all your shopping done before you start a cleanse. Make up the first day's worth of food so you are ahead of time and not tied to the kitchen preparing meals.

Remove trigger foods – any food that you normally turn to for a "fix" is best out of the way, so hide it or, better still, get it out of your home. If you can't see it, you won't want it.

Drink plenty of water – ideally, you'll want to quaff at least 2 litres of water per day.

Calm your mind – if you can clear your mind from work and problems, you will not only be helping your body to cleanse, but your brain will benefit from a clear-out too. Do whatever works best – read a book, meditate, or pay yourself some attention; many a good idea has come out of a cleanse, as your brain has some clear time to think differently. The foods you eat directly impact your mood, and drawing the toxins from your body during a cleanse will also improve your outlook and your brain's thought processes afterwards. Just think what great ideas you might have.

How you might feel and what might happen

If you have not undertaken a cleanse before, it's good to be warned that you might feel worse before you feel better. The process of drawing toxins out of your body creates classic symptoms, such as:

headaches
tiredness
irritability
skin break-outs
bloating
constipation

Extras for the ultimate cleanse

Any and all of the following suggestions will boost the success of your cleanse, so choose those that suit you.

Start the day with hot water and lemon
A glass of hot water with a lemon slice first thing in the morning helps to bring your body into an alkaline state after a night of detoxification.

Take a probiotic
These supplements help to reinvigorate your gut with good bacteria, making your digestive system work more efficiently again. What's more, probiotics also help with any bloating you might experience.

Take some artichoke extract
Tablets or drops containing concentrated artichoke extract can combat water retention and thus reduce the amount of bloating throughout the body. For this reason, it's also great if you're doing a lot of flying.

Drink herbal teas
Teas that facilitate your cleanse are: fennel, camomile, peppermint, and nettle.

End the day with magnesium flakes in a bath
Many people are deficient in magnesium, a mineral pivotal in regulating various body reactions, including energy production and nutrient absorption. As your skin can absorb magnesium directly, a magnesium-enriched bath not only helps you sleep and relax, but also helps support energy production, so come Monday morning you will be flying out the door, ready for anything the week can throw at you.

Cleanse your colon
The last thing to do before you go to sleep is to take a colon-cleansing supplement mixed with warm water. The fastest way to remove toxins from the body is via excretion, and this supplement gives nature a helping hand. It will also help if you have constipation from the change in diet. Be sure to follow the recommended dose.

disorder. It has only been in being "kind" to myself and finding my healthy approach to food that I have found a comfortable state where I can cleanse my body – and see it as enjoyable rather than as a chore or a frightening experience.

Cleansing affects your body in many ways, and if this is your first cleanse, be sure to look over the list of points in the "How you might feel" box (page 11). It's best to know what might happen so that you feel prepared rather than overwhelmed. Whichever symptoms you display, it's your body's reaction to the detoxification process; do know that they will pass and soon you will start to feel amazing. Remind yourself what a wonderful thing you are doing for your body – you are giving yourself a gift. I've also listed, from experience, top tips to make any cleanse go as smoothly as possible and what you can do to maximize its benefits.

Learn what works for you

One of the clients of my UK nationwide food delivery service, Fridge Fill, contacted me to say that she had been an insomniac for five years, but that after just two weeks on our alkaline cleanse, she was sleeping through the night – for the first time in years she finally felt energized! It's such a humbling feeling to know that something that was a healing journey for me is now helping other people. The amazing thing about eating great nutritious food on a daily basis is the educational aspect. Every day I am still learning about foods and combinations that help support me. For example, I find that when I am tired from work and/or stressed, I automatically reach for carbohydrates, which then sends me on that vicious circle of craving more, because the initial surge in my blood sugar has plummeted and then I need a top-up. Instead I make different choices. I reach for Broccoli or Almond-base pizza (see pages 198 and 211) or Asian noodle soup (see page 114) which really check a lot of boxes for me when I start to crave, and I always have rice noodles in the larder. The key, I find, is to acknowledge that the craving is happening and reach instead for a healthy alternative. For example, to deal with my urges for something sweet, I try always to have a batch of Gooey vegan brownies (see page 233) on hand and a carton of salted coconut ice cream in the freezer.

Another thing I've found is that when I'm feeling low or tired, a burst of exercise or activity just gets the "happy hormones" (aka endorphins) pumping around my body, and in that state I find that I naturally reach for healthier foods. What's more, research has shown that just eating healthy food can boost endorphins in the brain – so combine that with exercise and you'll double the hit. But – and there is a but – if you eat the same healthy food every day, then the endorphin levels plateau and can actually decrease. This makes total sense and explains why so many people on a "diet" fail after days of eating the same salad. Variety is therefore key to feeling better and healthier.

A holistic approach

Being healthy is not just about food and what you put in your mouth. You need to look at the bigger picture, too, just as you would in a business. If, for example, a company is losing money, you need to look at everything that isn't working: from the logistics to the marketing strategy, from staff training to the execution of the company's mission and vision. It's the same with health: you need to look at all the elements that make up your mind, body, and spirit, not just what is on your plate.

I have a mind coach who I speak to via Skype once a month, and he always starts the conversation by asking me

> Like the weather, your body and your mind change every day – what you needed yesterday to make you feel fantastic might well be the opposite of what you need today.

what my weather report is for that particular time in my life. I really love that idea.

I am sure you have heard the advice: "listen to your body." Well, it's true; it's not just a hippy saying. For me, the key is understanding what makes *you* feel great and what can help support you when you are too busy, tired, and emotional to return to your optimum. Could it be meditation, going for a walk in the park, having an intense workout, spending time with friends, listening to music, baking a cake, surrounding yourself with nature? What works for you? Ask yourself these questions:

How do I feel today right now?

How do I feel when I am at my best?

What would be the first step to take to get to that point?

How would I feel if I took that step?

Let me show you a couple of regular conversations that happen for me.

First example:

How do I feel today right now?

I am feeling really overwhelmed. I'm feeling unproductive and have so much to get done.

How do I feel when I am at my best?

Calm, secure, inspired, productive.

What can I do to feel at my best?

Tidy my desk so it's not cluttered. Go to the gym. Have a green smoothie in the mornings to give me energy. Take an hour for lunch and walk the dog in the park. Do my breathing exercises or yoga to calm my mind. Have an early night.

How would I feel if I took that step?

As if I have the space to get grounded so that I can approach the work I need to do.

Second example:

How do I feel today right now?

I feel fat and my clothes are too tight.

How do I feel when I am at my best?

Slim, toned, fit, sexy, comfortable in my clothes.

What would be the first step to take to get to that point?

Go to the gym for a workout, then go shopping to get healthy food in my fridge. Prep my week's lunches in advance.

How would I feel if I took that step?

Proud, organized, motivated, energized.

Cleansing timetable

Personally, I like to cleanse a couple times a year because it keeps my body feeling amazing. However, it's not just about the actual cleanse. The transition periods of going into and coming out of a cleanse are just as important. Make sure you are

```
When starting a business
you create a vision and
mission statement for your
company to keep you on
track, so why not create
one for your health?
```

Special equipment

Many of my recipes use a juicer, blender, or food processor, so if you need to buy these machines, here's what I'd recommend:

High-speed blender
Top-notch: Vitamix
Lower-price: Nutribullet

Food processor
Top-notch: Magimix
Lower-price: Kenwood

Juicer
Top-notch: Sage by Heston
Lower-price: Philips

You'll also need: a microplane grater, a spiraliser, a mandoline

Find more links to equipment and ingredients on the shop page of our website. www.honestlyhealthyfood.com

not planning a big night out the day you finish your cleanse. Put yourself in a situation that supports you and your decisions.

When embarking on a cleanse, remember the two Ps – plan and prepare. By sorting out your menu for the week and preparing as much as you can in advance, you'll make everything else so much easier and be better able to keep right on track. Feeling excessively hungry is not something I promote – it's not healthy to starve yourself. Don't let your blood sugar levels get to such a point that your cravings take over. Remember, it takes 21 days to form a habit and 21 days to break it – that's only three weeks to reprogram your brain!

Many of the recipes within each cleanse can be used within the other cleanses. Each of the cleanses is color-coded with dots that show you which recipes you can make within it. For example, in the #feelgood you can have a soup from

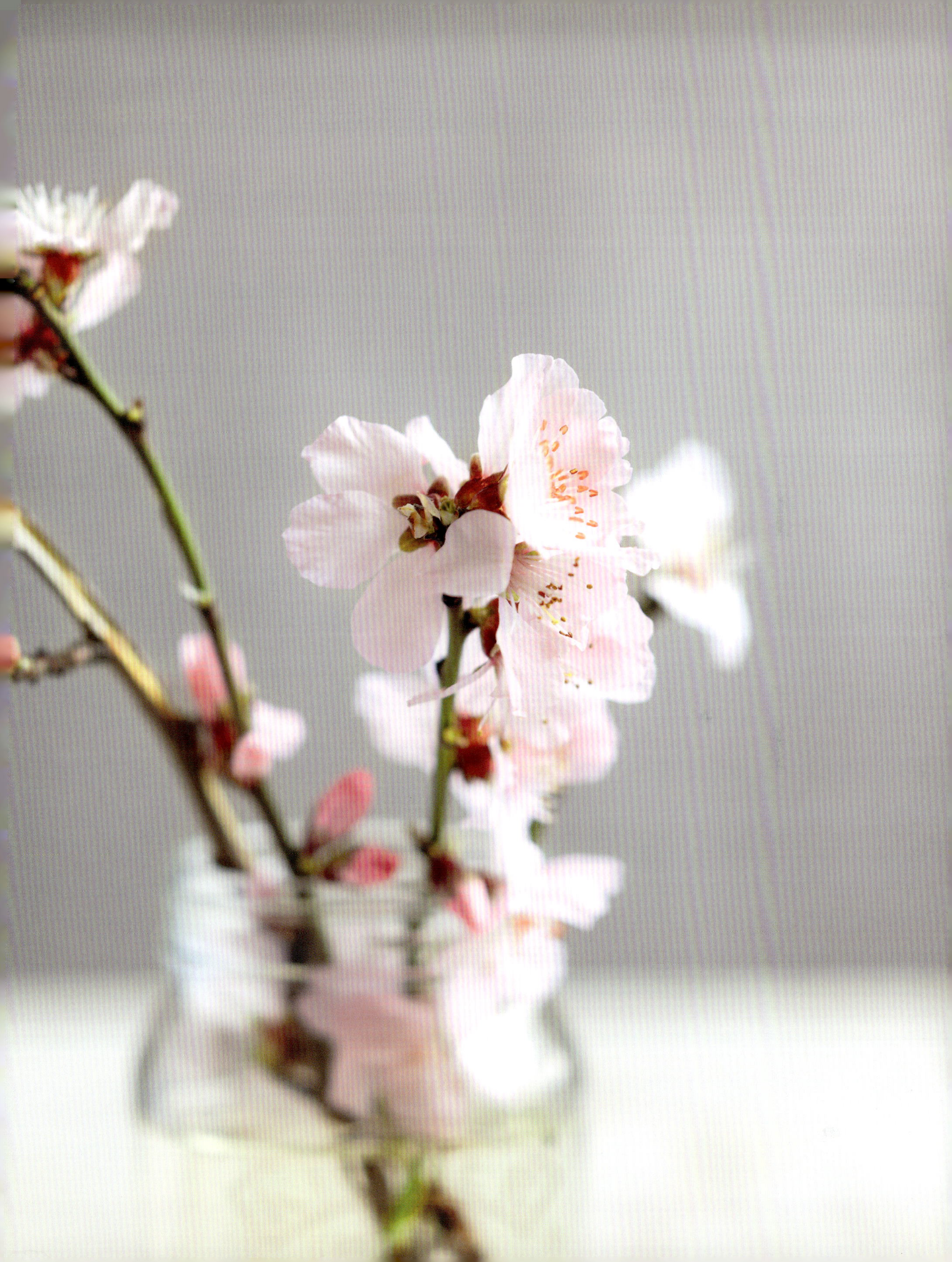

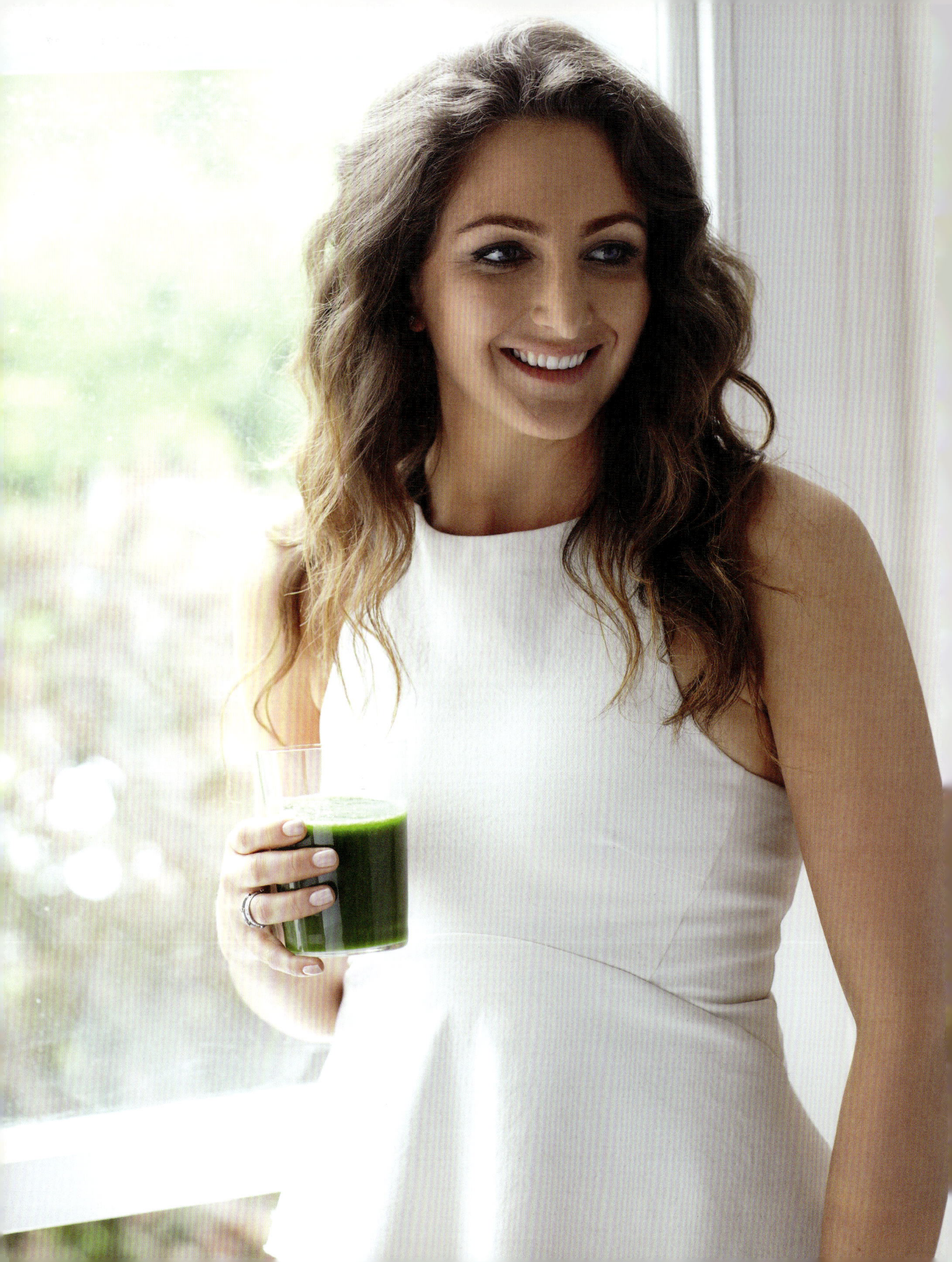

#slimdown. In the menu planners (see pages 27, 48, 86, and 162) you will see that some recipes are used in more than one cleanse.

One small step...

At a press breakfast in 2013, I was asked "What was the best thing about my brand and my business?" I can honestly say that seeing the photos that people post on social media means more to me than anything; it shows me that you are making the recipes, and I love seeing how well they turn out. It's so encouraging to think that when I am creating my recipes at home and trying them out on my friends and family that soon the #honestlyhealthy fans will be inspired to make them and, from experience, they like to tell me how good they taste! All my recipes are really simple to make. Like many of you, I don't have the time to be creating meals that take ages to prepare, so if I can make

them, you can too! I find that cooking is really meditative – a great transition from workday to evening – and perhaps this is something you'll find, too, once you've got the Honestly Healthy habit.

If you can do one thing for your health today, add one great nutritious ingredient to your diet. If you find doing an entire cleanse is going to set you up for failure, start slowly by adding one healthy meal to your day, and then steadily increase this each week. In this way it's a gentle transition for your mind, too, as at the end of the day it's only your mind you have to trick – your body really wants to be healthy.

Let me know how you get on by sending me your pictures over social media, and hashtag which cleanse you are on!

Tash x

#goodluck @honestlyhealthy

Cook's Notes

Unless stated otherwise:

Spoon measures are level.

Eggs are medium and preferably organic and free-range.

Pepper should be black and freshly ground.

Fruit and vegetables should preferably be organic, and washed and/or peeled before use.

The standard portion size should fill two hands cupped together.

Key

Each cleanse includes a suggested menu planner. You can also see which recipes are suited to which cleanse using the color-coded guide on each page:

#feelgood

#slimdown

#highenergy

#lifechanging

#glossary of ingredients

Acai powder – The acai berry, a rich purple fruit indigenous to the Amazon rainforest, has a unique flavor with hints of red wine and chocolate. The small berries are freeze-dried and ground into a powder that is packed with nutrients; the purple color originates from pigments known as anthocyanins.

Agave syrup – Also known as agave nectar, this sweetener is derived from the blue weber agave plant and is sweeter than refined sugar. Always buy organic raw agave and use it in small quantities. It has a low glycemic index, so doesn't cause swings in blood sugar levels.

Almond butter – Simply a paste of almonds; you can make it yourself or buy it in jars. Comes in smooth or crunchy versions.

Apple cider vinegar – The only alkaline vinegar; this condiment is made from the fermentation of apple cider.

Arame seaweed – Sold in packs as dried strips, arame has a slightly sweet and delicate flavor and is almost black in color.

Baobab fruit powder – The fruit of the baobab is dried on the tree, harvested, and then ground into a powder. This tangy powder is more potent than vitamin C and helps to keep you well year round.

Barley coffee – This naturally caffeine-free version of coffee was drunk by Italian peasants, as they couldn't afford genuine coffee. It's sold as a powder that's mixed with hot water and perks you up.

Bee pollen – This granular garnish is made by worker bees, who pack pollen into little granules with added honey or nectar. Sold in small jars, a little goes a long way; it's highly nutritious and adds great texture to salads and smoothies.

Bouillon powder – This vegetarian instant stock powder is made only from vegetables, so it has a pure veggie flavor. As such, it makes a great flavor enhancer and, what's more, is free from preservatives, artificial flavoring, GM organisms, and coloring.

Brown rice syrup – This natural sweetener is derived from ground brown rice and is naturally low on the glycaemic index. There are many adulterated versions around so be sure to choose an organic version of this product.

Brown rice vinegar – A delicious Japanese condiment, this is slightly sweet and doesn't have the acidity of other vinegars.

Chia seeds – Grown as a grain, originally in Mexico and Guatemala, these seeds are a rich source of energy. They have the highest level of omega-3 fatty acids of any seed and can absorb up to 15 times their own weight in fluids. They make a great thickening agent.

Coconut blossom syrup – This sweetener has a low glycemic index, so keeps blood sugar levels balanced. If you can't find it, substitute it with agave syrup.

Coconut manna – Similar to coconut butter or coconut cream, coconut manna can be used as a replacement for milk, cream, yogurt, or butter, or even eaten just as a dip with crudités.

Coconut milk yogurt – Totally different from coconut-flavored yogurt, this dairy-free and vegan yogurt is made from squeezing the cream from the white flesh of the coconut. It can be bought in cartons and is also available as ice cream.

Coconut palm sugar – More nutritious than ordinary sugar, but just as sweet, palm sugar is made from the sap of the coconut palm tree. It has a low glycemic index, but use it in small amounts to avoid getting hooked on its sweetness. Look for organic and unprocessed versions, and make sure it's a pure coconut palm product.

Coconut water – This delicious drink is packed with nutrients and rehydrates you faster than water. What's more, it's completely free of fat, sugar, and cholesterol. Be sure to buy 100% pure coconut water.

Freeze-dried plum powder – A nutrient-rich flavoring and coloring, this powder consists of ground, freeze-dried plums and can be added to a range of foods and drinks.

Hatcho miso – This type of miso is grain-free and takes at least two years to ferment, so it has a medicinal and deeply robust flavor. It is believed that fermented ingredients are important in healing the gut.

Himalayan pink salt – A rose-colored salt mined in the foothills of the Himalayan Mountains, this is an ancient product, first created thousands of years ago. It's high in iron, potassium, and magnesium, which are all vital for good health.

Kombu seaweed – Sold as wide, dried strips, kombu is a common flavoring in Japanese soups and stocks (dashi). It contains an amino acid that enhances other foods with an umami flavor. Also, when added to lentils, for instance, during cooking, kombu releases an enzyme that helps the digestive process and eliminates bloating.

Kuzu Root starch – This ancient Oriental starch is taken from the root of the kuzu plant. It's a natural thickener and can be used in baking, custards, and desserts.

Liquid chlorophyll – A dietary supplement that is the liquid form of chlorophyll found in plants. It works in the body in a way similar to hemoglobin, the pigment that carries oxygen around inside red blood cells. Drinking this amazing liquid will boost oxygen levels throughout your body.

Lucuma powder – The dried powder of the lucuma fruit from South America adds a certain maple syrup sweetness to foods or drinks and helps maintain blood sugar levels, as it has a low glycemic index. It's naturally rich in vitamins, protein, and zinc.

Maca powder – Also known as Peruvian ginseng, maca powder has been used in Peru for endurance and energy for over 2000 years. It adds a certain malty sweetness to smoothies and desserts.

Matcha – This green powder, sold in small cans, is made from green tea leaves that have been ground very finely. Traditionally drunk in Japan as part of the tea ceremony and by monks, matcha promotes alertness and focus. It imparts a pleasing green color and has a slightly bitter taste.

Millet – This little grain has a naturally hard, indigestible covering that is removed (or hulled) during processing. It looks like birdseed, and unlike most other gluten-free grains, is alkaline. Millet has a nutty flavor and adds interesting texture to dishes.

Mirin – This essential condiment used in Japanese cooking is a sweetened sake or rice wine with a light syrupy texture. It offers a wonderfully mild sweetness to dishes.

Miso – This traditional Japanese food usually comes as a paste, and in Japan is eaten at almost every meal as miso soup. It's made by fermenting soy beans with salt and a fungus, and sometimes rice or barley is added. Miso is high in protein and rich in vitamins and minerals.

Nori seaweed – Produced in sheets, nori is available toasted or untoasted, and is used for wrapping sushi or eating as a snack. It can be deep green or purplish in color and, as with all sea vegetables, is highly alkaline and full of amino acids.

Nutritional yeast – Sold in the form of flakes, this ingredient is made from a single-celled yeast, *Saccharomyces cerevisiae*, which is grown on molasses, then harvested, washed, and dried with heat to "deactivate" it. So, unlike yeast for making bread, it has no leavening ability. A sprinkle packs a nutritional punch and adds a certain savoriness to lots of dishes.

Psyllium – Sold as psyllium husks, capsules, and powder, this ingredient works well in all kinds of gluten-free baking and is highly beneficial to the colon and digestive function in general.

Quinoa flakes – This is essentially raw quinoa seeds that have been rolled flat to create thin flakes. Nutrient-rich and gluten-free, they're fast-cooking, due to their thinness.

Rapadura sugar – This is granulated cane sugar, but not as we generally know it. Rapadura is unrefined whole cane sugar which is made from the pure juice extracted from sugar cane. It has a unique caramel flavor and is a great sweetener for all manner of foods and drinks.

Red beet powder – This powerful powder is derived from beets and offers great color and natural sweetness. Sold in small packets.

Spirulina – Sold as tablets or a powder, spirulina is a blue-green algae that has a full spectrum of nutrients that nourish the body and mind.

Sprouts – Anyone can sprout seeds or beans on a windowsill or in a flower pot. These nutritious and delicious micro-greens come in as many kinds as there are seeds or beans. Popular ones include aduki bean, alfalfa, broccoli, mustard, and cress, mung bean, and rose sprouts.

Sumac – This tangy, lemony spice is often used in Mediterranean and Middle Eastern cooking. It's made from the berries of *Rhus coriaria*, which are bright red, so it has a vibrant color too.

Sweet miso – Historically sweet, miso was the preserve of the rich because it is made with lots of rice koji (mould spores), which made it very expensive to buy. This type of miso has a wonderful creamy richness and slightly salty sweetness.

Tahini – A thick paste made from ground sesame seeds, tahini is often used in Middle Eastern cooking. It packs a high-protein punch and is wonderfully versatile – it can be used in baking or dressings, for instance. It has a lovely nutty flavor.

Tamari – Essentially a wheat-free soy sauce, tamari can be used if you need to make a dish gluten-free. Its taste does differ slightly from regular soy sauce – it's less salty – and has a dark, rich color, but can be used in the same way.

Teff flour – Teff is a grain grown in certain African countries and is tiny – the size of a poppy seed. Flour made from teff makes a great gluten-free alternative to wheat flour and is packed with protein, calcium, and iron.

Tempeh – Although it looks a little like a small white cake or veggie burger, tempeh is made from cooked and slightly fermented soy beans. It has a unique taste and is highly nutritious. You can make your tempeh or buy it in Asian food stores.

Tofu – This soybean product is made from the "milk" of mature white soybeans (not the edamame you'll see in the recipes), which is pressed and then all the liquid is squeezed out. It's available in blocks of various levels of firmness (soft, medium, and hard), which are good to cut up and use in curries or stir-fries. There's also the silken type of tofu, which is soft and silky in texture and works well in blended sauces or smoothies. As with all soy products, choose an organic and non-GM version.

Turmeric – Quite a different thing from the ground version, fresh turmeric looks a bit like ginger root or a thin Jerusalem artichoke. Its flesh is bright orange (watch out, as it stains). It has an earthy, citrusy taste; and slight tongue-numbing qualities (rather like Sichuan pepper).

Umeboshi paste – This sweet condiment is used extensively in Japanese cuisine. It is made by slowly pickling the ume fruit in salt, and then extracting the purée that results from the breakdown and fermenting of the fruit. Its taste is tart and tangy, and it's very alkalizing on the body.

Vegan butter – This dairy-free spread is a mixture of oils that has a rich, buttery taste and can be used in just the same way as butter.

Wakame seaweed – Packaged as dried strips and flakes, this seaweed has tender, dark green fronds, a mild flavor, and is super-versatile. It's similar to kombu seaweed nutritionally.

Xanthan gum – This ingredient keeps your home baking gluten-free. It's made by fermenting sugar with the bacterium *Xanthomonas campestris* and is available in a powdered form. It can be used as a thickening agent.

Xylitol – Extracted from hardwood trees and the fibers of some fruits and vegetables, xylitol is a sugar alcohol. This natural sweetener contains far fewer calories than refined cane sugar and has a low glycemic index. It does, however, have a slight after-taste that some people find unpalatable.

Yerba mate – Available as leaves or a powder, yerba mate is a green tea from South America. It has an ability to naturally energize, focus, and rejuvenate the body, and is nutrient-rich. Used as tea or in smoothies to give a smoky edge.

Za'atar – A powerful blend of herbs and spices – sesame seeds, oregano, marjoram, sumac, sea salt, and cumin – za'atar is used in eastern Mediterranean and Middle Eastern cooking.

#feelgood

Nourishing your body while you rest

2-3 days of satisfying smoothies, fresh juices, and soothing soups.

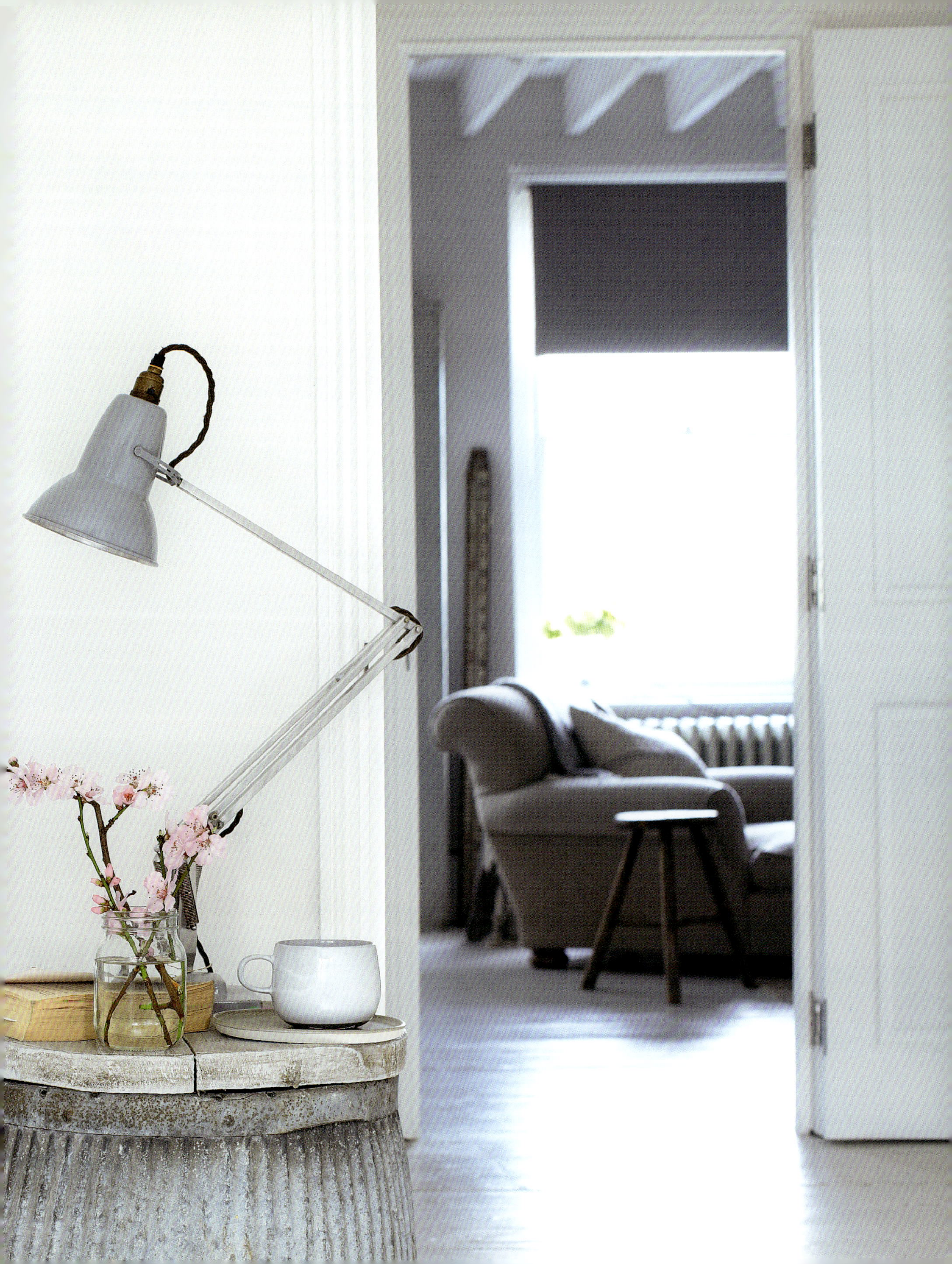

Feeling good for me means

nourishing my body. During a typical work week, it can be hard to stop and listen to what your body is telling you, so taking a weekend for yourself is one of the best ways to feel good and re-boot the system. Such weekend-only cleanses give you a chance for some "time out," and getting into the habit of doing them regularly can only do you more good. When I do the #feelgood cleanse I turn off my phone and my computer, get some great books and movies, and prepare for some "me time."

This cleanse is not only great for feeling good, but is also a perfect kick-start after an indulgent time. It has plenty of soups and smoothies to help soothe your digestive system and draw the toxins out of your body. I especially love this cleanse, as you end up with a super-flat tummy after just two days and are totally recharged.

Meditation

If you like to meditate, a weekend offline is a perfect opportunity to do so; and if you have never considered doing meditation, now is the time to start. Find a comfy sitting position and, for only 10 minutes, concentrate on the breath coming in and out of your nose. Your mind is sure to wander, but when you realize that, simply bring your focus back to your breath and the sounds and movements of inhaling and exhaling.

You will need # plenty of rest # a blender # ingredients for the recipes

What to expect . . .

This cleanse is perfectly designed for a weekend – ideally it would be three days, but two days works, too. As you'll have plenty of time to relax and pamper yourself, you can let the foods do their work without having to concentrate on anything apart from yourself.

The feelgood programme comprises smoothies, juices, teas, and soups – all designed to give your body a rest from digesting solid foods and to help draw out the toxins naturally.

Stay away from:

# caffeine	# meat
# solid food	# sugar
# alcohol	# wheat and gluten
# dairy products	# processed foods

All of the above are extremely acid-forming in the body (and not alkalizing). To rebalance your body towards a more alkaline state you need to cut these items out of your diet.

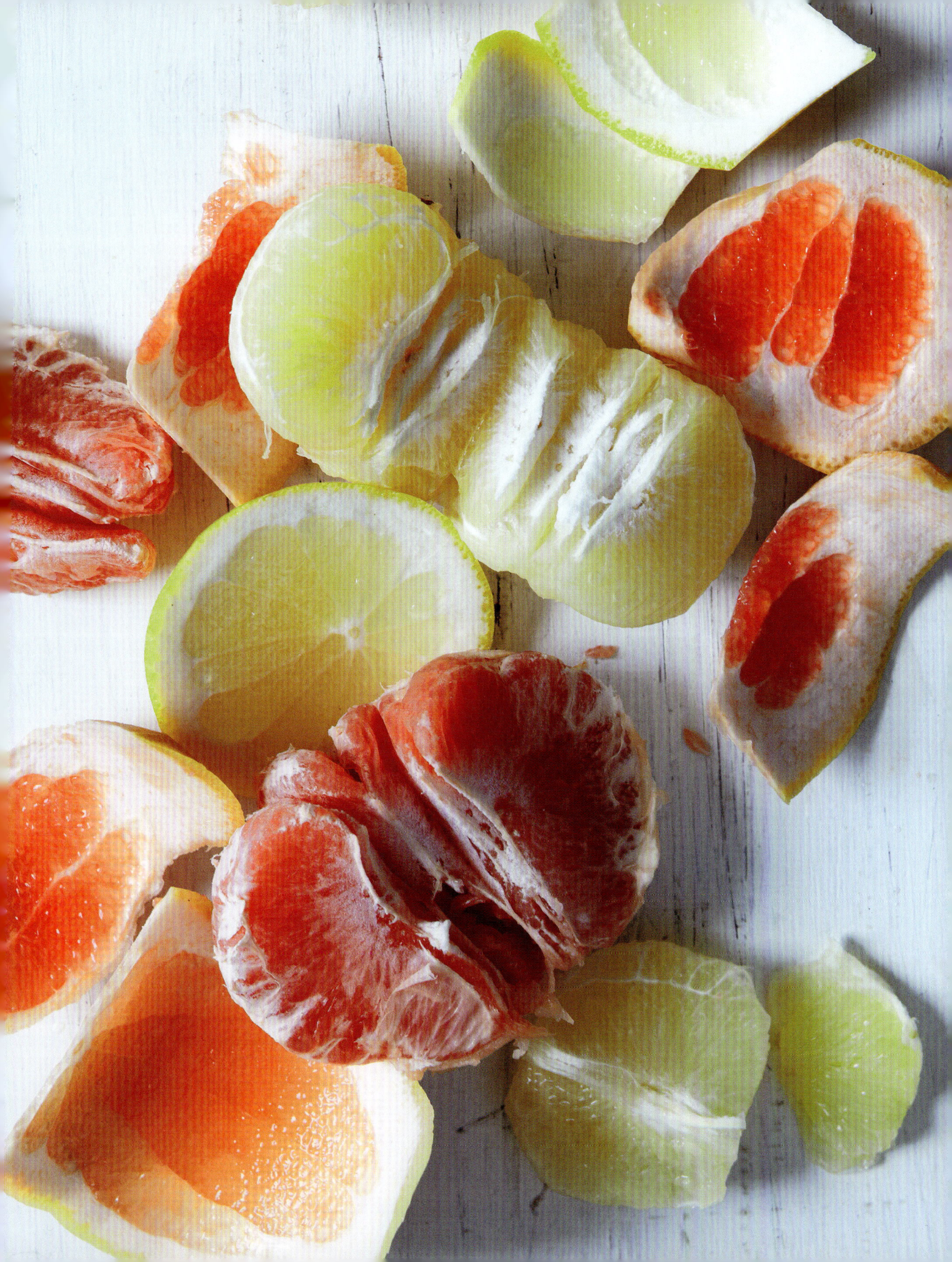

#feelgood menu planner

You can have up to three smoothies and juices and two soups per day. If you are finding it too much, you can drop one of the smoothies or juices, but make sure to have one green smoothie each day. We don't want you to get hungry, so listen to your body. Obviously you don't need to follow this menu planner exactly; if you want to make a big batch of say three soups over the 2-3 days of cleansing, just make sure that one of them is green.

Day 1

AM	Chlorophyll smoothie (page 31)
Mid-morning	Red juice (page 30)
Lunch	Cauliflower and pink peppercorn soup (page 38)
PM	Avocado smoothie (page 57)
Dinner	Carrot and lime soup (page 41)
Pre-bed	A cleansing and calming tea (page 36)

Day 2

AM	Carrot and turmeric smoothie (page 31)
Mid-morning	Green starter juice (page 30)
Lunch	Pumpkin soup (page 68)
PM	Chia green smoothie (page 33)
Dinner	Broccoli, celery, and dill soup (page 42)
Pre-bed	Rose, ginger, and star anise tea (page 36)

Day 3

AM	Acai smoothie (page 50)
Mid-morning	Energizing tea (page 58)
Lunch	Cauliflower and pink peppercorn soup (page 38)
PM	Kale and oat smoothie (page 56)
Dinner	Broccoli, celery, and dill soup (page 42)
Pre-bed	A cleansing and calming tea (page 36)

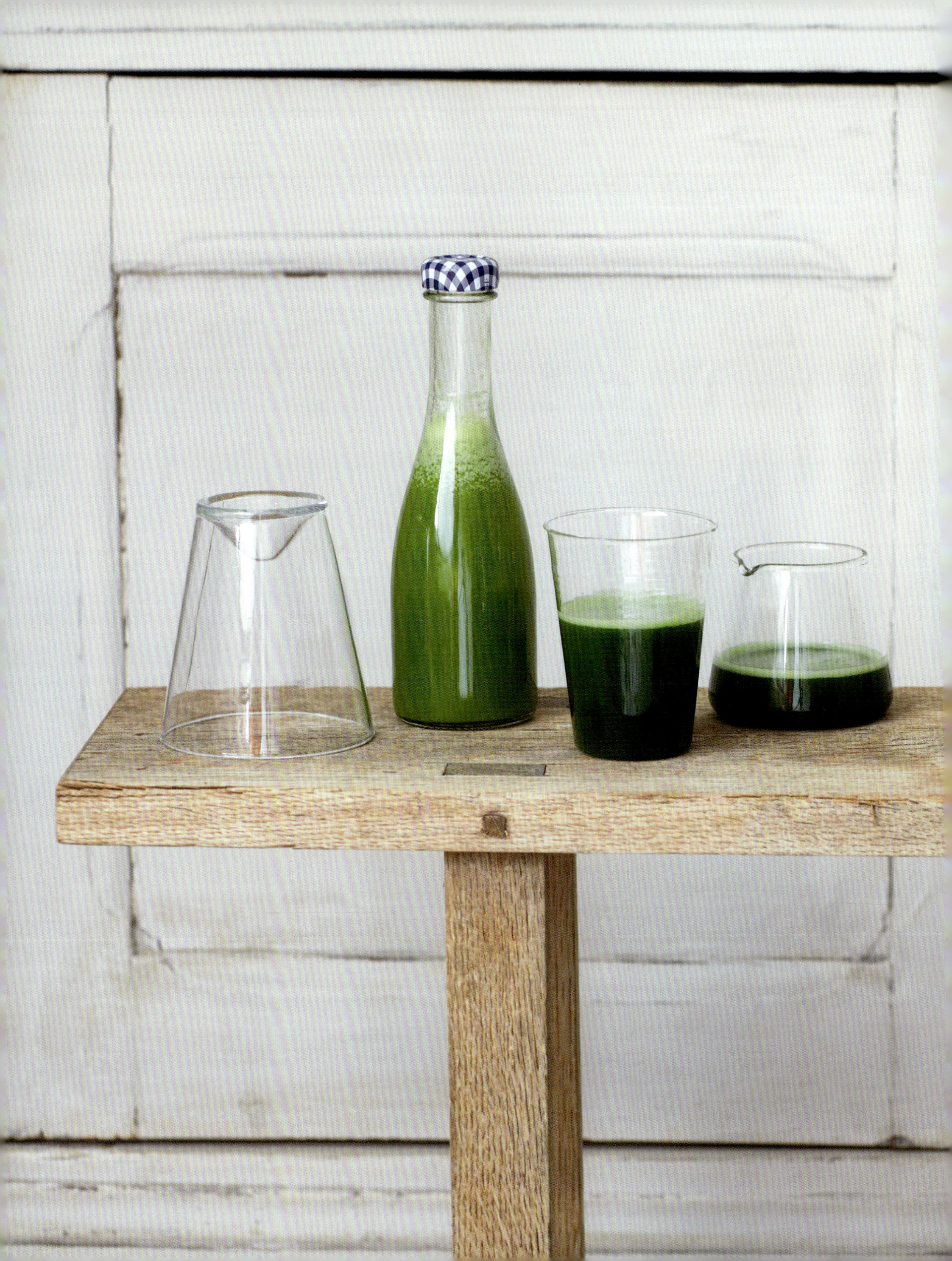

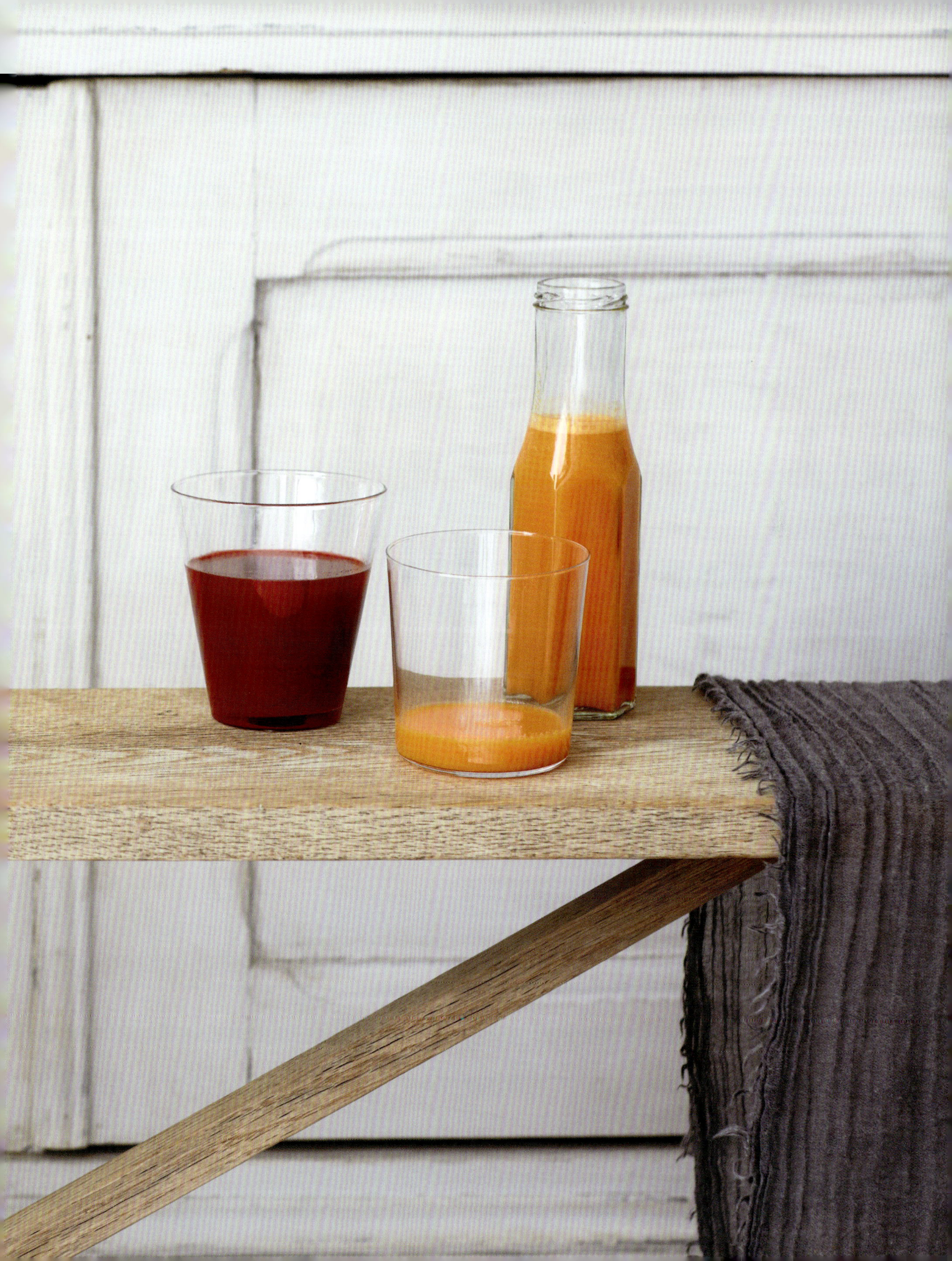

Red juice

This juice is such a beautiful color. It looks good and does you good – it's packed with minerals and vitamins. What better way to start your day? You can buy fresh turmeric from local Asian supermarkets or online.

serves 1

3⅛ cups (160g) raw beet

2 cups chopped (250g) carrots

¾ cup (135g) ripe tomatoes

4 radishes

1 blood orange, peeled

9 × 1in (2.5cm) slices (20g) fresh turmeric (if you can't find fresh, blend in 1 tsp ground turmeric right at the end)

Put all the ingredients through a juicer. Keep the pulp to make the raw crackers (see page 32) and drink the liquid.

Photo on previous page (left-right): Chlorophyll smoothie, Green starter juice, Red juice, Carrot, and turmeric smoothie

Green starter juice

For me, the best color in the world is green! Drink it, eat it, whichever way you decide. Just be sure to get some fresh, gorgeous greenness into your system. This vegetable-based green juice doesn't taste too earthy, so makes a great introduction to the world of green.

serves 1

1⅔ cups (150g) broccoli

1⅛ cups (150g) cucumber

1 cup chopped (65g) kale

1¾ cups (130g) fennel

3 sticks celery

Put all the ingredients through a juicer. Keep the pulp to make the raw crackers (see page 32) and drink the liquid.

Chlorophyll smoothie

This green smoothie has added chlorophyll – the pigment that gives leaves their green color; it's like a plant's blood. Chlorophyll works in the body similar to hemoglobin, the pigment that carries oxygen around your body inside red blood cells. Drinking this amazing liquid will boost oxygen levels throughout your body. What's more, green leafy vegetables are highly alkaline, helping the body to reduce toxins and toxic waste. What better way to start taking chlorophyll than with this delicious green smoothie?

makes 4 cups (1 litre)

½ cup chopped (35g) kale

¾ cup chopped (70g) broccoli

1 apple (¾ cup chopped, about 100g)

⅛ cup (10g) flat leaf parsley

½ grapefruit (⅓ cup/about 80g)

1 tbsp liquid chlorophyll (I use Dr. Young's pH Miracle Greens)

2⅛ cups (500ml) coconut water

Simply put all the ingredients into a blender and blend until smooth. The smoothie is best drunk right away, but you can always put it in a jar and take it out with you to drink as soon as you can during the day.

Carrot and turmeric smoothie

Turmeric is one of the most amazing spices, originally the king spice of Asian cooking. It provides potent antibacterial, antiviral, and antifungal properties, so is great for warding off seasonal colds and flu. It does have a strong taste, so it's definitely a case of "less is more" at the beginning. It is also a natural stimulant, so who needs coffee when you can kick-start your day with this smoothie?

serves 2

¾ cup (170ml) carrot juice

juice of 1 orange

juice of 1 lime

¾ cup sliced (65g) fennel

¼ tsp ground turmeric (or to taste)

Simply put all the ingredients into a high-speed blender and blend until completely smooth. The smoothie is best drunk right away, but you can always put it in a jar and take it with you to drink as soon as you can during the day.

Green and red raw crackers

Don't throw anything away! Use the pulp from your green and red juices to make these savory crackers. In fact, you can try this recipe using the pulp of other juices to experiment with those flavors.

Preheat an oven to its lowest temperature or preheat a dehydrator to 37°C (98.6°F). Line a baking sheet with parchment paper.

When the Chia seeds have become thick and gloopy, put them and all the remaining green cracker ingedients into a bowl. Mix well, then spread out onto the prepared baking sheet – the mixture should be about 3mm thick.

Combine all the red cracker ingredients in a clean bowl and mix well. Spread onto the prepared sheet as before.

Bake in the oven for 6–7 hours or place in the dehydrator for 10–12 hours until dry and crisp. These crackers will keep for 5 days in an airtight container.

Enjoy with dips or nut butters, or nibble just as they are.

makes enough to fill a baking tray (about 6–8 portions)

for the green crackers:

2 tbsp ground chia seeds soaked in 6 tbsp water for 10 minutes

pulp from the green juice (see page 30)

1 tbsp sesame oil

¼ tsp salt

2 tbsp za'atar

1 tbsp raw sesame seeds

juice of ½ lemon, or to taste

for the red crackers:

pulp from the red juice (see page 30)

finely grated zest of 1 blood orange

1 tsp tamari

¼ tsp ground ginger

1 tbsp sweet white miso

2 heaping tbsp radish sprouts

Spirulina smoothie

I think the perfect way to start any day is with a green smoothie that includes spirulina powder. This smoothie has such a gorgeous color and is incredibly rich in essential nutrients; some researchers say that spirulina is one of the most nutritious food sources in the world, which is why it is called a superfood. If you're new to spirulina, start with just a small amount, as it can be very detoxing for the liver, and work your way up to the levels in the recipes over time. Nowadays, spirulina is much more available; you can buy it from most supermarkets, healthfood stores and online. *Photo overleaf (right)*

serves 2

¾ cup (25g) spinach leaves

½ cup shredded (55g) iceberg lettuce

1 tsp spirulina

1 large ripe peach

1½ cups (360ml) filtered water or coconut water

Simply put all the ingredients into a high-speed blender and blend until completely smooth. The smoothie is best drunk right away, but you can always put it in a jar and take it with you to drink as soon as you can during the day.

Chia green smoothie

Chia seeds are an ancient seed from Mayan times and the Mayans used them for energy. These wondrous little seeds are also full of protein and healthy fats, such as omega-3, which will make your skin glow and help you bounce out of bed in the morning. If you can't get your hands on coconut milk yogurt, add the same amount of the "cream" on the top of a can of coconut milk; it will give the same taste and texture. *Photo overleaf (left)*

serves 2

⅓ cup chopped (25g) kale

¾ cup shredded (55g) pak choi

1 tbsp chia seeds

⅔ cup diced (100g) honeydew melon

4 tbsp coconut milk yogurt

1½ cups (360ml) water

Simply put all of the ingredients into a high-speed blender and blend until completely smooth. The smoothie is best drunk straight away, but you can always put it in a jar and take it with you to drink as soon as you can during the day.

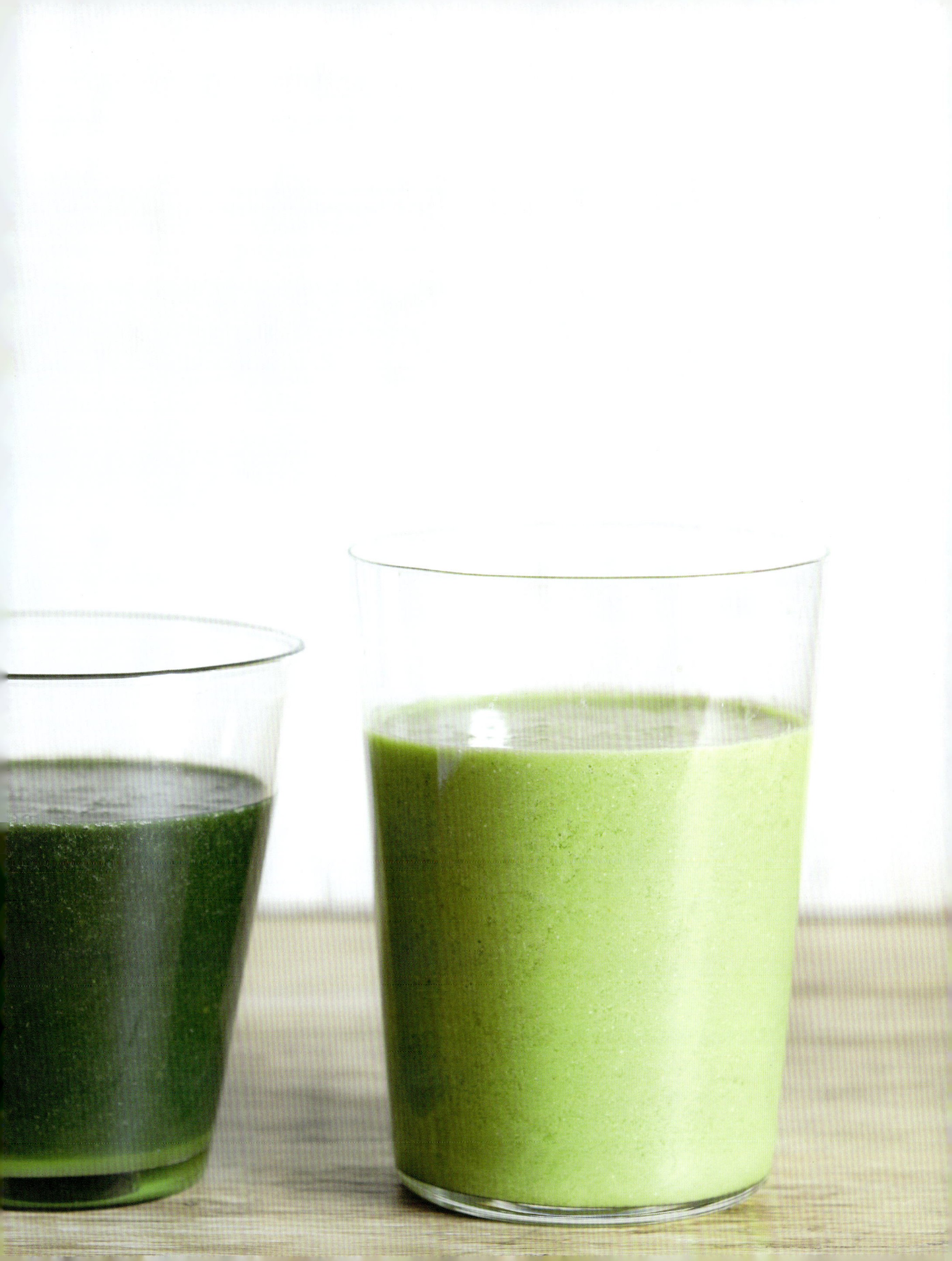

Rose, ginger, and star anise tea

This is one of my all time favorite teas; I love to make it when I am having some "down time." It's so comforting and calming to your body that it really allows you to rejuvenate.

makes 4 cups (1 litre)

5 rosebuds

2in (5cm) piece of ginger, sliced

2 star anise

4 cups (1 litre) boiling water

Put all the ingredients into a teapot and leave to infuse for 5 minutes. Enjoy as a calming and cleansing tea.

A cleansing and calming tea

The essential oils in lavender and camomile help you to relax and sleep, and they do the same in this tea. The fennel seeds provide the cleansing element and they help to reduce water retention. Some people find the taste of lavender a bit strong, so if you prefer, reduce the amount a little. This tea works all year round: drink it hot in the colder months and over ice when it starts to get warmer.

makes 4 cups (1 litre)

1 tbsp fennel seeds

1 tbsp lavender flowers

1 tbsp camomile flowers

4 cups (1 litre) boiling water

Put all the tea ingredients into a teapot and leave to infuse for 5 minutes. Drink this soporific tea before bed for a good night's sleep, or when you want to relax and unwind.

You can also put some of the lavender in your bath with magnesium flakes before bedtime. It will give you the best night's sleep of your life!

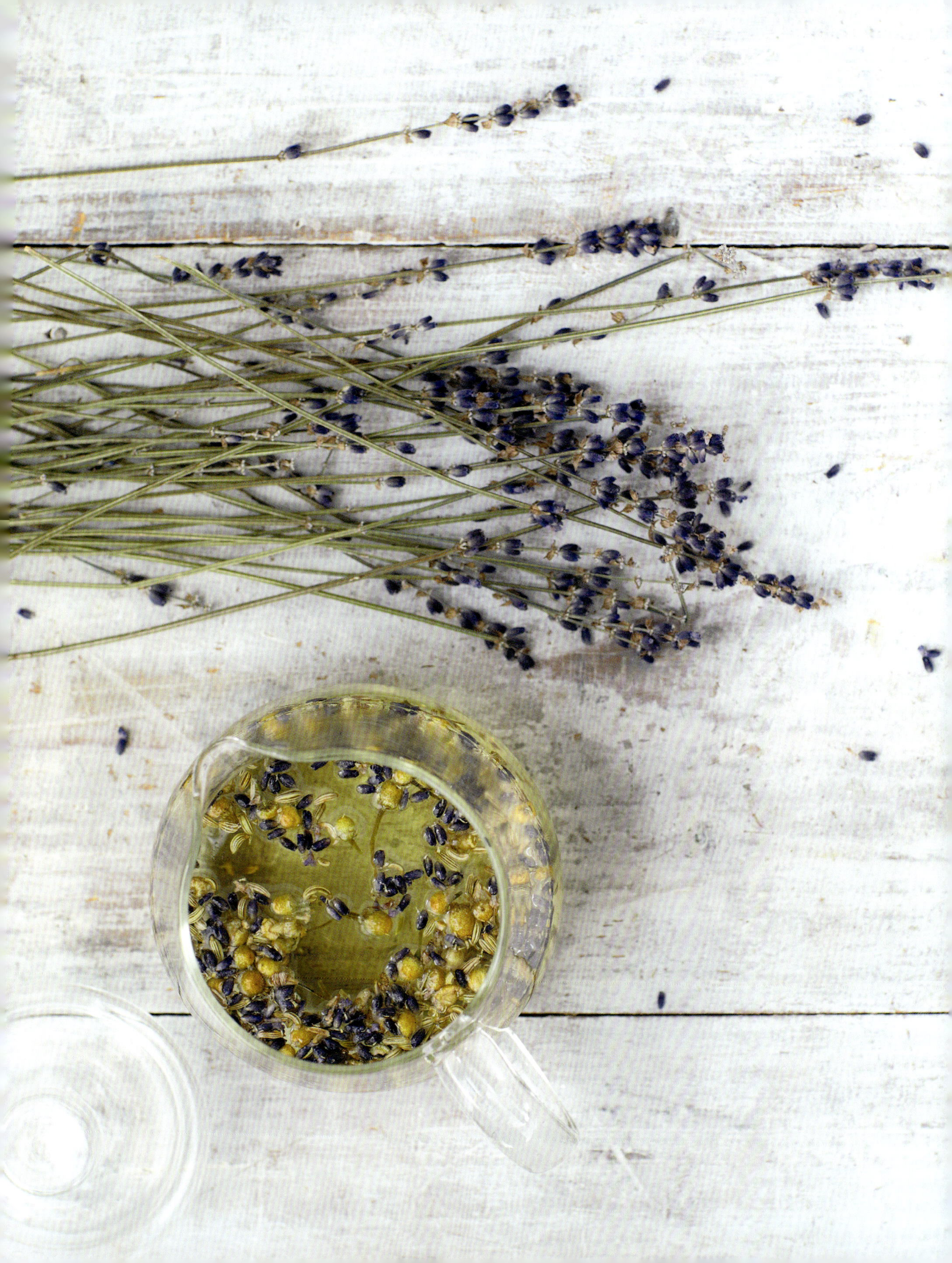

Cauliflower and pink peppercorn soup

I love nothing more than a velvety soup to warm me up and to feel like I am cleansing my body from the inside out. Here, I like to use the umeboshi paste for its natural saltiness and its alkalinity. I also love to add nutritional yeast to this soup to give it a deeper flavor, but that is optional. I always keep this in my larder as it has a delicious flavor and is so good for you. I buy the brand that has added vitamin B12, as it can be hard to get adequate amounts of this vitamin if you're following a vegetarian diet.

In a medium-sized pan, heat the coconut oil and sauté the sliced shallot and garlic for 2 minutes. Add the sumac, ground coriander, pink peppercorns, and oregano. Add the cold water, bring to the boil, then simmer for a further minute.

Add the leek and cauliflower pieces to the pan and be sure to stir well so all the flavors can mingle. Add the boiling water and leave to cook on a medium heat for about 10 minutes. You will know it's ready as the cauliflower will start to break up into much smaller pieces and will be soft to the point of a knife.

Add the umeboshi paste and stir well. Transfer the contents of the pan to a blender and whizz until very smooth. If you are going to add the nutritional yeast stir it into the soup once it's blended.

Serve the soup hot with a garnish of oregano and a sprinkle of sumac or a few pink peppercorns on top.

serves 2–3

1 tbsp coconut oil

1 shallot, sliced

1 clove garlic, sliced

2 tsp sumac, plus extra to garnish

¼ tsp ground coriander

10 pink peppercorns, plus extra to garnish

⅓ cup (5g) oregano leaves, plus extra to garnish

1 cup (250ml) cold water

1 leek, chopped into 1–2in (2.5–5cm) chunks

1 whole cauliflower, chopped into 1–2in (2.5–5cm) chunks

3⅓ cups (800ml) boiling water

½ tsp umeboshi paste

2 tbsp nutritional yeast (optional)

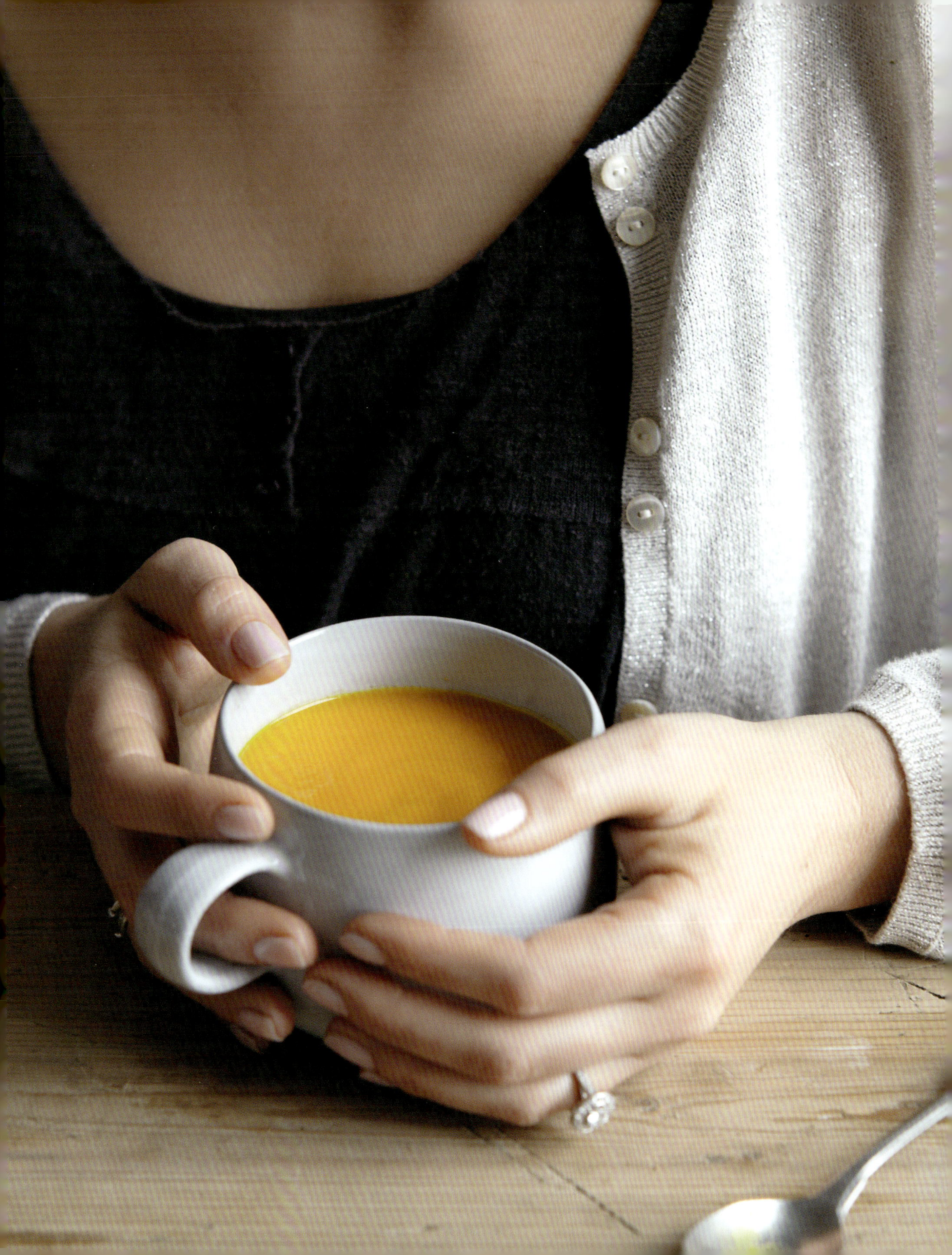

Carrot and lime soup

Carrots are a wonderful source of vitamin C and also naturally sweet and delicious. The turmeric is brilliant at boosting the immune system and can be antiviral. So all in all, this is probably one of the healthiest soups that will warm you up and keep you nourished.

In a medium-sized pan, heat the coconut oil and sauté the onion and garlic gently for 2–3 minutes until soft.

Add the carrots, celery, turmeric, lime zest, and ginger and continue to sauté for a further 2 minutes.

Dissolve the bouillon powder in the boiling water, stir well, and add to the pan. Simmer over medium heat until you can crush the carrot with the back of a spoon.

Transfer the contents of the pan to a high-speed blender and process until velvety smooth. Lastly, stir through the lime juice and serve.

serves 4

2 tbsp coconut oil

1 red onion, finely sliced

1 clove garlic, finely chopped

2¼lbs (1kg) carrots, cut into ¾in (2cm) cubes

2 sticks celery

1 tsp ground turmeric

finely grated zest and juice of 1 lime

1in (2.5cm) piece of ginger, finely grated

2 tbsp bouillon powder

5⅛ cups (1.2 litres) boiling water

Just before blending try adding a tablespoon of coconut oil for an extra creamy texture.

Broccoli, celery, and dill soup

I love to make soups, especially when I'm cleansing, as they fill you up with their delicious nutritious goodness. This soup is a perfect alkalizing meal in a bowl. I'm a big fan of dill, but if you're not, try using cilantro or parsley here instead.

In a medium-sized pan, heat 1 tablespoon of the coconut oil and sauté the garlic and scallion with the caraway seeds and ground coriander for 2½ minutes, then add ½ cup (100ml) of the boiling water.

Next, add the celery along with the zest and juice of the lime and leave to simmer for 7 minutes so that the liquid reduces.

Add another 1⅔ cups (400ml) of water and return to the boil. Drop in the broccoli and pour in the remaining water, add the spinach and let it wilt.

Transfer the contents of the pan to a blender. Add the avocado, dill, salt, and remaining coconut oil and blend until smooth.

Serve the soup hot with an extra garnish of dill if you like.

serves 2

2 tbsp coconut oil

1 clove garlic, crushed

1 scallion, chopped

¼ tsp caraway seeds

½ tsp ground coriander

3 cups (700ml) boiling water

3 sticks celery, chopped

finely grated zest and juice of ½ lime

1⅓ cups (100g) broccoli, broken into florets

3⅓ cups (100g) spinach leaves

¼ avocado

⅔ cup (6g) dill sprigs, plus extra to garnish

¼ tsp Himalayan pink salt

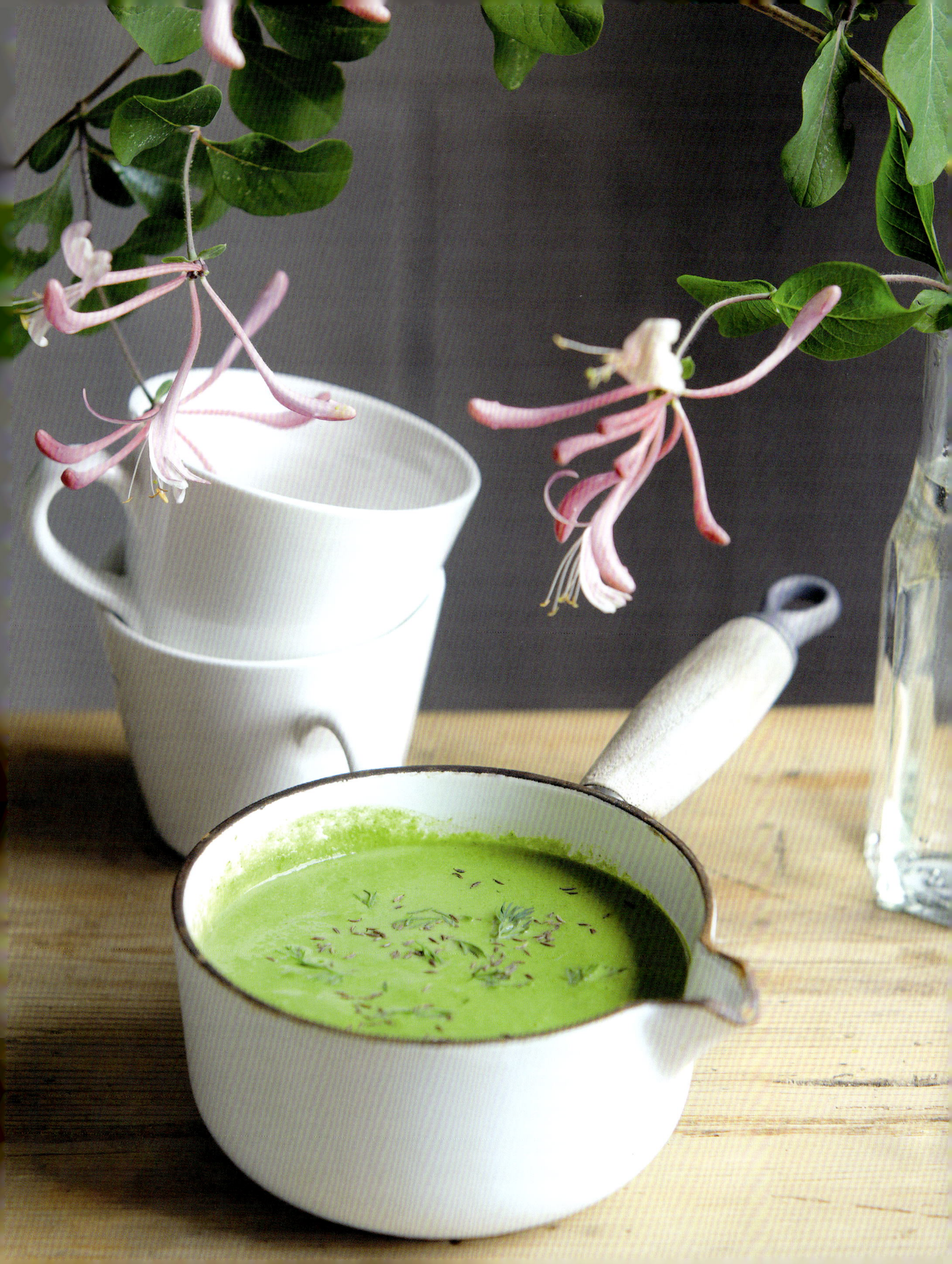

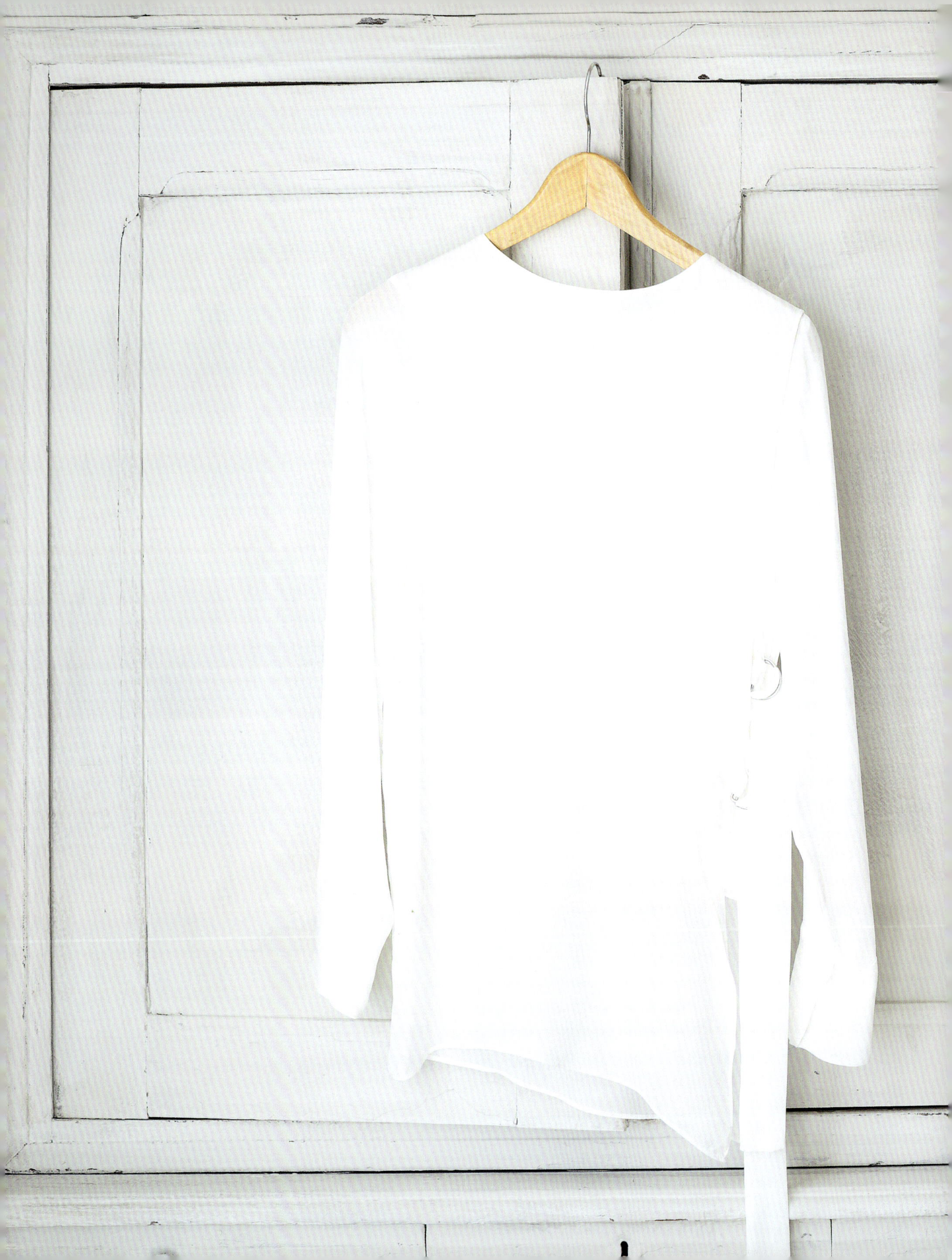

#slimdown

Helping you feel refreshingly light

6 days of wholesome soups, vibrant raw salads, and revitalizing smoothies.

This cleanse is a six-day gentle kick-start to lose any extra pounds before a party, holiday, or special event. I find that if I reduce the amount of grains and beans in my daily diet, the weight just drops off and I feel fantastic at the same time. As with any cleanse, if you're cutting down on certain foods, you still need to achieve a good nutritional balance, so be sure to include enough protein every day, especially if you are exercising. On this cleanse, some exercise is good, but don't overexert yourself, as you'll divert your body's attention from cleansing itself – body and mind – to fueling the activity. As always, listen to your body.

The food that you will be creating in the kitchen for this cleanse consists of delicious soups and smoothies, nourishing salads, life-changing tarts and baked goods, and even a "risotto"! Each recipe is packed full of nutritious ingredients so that you'll feel amazing throughout the cleanse.

Start each morning with either a smoothie or chia porridge, followed by a delicious salad for lunch, and heart-warming soup for dinner.

I think of this cleanse as one step up on from the #feelgood, as it includes some solid food for lunch. If you prefer, you could super-boost your body's cleansing by following the #feelgood cleanse for two or three days and then go straight into this six-day #slimdown – a wonderful way to ease yourself back into the normal pattern of eating, and to feel utterly fantastic.

You will need # plenty of rest # ingredients for the recipes # spiralizer # food processor or blender

What to expect ...

This cleanse is perfectly designed for you to carry on with your day-to-day life, as you'll have plenty of energy and be able to focus on life and work. If you have never done a cleanse before, eliminating sugar and caffeine can mean you might experience withdrawal symptoms such as headaches, and so starting your cleanse on a Saturday might help you ease into it over a relaxing weekend. By the time Monday comes, you'll be feeling vibrant, full of energy, and ready for the week ahead.

The #slimdown programme comprises six days of smoothies, juices, tea, and soups, as well as some delicious main meals for lunch – all designed to give your body optimal nourishment while allowing it to a rest from digesting grains, and helping to draw out the toxins naturally.

Stay away from:

caffeine   # sugar

alcohol   # wheat and gluten

dairy products   # processed foods

meat

All of the above are extremely acid-forming in the body (and not alkalizing, which is what this cleanse is all about). To rebalance your body towards a more alkaline state you need to cut these items out of your diet.

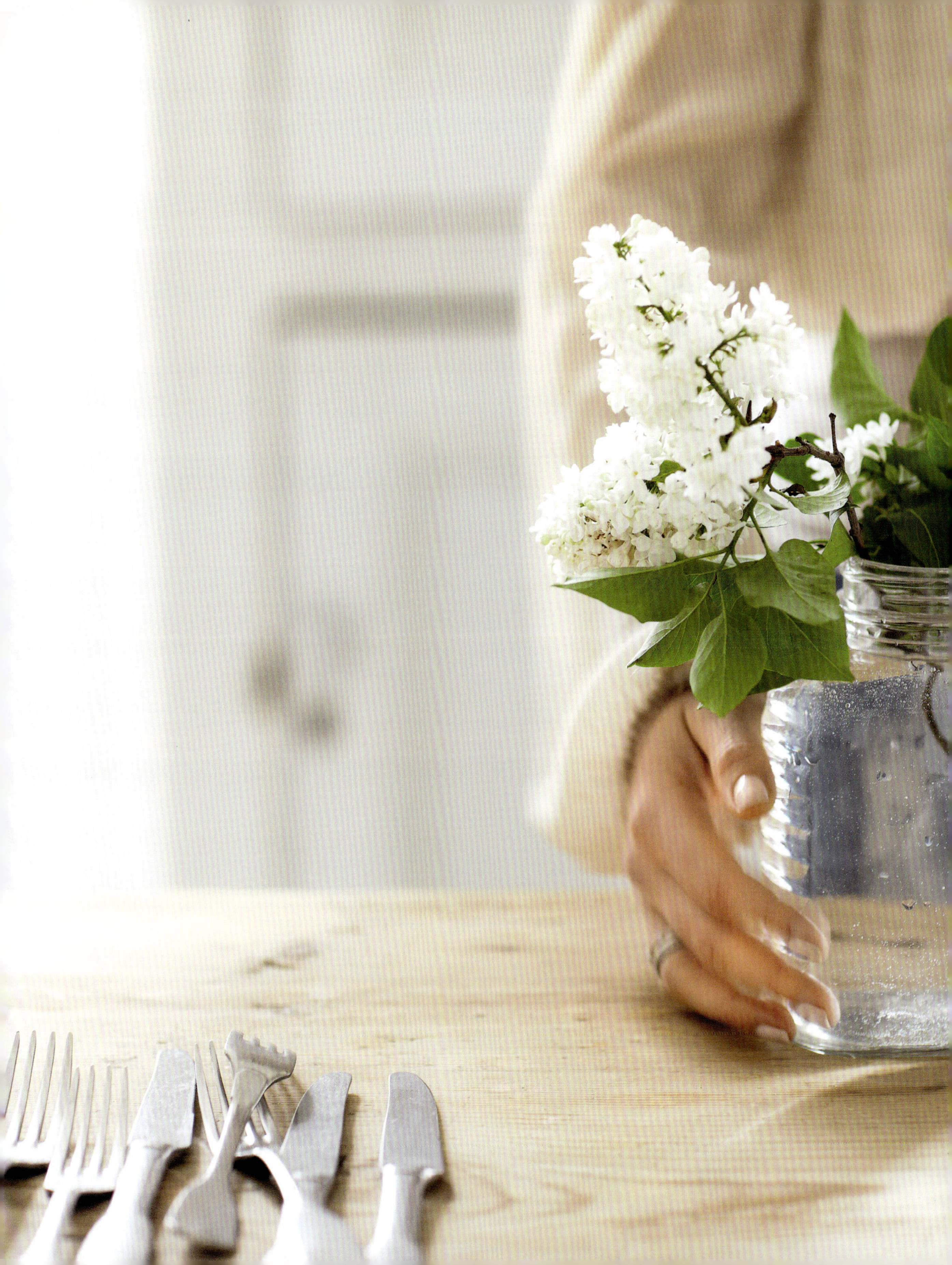

As I said in the introduction to the book, none of these cleanses are meant to make you feel hungry – each is designed to nourish your body, so make sure you are getting enough food. Remember, your portion size should fill your two hands cupped together.

From past experience I have found that when starting a cleanse like this I can get myself into a state of panic thinking that this cleanse is going to solve all my problems, and I'll be my perfect image by the end of it. Putting that much pressure on anything will only set you up for failure – it's a recipe for disaster! When entering any sort of cleanse it's so important to be kind to yourself. If you are not used to eating like this, then it will most likely be a challenge at the beginning, but try to look at it like a

#slimdown menu planner

Start your day with a smoothie, have a main meal for lunch, and soup for dinner. In between you can have a juice or smoothie, if you find yourself getting hungry, and have your delicious cleansing teas before bed.

Day 1

AM	Chlorophyll smoothie (page 31)
Lunch	Raw green sea salad (page 60)
Bites	Green starter juice (page 30) / A cleansing and calming tea (page 36) / Beet chips (page 148)
Dinner	Pumpkin soup (page 68)

Day 2

AM	Beet and blueberry smoothie (page 56)
Lunch	Carrot "noodles" with avocado dressing (page 72)
Bites	Maca almond milkshake (page 92) / Rose, ginger, and star anise tea (page 36)
Dinner	Broccoli, celery, and dill soup (page 42)

Day 3

AM	Carrot and turmeric smoothie (page 31)
Lunch	Pea, fava bean, and pine nut salad (page 220)
Bites	Edamame and avocado temaki (page 145) / Energizing tea (page 58)
Dinner	Cauliflower and pink peppercorn soup (page 38)

game. Just get through each day and congratulate yourself on getting that far, then take the next step which is the next day.

If you break the cleanse, just make sure you get back on it for the next meal you have. Don't panic!!! These things can take time to accomplish – trust me, it took me about fifteen years to get to a point where I am level-headed with my approach to food. Never give up, because when you find that one cleanse that inspires you to be healthy all the time, and helps you to accept yourself for who you are, it will change your outlook on food forever, and I hope that the alkaline way is your inspiration, as it was for me.

Day 4	AM	Avocado smoothie (page 57)
	Lunch	Cucumber and tempeh salad (page 65)
	Bites	Red juice (page 30) / Broccoli pesto with crudité (page 142) / Energizing tea (page 58)
	Dinner	Carrot and lime soup (page 41)

Day 5	AM	Acai smoothie (page 50)
	Lunch	Arame broccoli salad on a bed of celery "noodles" (page 121)
	Bites	Chia green smoothie (page 33) / Red raw crackers (page 32) / Rose, ginger, and star anise tea (page 36)
	Dinner	Chunky root soup (without the millet) (page 71)

Day 6	AM	Rooibos and blueberry chia porridge (page 52)
	Lunch	Lime sprouted salad (page 74)
	Bites	Green starter juice (page 30) / Rose, ginger, and star anise tea (page 36) / Ginger-tamari-dressed edamame (page 224)
	Dinner	Pumpkin soup (page 68)

#morning time

Acai smoothie

I first fell in love with acai, a South American superfood, while traveling around Brazil, where I had the most amazing smoothies made from freshly frozen pulp. Well, this smoothie is the next best thing! Throw in a few ice cubes and you will get a deliciously cold smoothie that will freshen up your day to no end and nourish your body with its supply of antioxidants and immune-boosters.

Put all the ingredients into a high-speed blender and blend until completely smooth. Serve either in a bowl or in a glass, with a garnish of bee pollen or raw cacao nibs for extra crunch. The smoothie is best drunk right away, but you can always put it in a jar and bring it with you to drink as soon as you can during the day.

serves 2

1 small banana (⅔ cup sliced/about 100g)

¾ cup chopped (100g) cucumber, peeled

3 tbsp acai powder

½ cup chopped (80g) mango

1 cup (200ml) water

bee pollen or raw cacao nibs, to garnish (optional)

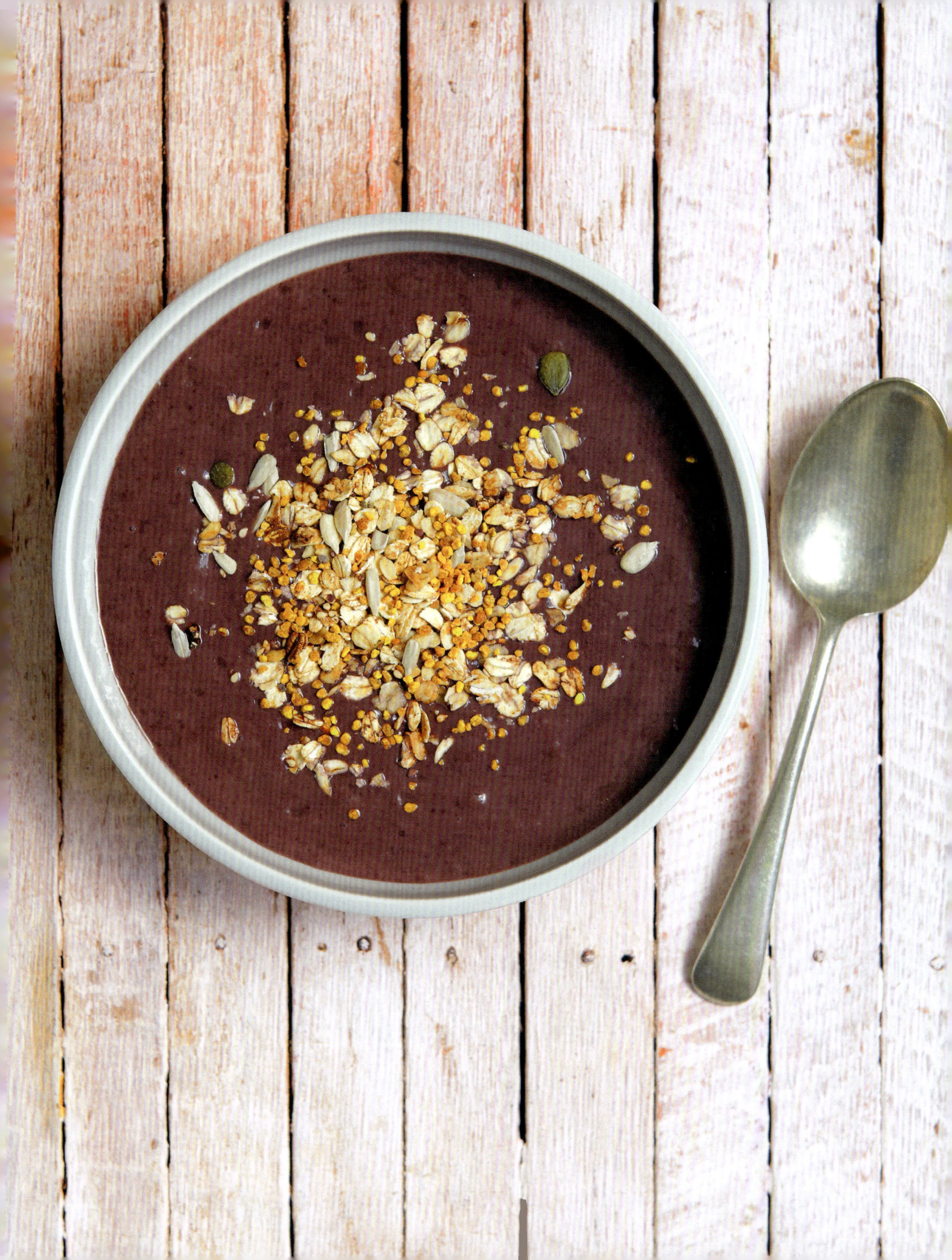

Rooibos and blueberry chia porridge

I like to think of this as a gentle twist on the usual chia porridge made with dairy-free milk. Chia seeds are gathering such great press as a fashionable superfood, but they really do live up to their reputation, with their great omega-3 levels, fiber content and cholesterol-lowering properties. This grain-free breakfast will keep your energy levels up and your blood sugar levels balanced. I think the best thing about this porridge is the blueberries – they just burst in your mouth! Delicious.

Soak the chia seeds in the measured water and give them a good stir, so they don't stick or get hard, then leave to soak for 20 minutes.

Make the rooibos tea and allow to infuse for 10 minutes until it's strong. Remove the teabag and discard.

In a pan, put the blueberries, maca, cinnamon, and half of the rooibos tea. Cook on medium heat for 3 minutes until the water is nearly absorbed and the blueberries are softened – the liquid will become a dark purple color.

Strain the mixture, reserving the blueberries in a sieve and returning the strained liquid to the pan. Add the remaining tea and the soaked chia seeds. Stir well and let the mixture bubble over medium–low heat for 4 minutes until the chia seeds start to grow in size and the sauce thickens.

Pour the porridge into 2 bowls and serve with the strained blueberries and a scattering of pumpkin seeds on top. Alternatively, keep the second portion to eat cold the next day.

serves 2

2½ tbsp (25g) chia seeds

⅛ cup (50ml) water, for soaking

¾ cup (120g) blueberries

½ tbsp maca powder

¼ tsp ground cinnamon

⅛ cup (20g) pumpkin seeds, for garnish

for the tea:

1 rooibos teabag

¾ cup (200ml) boiling water

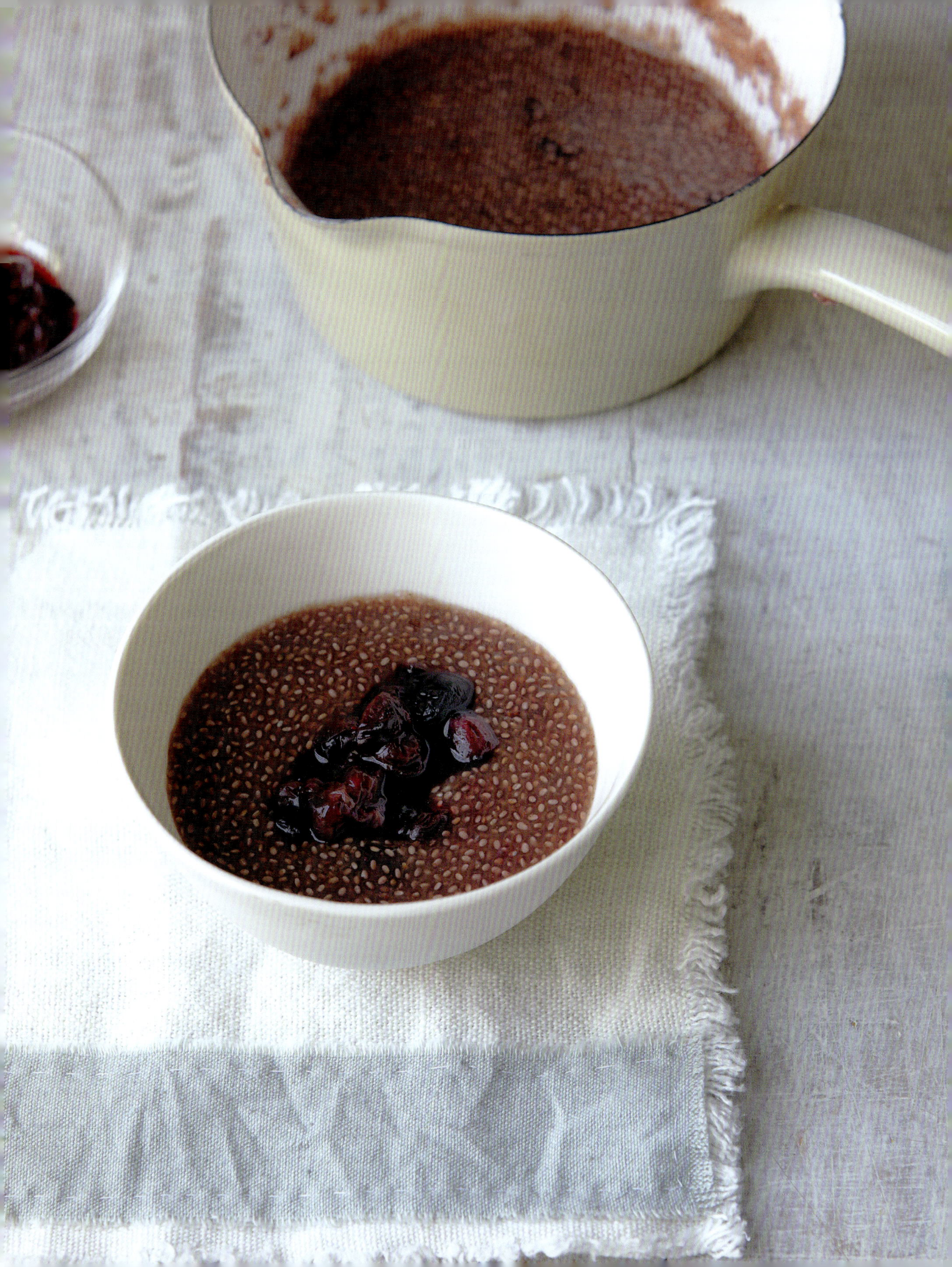

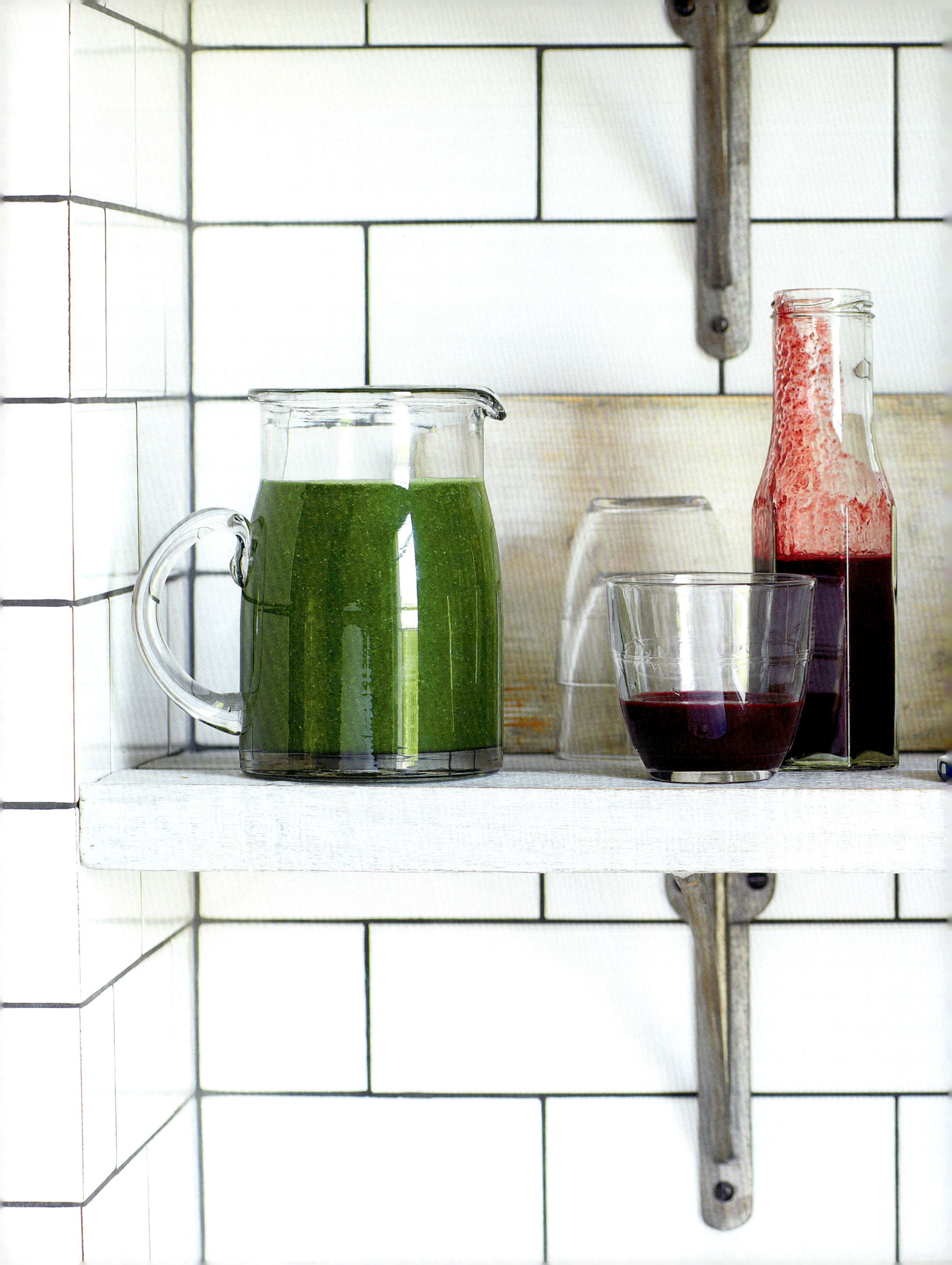

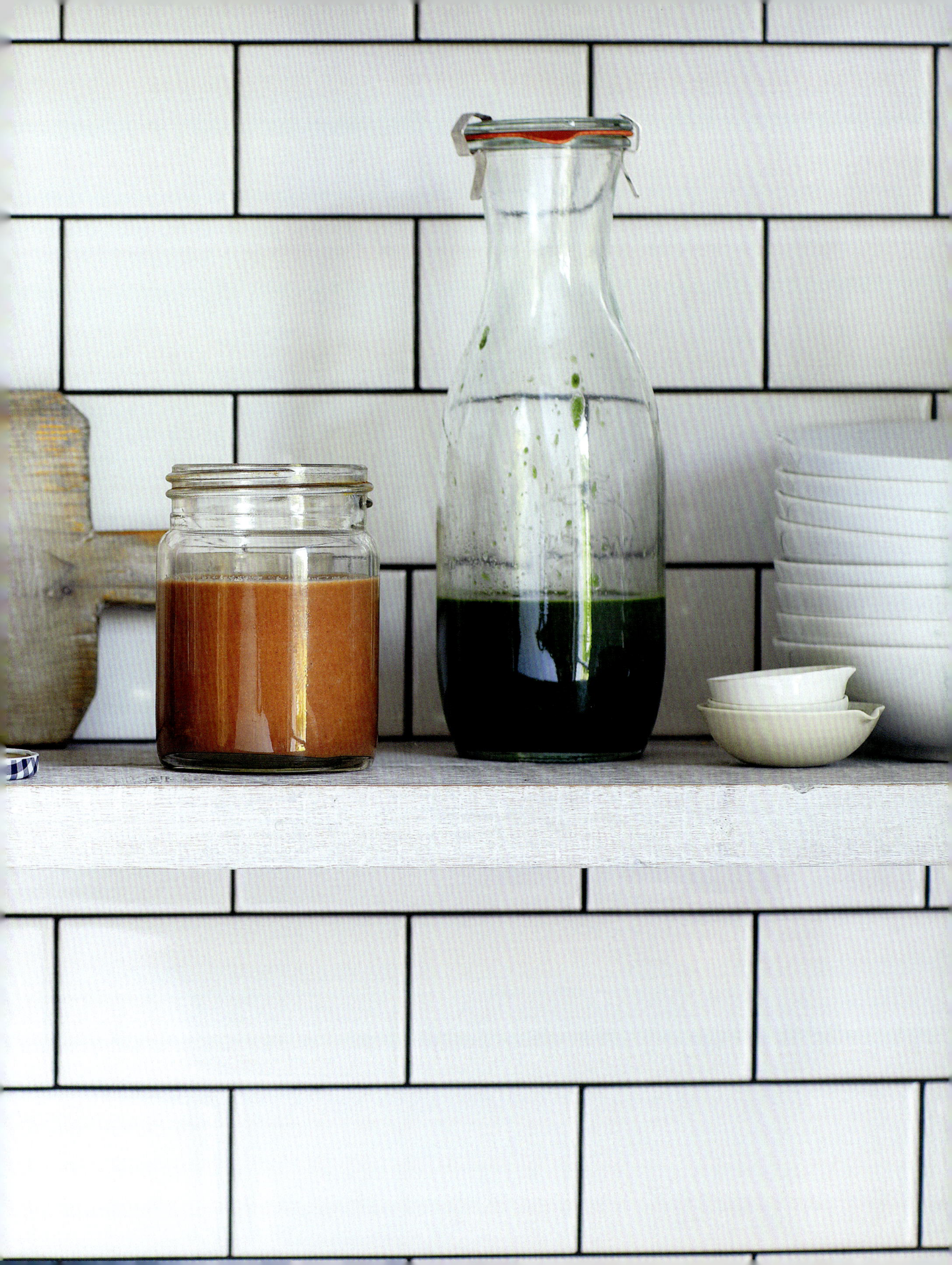

Kale and oat smoothie

This is an energy-creating smoothie – the oats are fantastic for releasing energy slowly and so this smoothie will keep you full until lunch.

serves 1 as a breakfast, 2 as a bite, or 1 as an accompaniment to a solid breakfast

1 cup cubed (150g) pear, cored

⅔ cup chopped (45g) kale

¾ cup chopped (115g) cucumber

½ cup (40g) gluten-free oats

2 cups (480ml) coconut water

1 tsp spirulina powder

Put all the ingredients into a blender and blend until completely smooth. The smoothie tastes best when you drink it right away, but you can always put it in a jar and take it with you to drink as soon as you can during the day.

Photo on previous page (left-right): Kale and oat smoothie, Beet and blueberry smoothie, Cacao, cinnamon, pear, and fennel smoothie, Avocado smoothie

Beet and blueberry smoothie

Eating raw vegetables on a daily basis is essential for your health and wellbeing, especially when you are cleansing. This gorgeous-colored smoothie is earthy and sweet at the same time. If kale is out of season, you can use spinach instead; and why not experiment with blueberries or raspberries instead of blackberries?

serves 1

¾ cup (180ml) fresh beet juice

¼ cup (30g) frozen blueberries

¼ cup chopped (15g) kale

¼ cup sliced (30g) banana

Simply put all the ingredients into a blender and blend until completely smooth. The smoothie tastes best when you drink it right away, but you can always put it in a jar and take it with you to drink as soon as you can during the day.

Cacao, cinnamon, pear, and fennel smoothie

Two of my favorite ingredients to put together are pear and fennel. And if you tried the pear and fennel soup in my first book, you'll already be converts. Here I thought I'd add just a touch of chocolate to concoct a supremely heavenly combination.

serves 1

1 cup cubed (170g) pear, cored

½ cup sliced (50g) fennel

1 tbsp raw cacao powder

1 cup (240ml) almond or rice milk

¼ tsp ground cinnamon

Simply put all the ingredients into a blender and blend until completely smooth. The smoothie tastes best when you drink it right away, but you can always put it in a jar and take it with you to drink as soon as you can during the day.

Avocado smoothie

Avocado is one of my go-to ingredients. It's an incredibly rich source of vitamin E, which gives your skin an amazing glow and keeps those wrinkles at bay. When blended in a smoothie, avocado also gives it a delicious creamy texture – so if you are looking for a substitute for a banana, then look no more.

serves 1

⅓ cup sliced (50g) mango

¼ cup chopped (30g) celery

¼ cup chopped (30g) cucumber

½ cup (15g) spinach

⅛ cup (2g) mint leaves, lightly packed

¼ avocado

juice of ½ lemon

½ cup (115ml) water

juice of 1 orange

1 tsp spirulina

Simply put all the ingredients into a blender and blend until completely smooth. The smoothie tastes best when you drink it right away, but you can always put it in a jar and take it with you to drink as soon as you can during the day.

Energizing tea

If you're feeling in need of a pick-me-up, try a cup of this energizing tea. Yerba mate is amazing for giving you energy and kick-starting your metabolism, so it can aid weight loss, too. This tea will definitely get you going; just make sure you don't drink it after 4pm or you might not be able to sleep that night!

Put all the tea ingredients into a teapot and leave to infuse for 5 minutes. Drink this energizing tea after a workout or first thing in the morning, if you're feeling lethargic. As with other teas, you can drink this hot, or cold over ice – the choice is yours.

makes 4 cups (1 litre)

1 tsp yerba mate powder (if unavailable, use matcha powder instead)

1 tbsp mint tea mixture, from a teabag

¾in (2cm) piece of ginger, sliced

4 cups (1 litre) boiling water

Always try to use water no hotter than 176°F/80°C when making green or yerba mate-based tea.This helps to retain vital anti-oxidants and nutrients as well as avoiding a bitter taste.

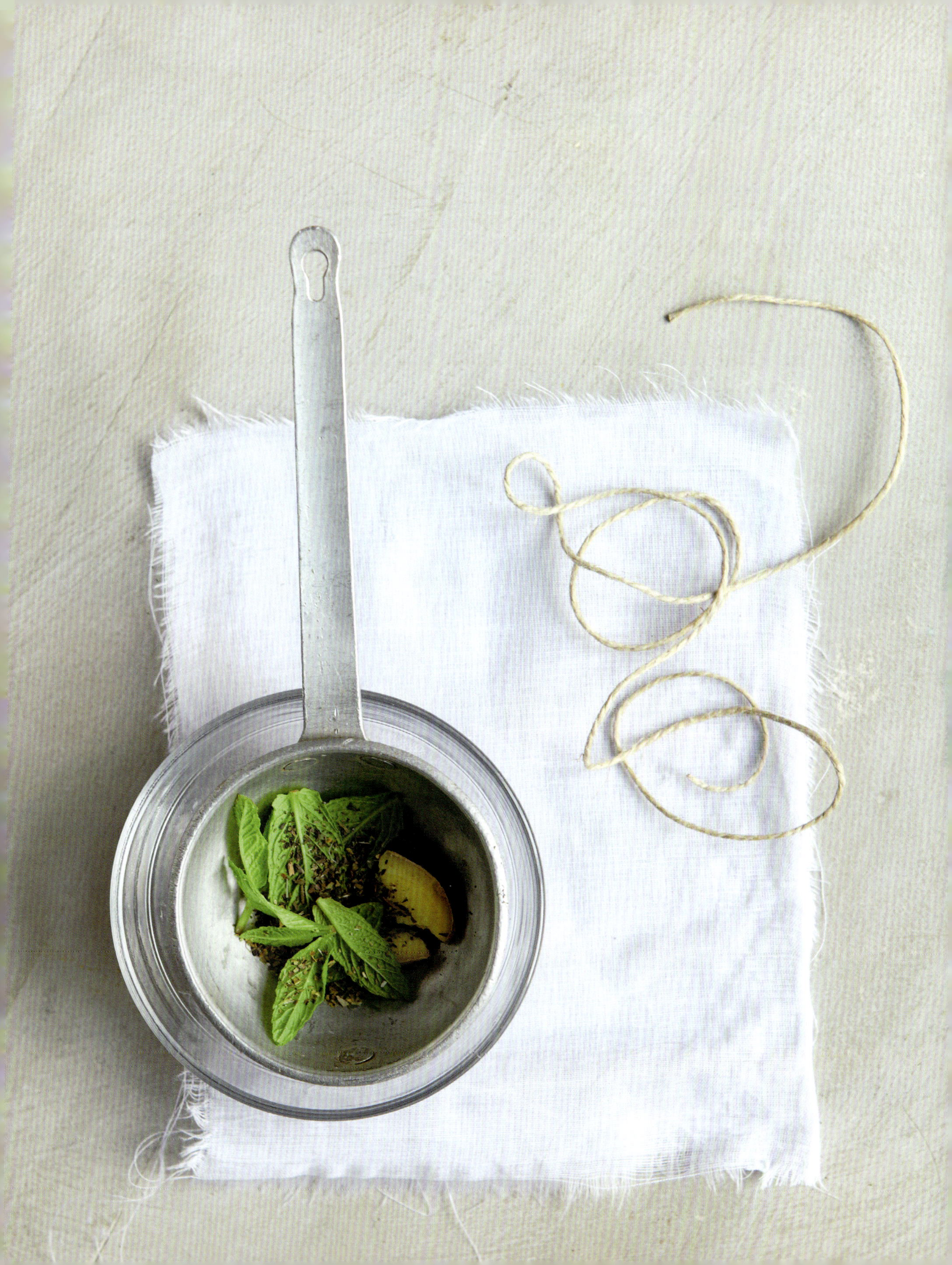

#meals

Raw green sea salad

One of the most important things that I encourage people to do is to have an abundance of color on every plate you eat. This rainbow of a dish is low in carbs and high in magnesium (from the beet), helping to detox the liver. Here I like to use hatcho miso, which is is grain-free and takes at least two years to ferment, so it has a medicinal and deeply robust flavor. Fermented foods are important in healing the gut.

Put the wakame in a bowl, cover with boiling water, and set aside to expand.

Put the kale in a large bowl, squeeze the lemon juice over it and massage the leaves until they start to "cook" and wilt.

Drain the wakame, then slice off and discard the "stalks."

On a plate, make a bed of the seaweed and kale, then place the remaining vegetables over the top.

Make the dressing by mixing all the ingredients together in a glass until fully incorporated. Then drizzle over the salad and finish off with a sprinkling of lemon zest.

serves 1

1 cup (20g) wakame seaweed

½ cup chopped (30g) kale

finely grated zest and juice of 1 lemon

1⅛ cups (70g) sugar snap peas, sliced diagonally

½ of a 2in diameter (20g) raw candy-striped beet or regular beet very finely sliced (I use a mandoline)

1 cup (70g) broccoli florets

for the dressing:

1 rounded tbsp (20g) hatcho miso

2 tbsp hot water

1 tsp rice vinegar

1 tsp pumpkin oil

Cauliflower and coconut tart

I made this dish for a dinner party and I have to say it was a huge hit with my guests. The crust itself turned out a bit like bread, so one slice is really filling. If you don't have coconut cream, you could use a dairy-free milk alternative instead.

Preheat the oven to 325°F/170°C/gas mark 3, and line a 9in tart pan with parchment paper.

First make the pastry. Put the cauliflower florets in a food processor or blender, and blend until they look a bit like rice. Alternatively, chop them by hand as finely as possible. Transfer to a bowl and add the ground almonds, nutmeg, lemon zest, salt, and the egg. Mix together until a dough forms.

Press this mixture into the prepared tart pan, pressing it up the sides, too, then bake in a preheated oven for 15 minutes.

Meanwhile, massage the kale with the lemon juice until it wilts. Set aside.

To make the filling, beat together the eggs, coconut cream and salt until smooth and evenly mixed.

Once the pastry is out of the oven, arrange a layer of the kale in the bottom. Cover with the zucchini ribbons, then pour the egg and coconut mixture on top.

Return to the oven for 20 minutes until it is cooked through.

serves 8

2 eggs

⅔ cup (160ml) coconut cream

¼ tsp Himalayan pink salt

½ cup chopped (30g) kale

juice of ½ lemon

½ zucchini, sliced into ribbons

for the pastry:

3 cups (300g) cauliflower, broken into florets

¾ cup (75g) ground almonds

3 good gratings of nutmeg

finely grated zest of ½ lemon

a pinch of Himalayan pink salt

1 egg

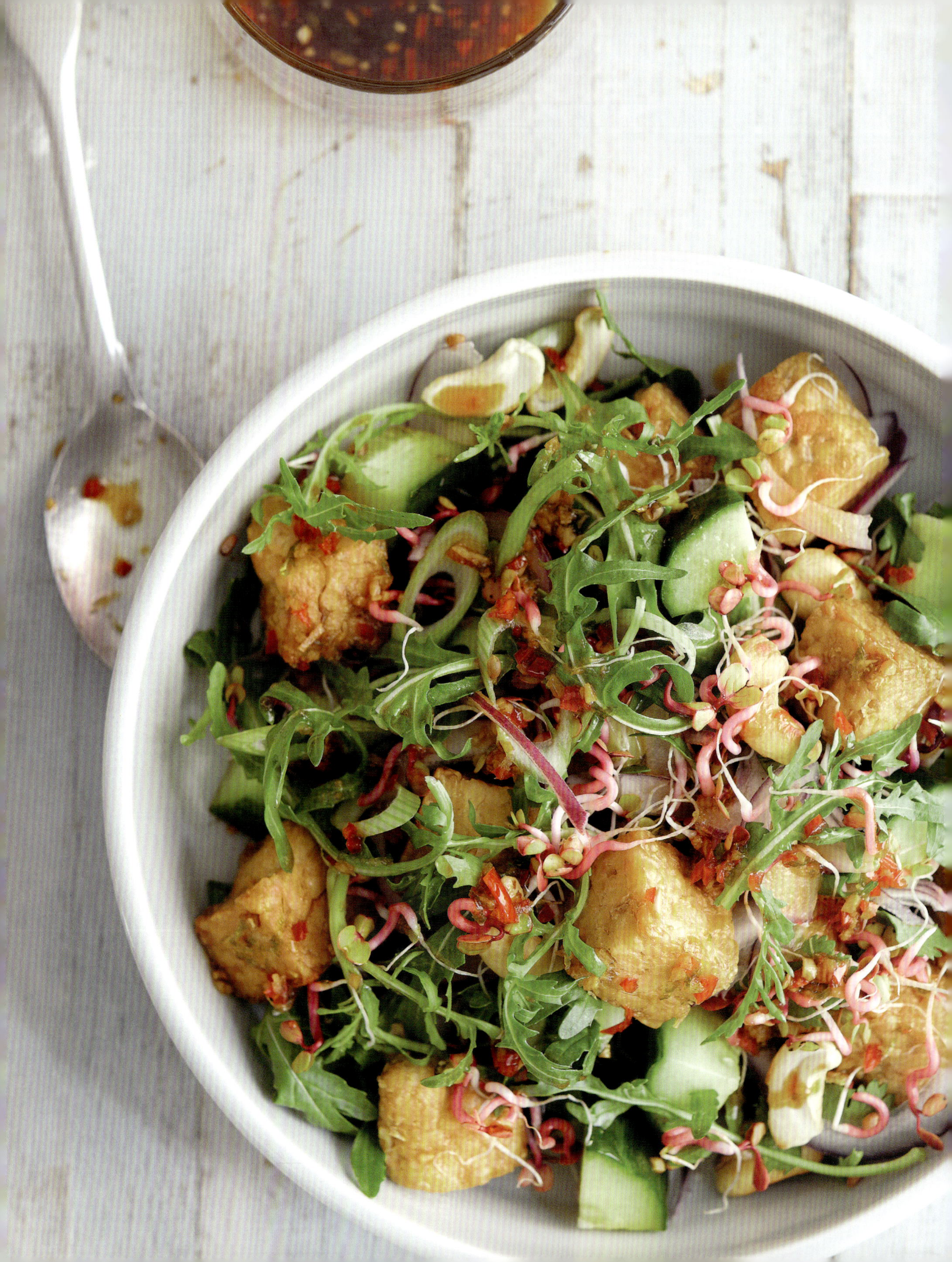

Cucumber and tempeh salad

This nutritious dish is one of my favorite Asian-flavored salads. If you can get your hands on some mizuna leaves, you can use them in place of the arugula for a super-summery taste. As tempeh is a great source of protein, you can add a handful to any salad for a fantastic post-workout protein kick.

First make the dressing. Put all the ingredients for the dressing, except for the lime juice and zest, in a saucepan and heat very gently for 3–4 minutes. Remove from the heat and set aside to allow the flavors to infuse.

Dry-toast the cashews then transfer them to a bowl, along with the cucumber, sprouts, arugula, onion, scallions, and cilantro.

Return the frying pan to the heat and cook the tempeh cubes in the sunflower oil until golden brown on all sides.

Add the tempeh to the bowl of salad and then add the lime juice and zest to the dressing in the saucepan.

Toss the salad together, transfer to a platter, and then drizzle over the dressing.

serves 3–4

½ cup (75g) cashews

1 cup (150g) cucumber, cut into ¾in (2cm) cubes

1 large handful sprouts

2 large handfuls arugula

¼ red onion, finely sliced

2 scallions, finely sliced at an angle

2 tbsp chopped cilantro

1 cup (150g) tempeh, cut into ¾in (2cm) cubes

1 tsp sunflower oil

for the dressing:

⅛ cup (30ml) rice vinegar

a pinch of Himalayan pink salt

1 tsp agave nectar

1 tsp toasted sesame oil

1 clove garlic, finely chopped

¼ large red chili pepper, finely chopped

1 tsp tamari

juice of 1 lime and finely grated zest of ½

Spinach pesto with raw noodles

Once you've had this gorgeous greenness, you'll find you want to eat it often; use it as the base of any meal or just eat on its own. I like to add a piece of chifu (see page 129) on top or sprinkle it with some Tamari-toasted seeds (see page 78). I love this dish on a Sunday night, if I've had an indulgent weekend, as it's quick to make and I know that by Monday morning my body will feel totally cleansed and ready for the week ahead.

Boil a kettle and pour the water over the spinach in a sieve. Squeeze out the water once it has cooled enough to touch. Transfer to a blender along with the cilantro, salt, and olive oil. Blitz into a paste.

Mix through the zucchini "noodles" and serve right away.

serves 2

6⅔ cups (200g) spinach

2 cups (30g) cilantro

a generous pinch of Himalayan pink salt

4 tbsp olive oil

2 zucchini, spiralized

I use a spiralizer here as it makes fantastic long noodles out of vegetables like zucchini and carrots. If you don't have one, you could use a peeler to make long strips and then slice these into noodles. If you feel like a warm dish, you could also lightly sauté the noodles before serving.

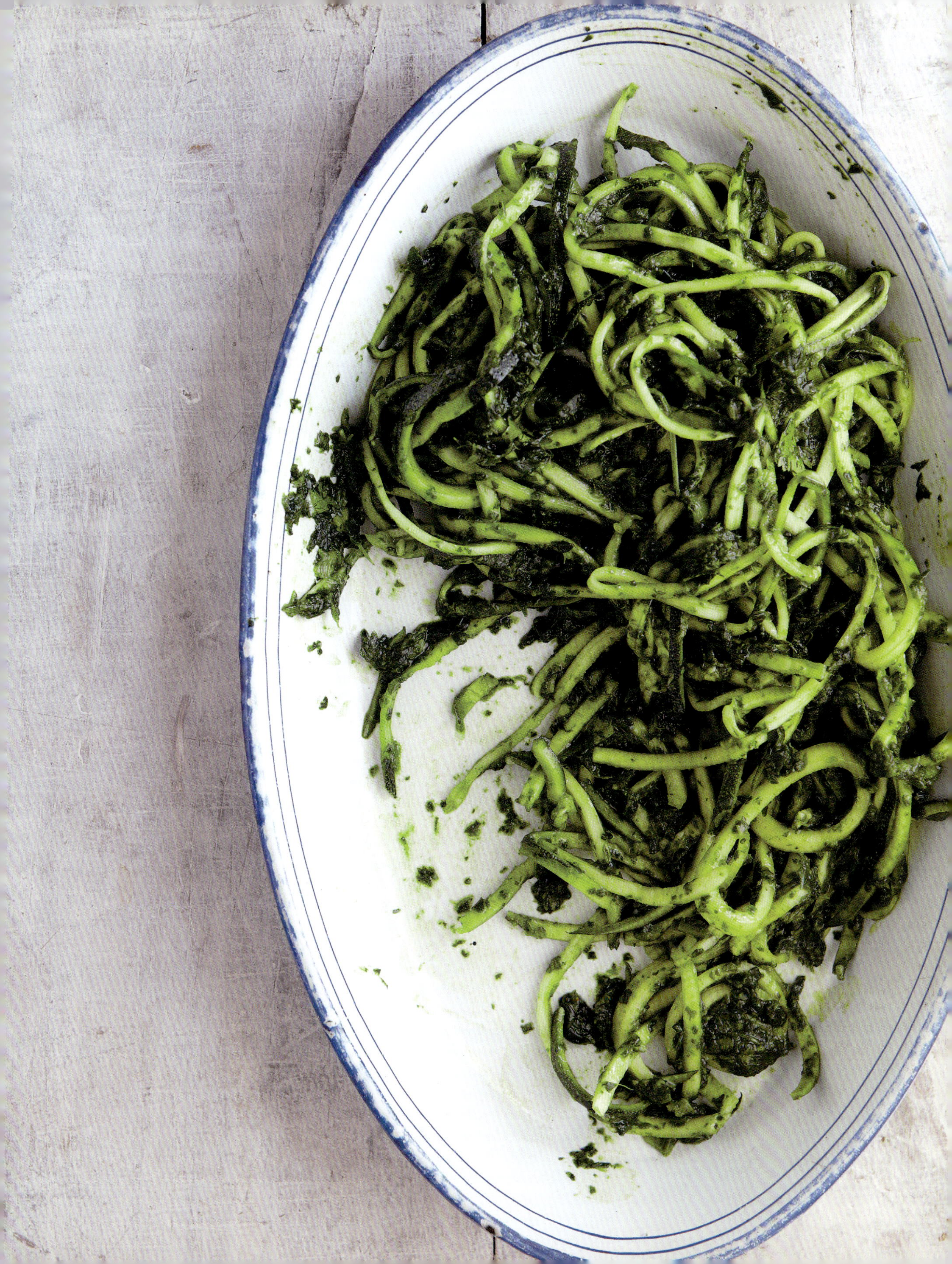

Pumpkin soup

Soup fills me with joy – it's not only easy to make, but it's packed with nutrients too, so every delicious mouthful does you good. This pumpkin soup is very alkaline and the ingredients are inexpensive, too! If pumpkins are out of season, use butternut squash instead – I find it works just as well.

Heat the coconut oil in a large saucepan and sauté the onion, garlic, and ginger. Simmer over medium heat for 1 minute. Once the oil starts to be absorbed add 4 tablespoons of the water along with the coriander seeds and continue to cook for another minute.

Add the remaining water, the pumpkin, and salt. Simmer over medium heat for 20 minutes.

Meanwhile, combine all the ingredients for the tahini swirl in a bowl.

Transfer the contents of the saucepan to a blender, process until very smooth and split between 2 bowls. Lastly, swirl a spoonful of the tahini mixture over the top. Sprinkle with a few coriander seeds and serve immediately.

serves 2

2 tbsp coconut oil

½ red onion, sliced

1 clove garlic, sliced

⅛ cup (10g) ginger, sliced

2⅛ cups (500ml) water

½ tsp coriander seeds, plus extra to garnish

4 cups (450g) pumpkin, chopped into 1–2in (2.5–5cm) cubes

⅛ tsp Himalayan pink salt

for the tahini swirl:

1 tbsp tahini

a generous pinch of ground cumin

juice of ¼ lemon

1½ tbsp water

a pinch of Himalayan pink salt

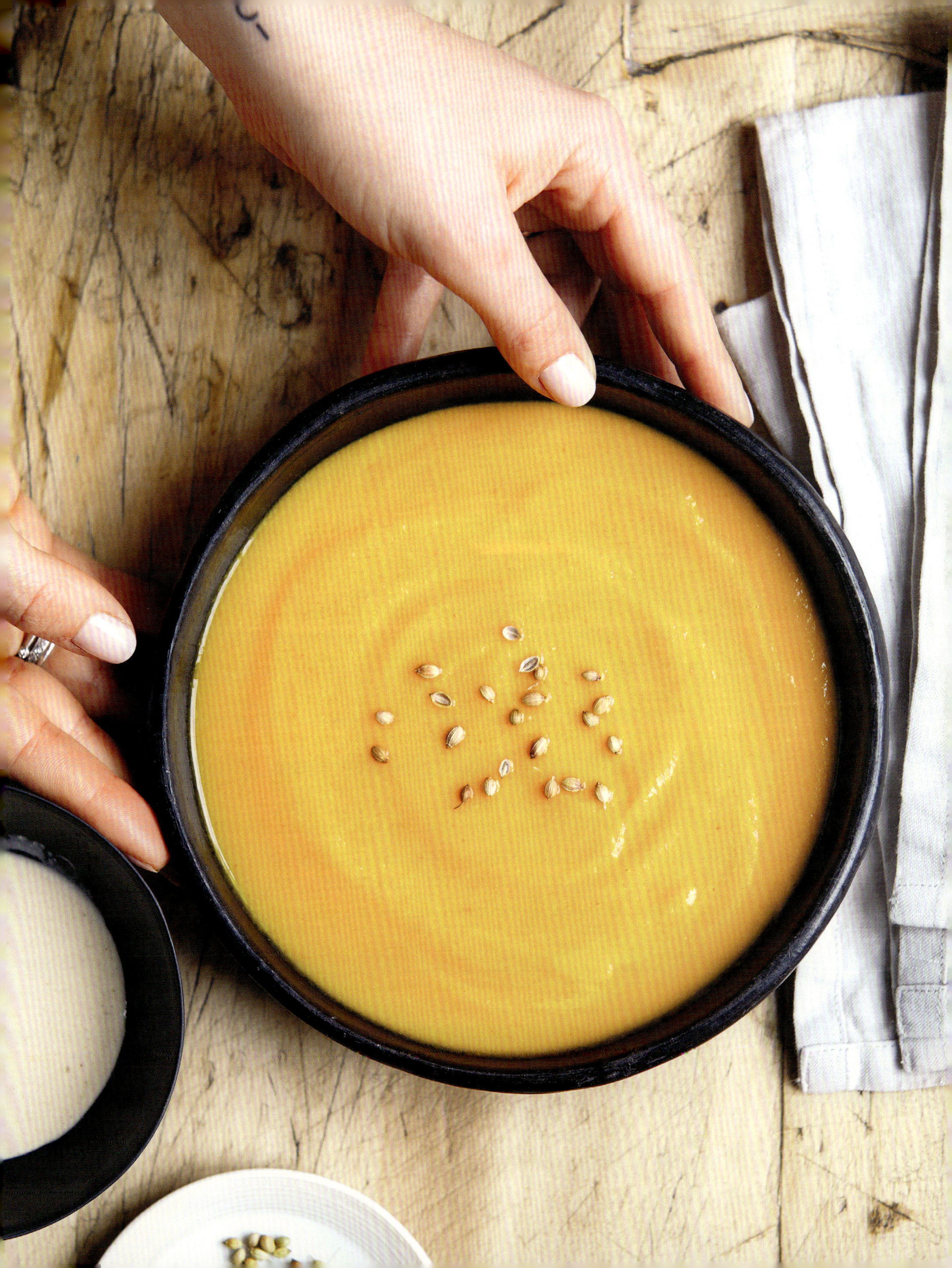

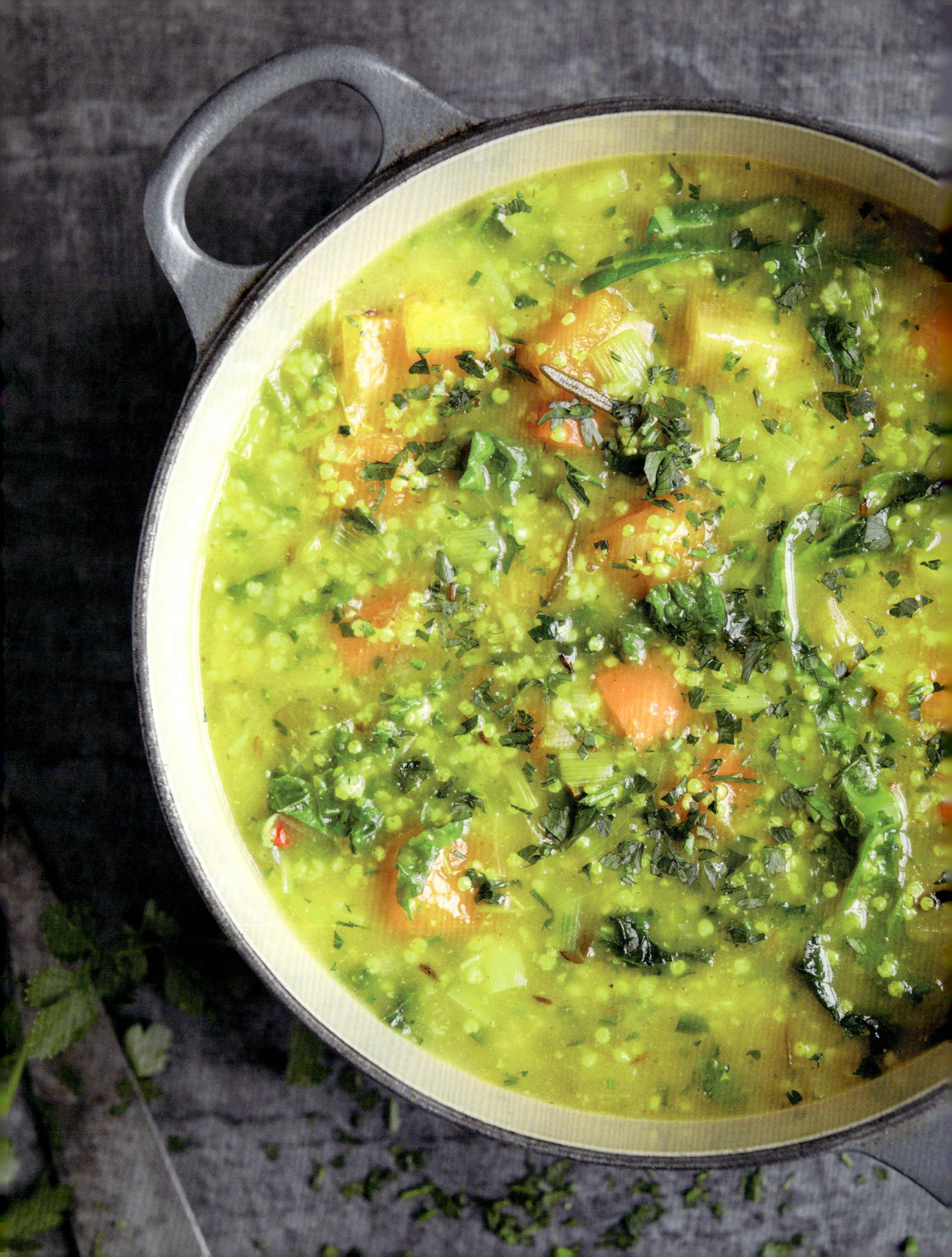

Chunky root soup with millet

This hearty and warming soup can be made with or without the millet. Skip the millet if you're on the #slimdown cleanse (except if you've exercised that day) and double the quantity of butternut squash, carrot, and beet. On the other hand, include the millet if you're on the #lifechanging plan. I steer clear of lots of grains, but love millet, because it doesn't make you feel bloated like some other grains do.

In a deep, medium-sized pan, heat the coconut oil and sauté the shallot and garlic for 1–2 minutes, until they start to soften. Add the leek along with the cumin, coriander, and turmeric and sauté for another minute. Stir in 2 tablespoons of water to add some moisture.

Next, add the millet, stir the spices through the grains and cook for another 30 seconds to help bring out its nutty flavour. Pour in 2¼ cups (500ml) of the water, along with the bouillon powder, lemongrass, and rosemary and cook for 4 minutes.

After 4 minutes cooking time, add the carrot and beets along with the 2¼ cups (500ml) water. Put the lid on and simmer for 10 minutes.

Remove the lid and add the butternut squash, rutabaga, umeboshi paste and the chili pepper, along with the remaining 1 cup (200ml) of water and simmer for a further 5 minutes.

Take the pan off the heat and stir in the kale and parsley.

Serve in bowls with some grated pecorino cheese and a large spoonful of yogurt, if you like.

serves 2–3

1 tbsp coconut oil

1 shallot, chopped

1 clove garlic, chopped

1 leek, thickly sliced

½ tsp cumin seeds

1½ tsp ground coriander

¼ tsp ground turmeric

½ cup (110g) hulled millet

5¼ cups (1.25 litres) water

1 tsp bouillon powder

½ lemongrass stalk, bashed with a rolling pin

1 sprig rosemary

1 carrot, cubed

2 × 2in diameter (160g) golden beets, cubed

1¼ cups (180g) butternut squash, cubed

1⅛ cups (150g) rutabaga, cubed

1 tsp umeboshi paste

1in (2.5cm) piece of red or green chili pepper

1 cup (60g) kale, finely chopped

½ cup (25g) flat leaf parsley, finely chopped

coconut milk yogurt or sheep's milk yogurt, to serve (optional)

pecorino cheese, grated, to serve (optional)

Carrot "noodles" with avocado dressing

This wonderfully cleansing dish is incredibly alkalizing too –
which is such a bonus! I love the creaminess of the avocado
dressing here, it really transforms a few humble ingredients
into a delicious meal.

Place the carrots in a bowl.

Put the avocados, lemon juice, sweet miso, garlic, and salt in a blender and
blend until completely smooth.

Pour this dressing over the carrot "noodles" and mix in – using your hands
is best I find – then stir in the red onion and cilantro.

Divide the pea shoots between 2 plates, add a pile of the "noodles" on top,
garnish with the tamari-toasted pumpkin seeds and lime zest, and drizzle
the pumpkin oil over the top.

serves 2

*2–3 carrots, spiralized
(see page 66)*

*2 ripe avocados,
roughly chopped*

juice of 1 lemon

1 tbsp sweet miso

*1 small clove garlic,
grated*

*a pinch of Himalayan
pink salt*

*½ small red onion,
finely chopped*

*1 cup (15g) cilantro,
chopped*

⅔ cup (40g) pea shoots

to garnish:

*Tamari-toasted seeds
(see page 78)*

*finely grated zest
of 1 lime*

1 tbsp pumpkin oil

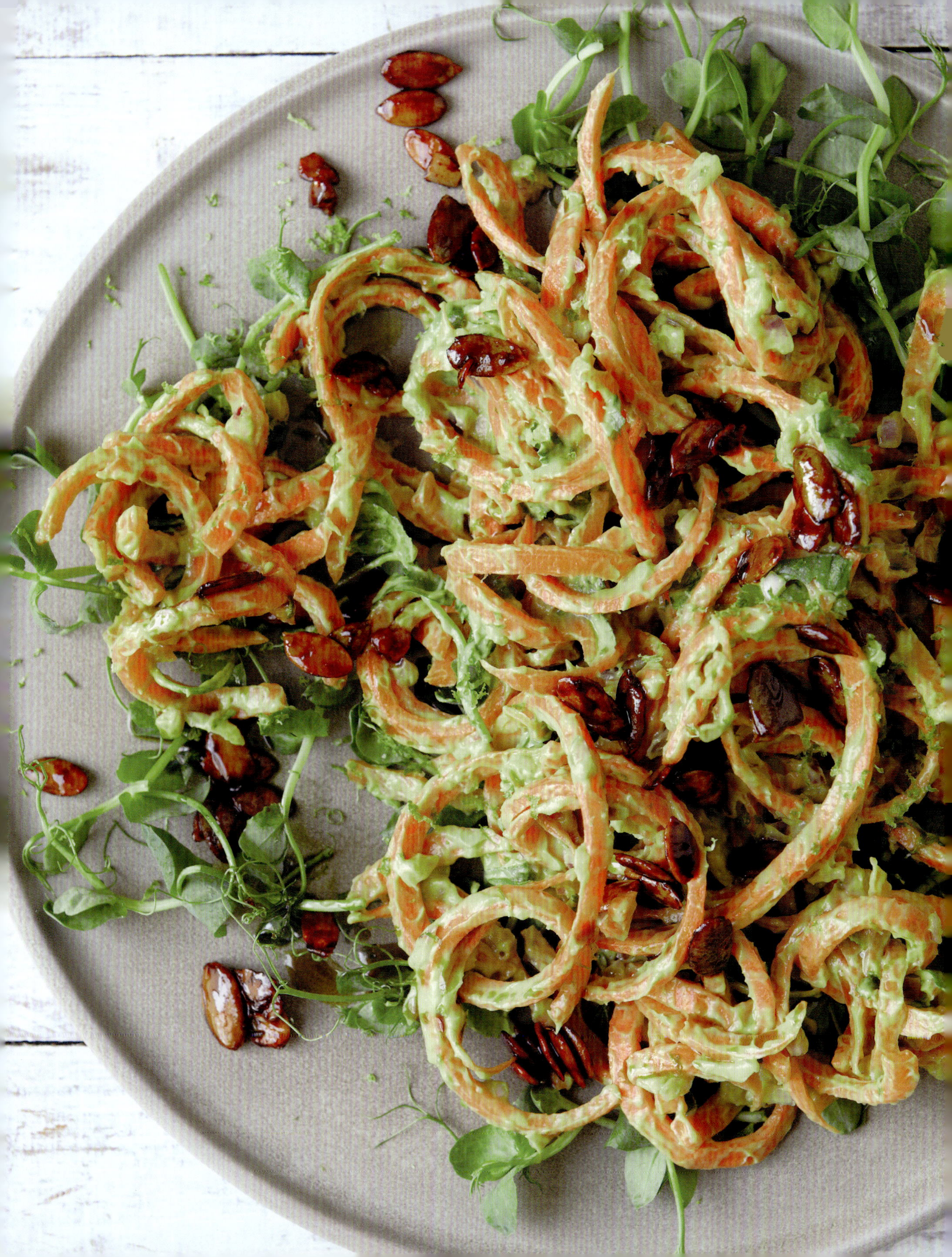

Lime sprouted salad

This wonderfully filling and nutritious salad is all wrapped up in a high-protein dressing. I can't get enough of the dressing – and you're sure to be fans of it, too, once you've tried it. And if you can't source broccoli sprouts, why not have a go at making them yourself at home? Check out honestlyhealthyfood.com for tips.

Put the kale in a large bowl and squeeze half the lemon juice over it. Sprinkle over the sesame oil and salt, and massage the leaves until they start to "cook" and wilt.

Squeeze the other half of the lemon juice over the top of the avocado slices.

Make the dressing by putting the cashew butter, water, and lime juice into a blender and process until smooth.

Add the salad greens and parsley to the kale, and toss with the dressing. Garnish with the lime zest, broccoli sprouts, and sesame seeds.

serves 2

1½ cups chopped (100g) kale, ribs removed

juice of 1 lemon

1 tsp sesame oil

a pinch of Himalayan pink salt

1 avocado, sliced

1¾ cups (60g) wild or mixed salad greens

1 tbsp (4g) flat leaf parsley

for the dressing:

6 tbsp cashew nut butter

2 tbsp water

juice of 1–2 limes

to garnish:

finely grated zest of 1 lime

⅔ cup (20g) broccoli sprouts

1 tsp sesame seeds, toasted

Broccoli sprouts are nutrient-rich and packed full of cancer-fighting antioxidants, vitamins, minerals, and even protein.

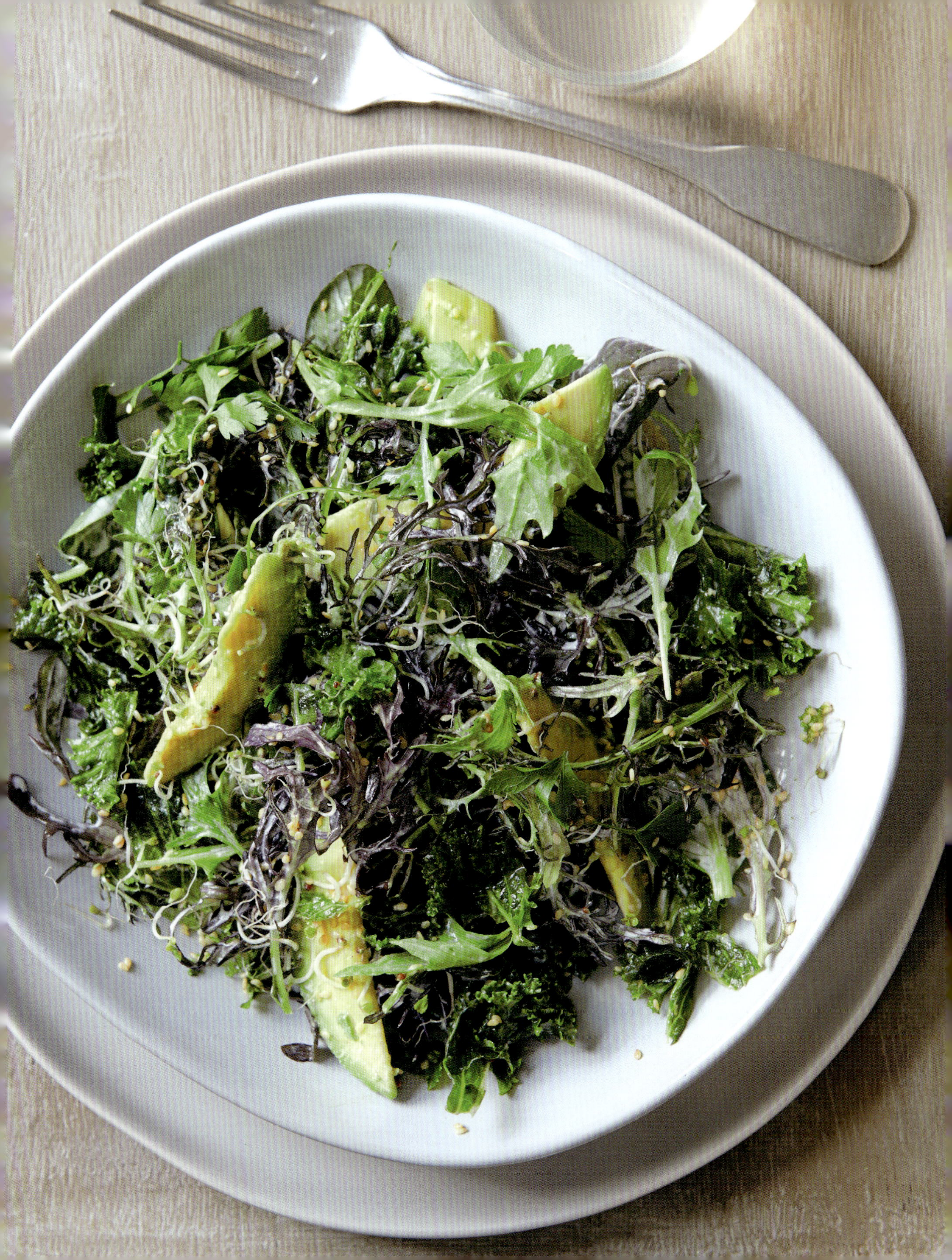

Green cauliflower "rice" risotto

If you love risotto, but are trying to avoid grains and cut back during a slimdown, then this is the risotto for you. It uses cauliflower to mimic the texture of rice and so is a fantastic grain-free alternative to rice-based risotto. To vary the flavors, use the same method for the "risotto," but stir in different flavored pestos at the end (see pages 66, 142 and 226).

Put the cauliflower florets in a food processor or blender and process until it looks a bit like rice. Alternatively, chop the cauliflower by hand as finely a possible. Transfer three-quarters of the cauliflower to a bowl and continue processing the remaining quarter until you end up with a paste.

Combine the bouillon powder and boiling water in a measuring cup.

In a medium pan, sauté the onion and half the garlic in 1 tablespoon of sunflower oil. When translucent add the coriander and za'atar and stir for 1 minute. Next, add the cauliflower paste followed by the cauliflower "rice" and cook for 1 minute until all the spices coat the "rice." Pour in the hot bouillon and simmer for 10 minutes.

Meanwhile, make the pesto. Put the watercress, olive oil, salt, and garlic in a blender and blend together.

Once the 10 minutes is up, add the polenta and water and cook for another 7 minutes.

Meanwhile, sauté the broccoli in the remaining sunflower oil with the remaining grated garlic for 2–3 minutes until soft, then set aside.

Once the "risotto" is ready, quickly stir in the pesto and nutritional yeast.

To serve, divide the "risotto" between 4 bowls, lay the broccoli over the top, and sprinkle each serving with toasted pumpkin seeds. Add a little wild salad on the top, if using, for a beautiful garnish.

serves 4

6 cups (600g) cauliflower, broken into florets

1 tbsp bouillon powder

2¼ cups (500ml) boiling water

½ red onion, diced

4 cloves garlic, grated

2 tbsp sunflower oil

¼ tsp ground coriander

¼ tsp za'atar

4 tbsp fine polenta

1 cup (240ml) water

½ bunch (100g) broccoli

1 heaping tbsp nutritional yeast

1 heaping tbsp (10g) toasted pumpkin seeds

¼ cup (10g) wild salad greens, to garnish (optional)

for the pesto:

1¾ cups (60g) watercress

2 tbsp olive oil

¼ tsp Himalayan pink salt

½ clove garlic, grated

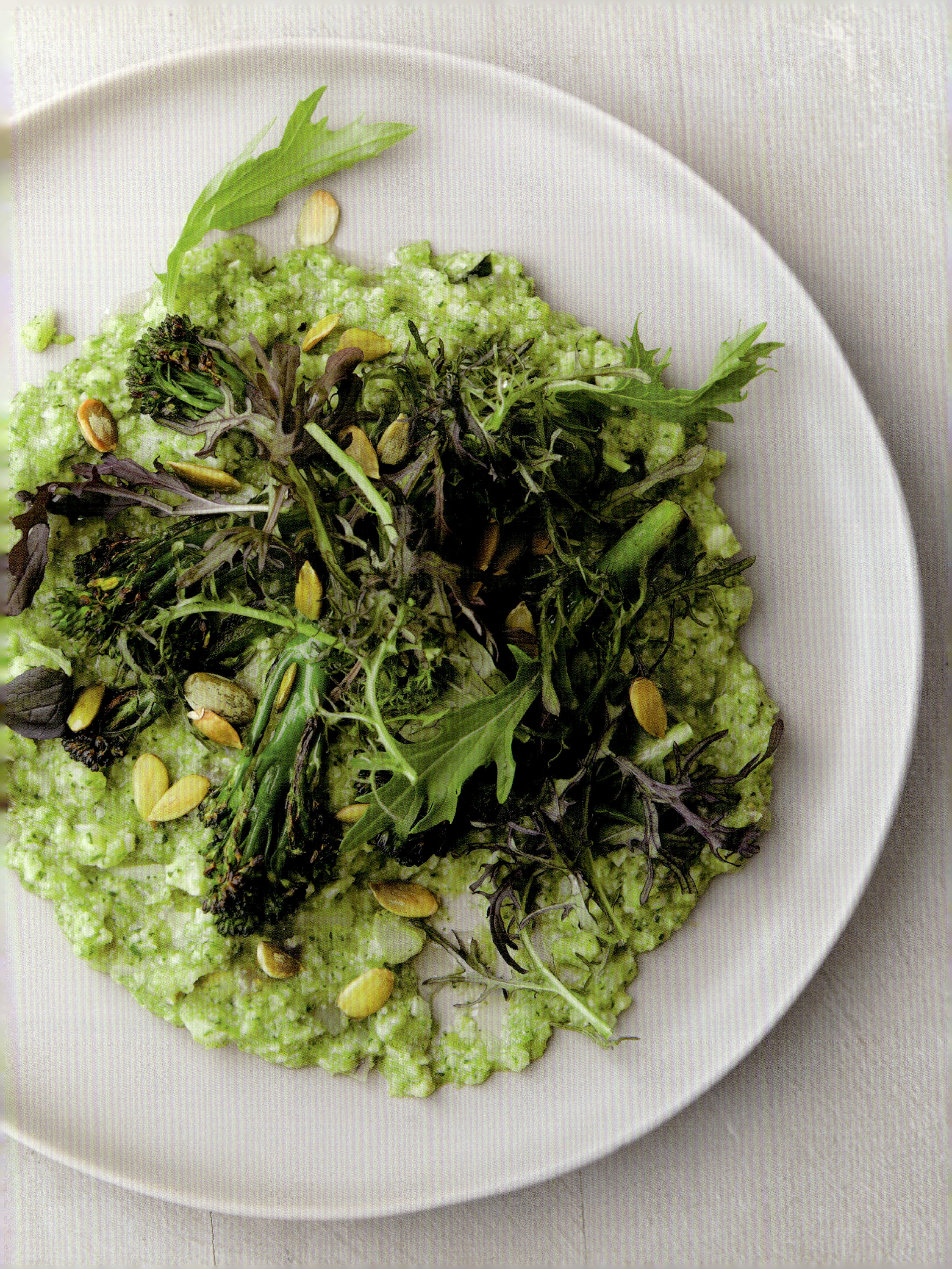

#bites

Tamari-toasted seeds

Here's my go-to recipe to transform a salad – really easy to make and delicious – also perfect as a snack. Packed full of protein, these little salty seeds are great for adding to any recipe.

serves 1 as a snack

1 tbsp sesame oil

1 tbsp tamari

¼ cup (30g) pumpkin seeds

Put the sesame oil, tamari, and pumpkin seeds in a pan over medium heat and toast for 1 minute. Set aside to cool.

Roasted red bell pepper dip

Finding an alternative to the usual hummus is a breath of healthy fresh air. You could make this scrumptious roasted red pepper dip with pine nuts or Brazil nuts in place of the walnuts for a different nutty flavor. *Photo overleaf.*

serves 4–5 as a dip

¾ cup (80g) raw walnuts

½ cup (120ml) water

2 red bell peppers

1 tbsp sweet miso

1 clove garlic, grated

⅓in (1cm) piece of fresh chili pepper, chopped

¾ cup (20g) basil leaves

Preheat the oven to 325°F/170°C/gas mark 3.

Soak the walnuts in the water for 45 minutes.

Meanwhile, put the whole red bell peppers on a baking tray into a preheated oven to roast for 25 minutes.

Remove the peppers from the oven and handle them carefully – they are mighty hot. Allow the peppers to cool for 15 minutes, then pull out the stalks and watch as the seeds come out with them.

Place the peppers in a blender along with the soaked walnuts, their soaking water, the sweet miso, garlic, chili pepper, and basil and blend to combine and until you get a chunky texture.

Serve as a dip with either gluten-free crackers (see page 32) or raw vegetables.

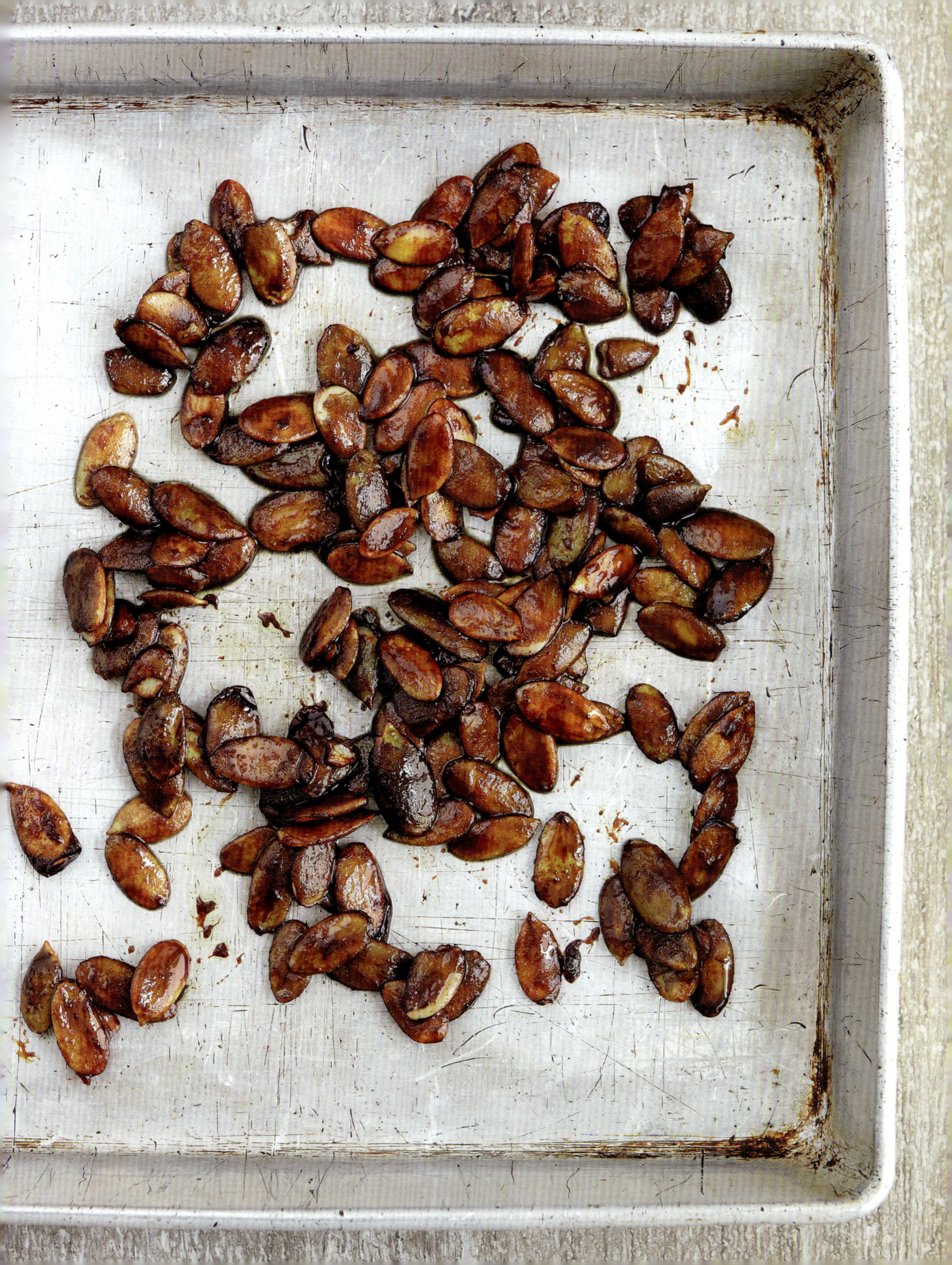

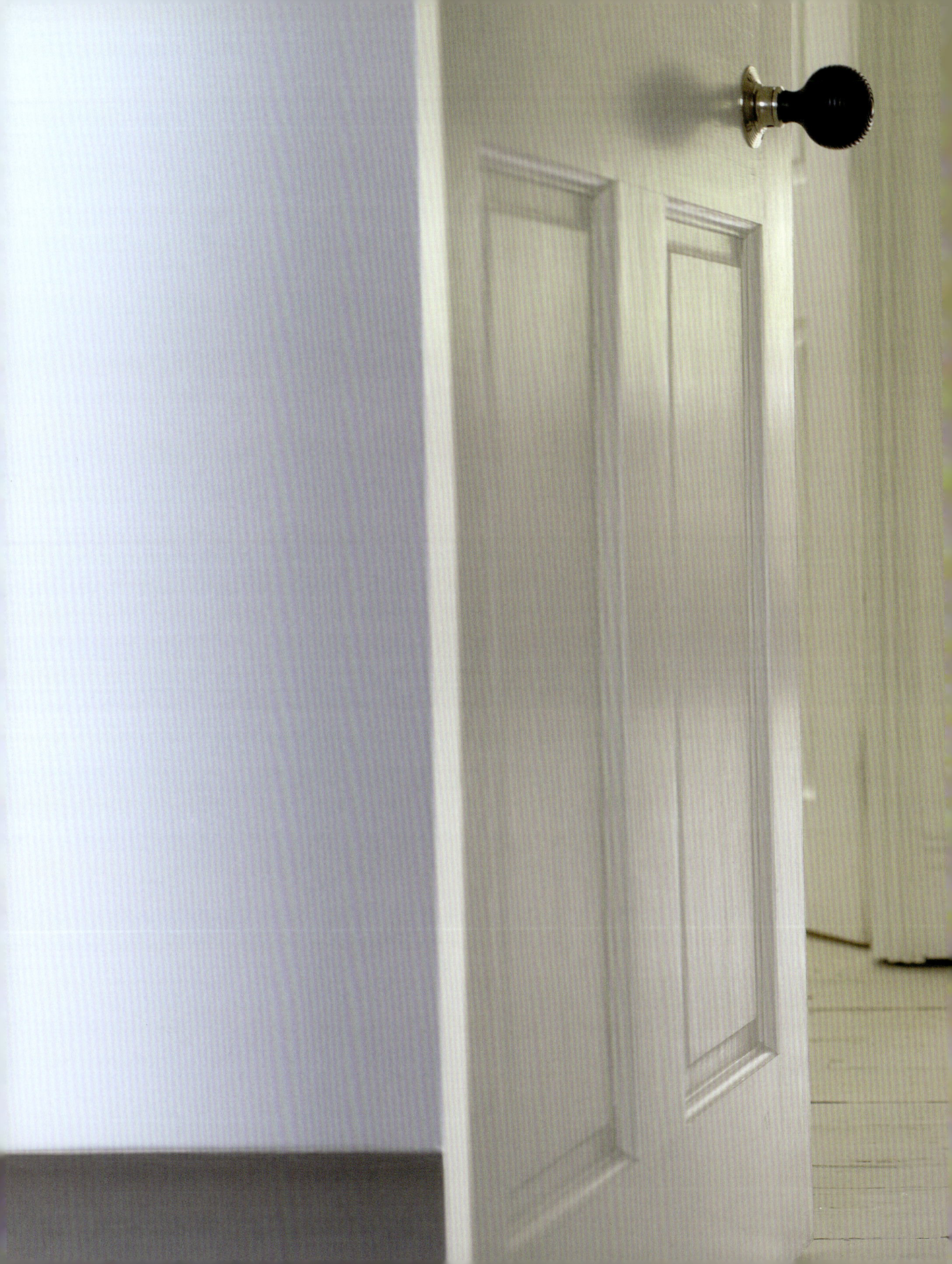

#highenergy

Nourishing your fitness

6 days of protein-rich balanced meals,
soups, and smoothies

The **#highenergy** cleanse is a six-day program designed for people who are exercising a lot, who want to find out how to get more vegetarian protein into their daily diet and cleanse their body at the same time. I exercise three to four times a week, and on the days when I do more cardio-based activities, I make sure I have a high-protein meal. Finding a good protein shake is also a great way to supplement your diet if you're lacking energy. When looking at the brands of shake available, be sure to choose one without whey protein, as this is cow's milk and, as such, is acid-forming in the body. I like the Sunwarrior brand as it is vegan and sugar-free.

One recipe that I am extremely excited by in this book is my "chifu," a tofu-like food that I've created using chickpea flour (see page 129). It's not quite as high in protein as regular tofu, but it's so much healthier for you. As with all soy-based produce, do be wary when buying regular tofu as so much soy is genetically modified these days. Choose an organic one if possible, or make some of my chifu and use that instead.

Afternoon snacks are your friends on this cleanse. I find that when I follow the #highenergy cleanse, I need a little pick-me-up in the afternoon. There's no need to be hungry – if you drive yourself to the point of hunger, you are likely to reach for the nearest food and that might not be a healthy one. So arm yourself

You will need # a gym membership or home workout program – try our high-intensity interval training as part of the downloadable 30-day slimdown on the Honestly Healthy website for a six-day home workout # ingredients for your recipes # food processor or blender

What to expect ...

This cleanse is designed to detoxify your body while supporting you with plenty of energy-rich foods so you can continue your highly active life. In my experience, it's hard to find cleanses that support an active lifestyle, so I'm delighted with this one – it's worked wonders for me!

The #highenergy program comprises six days of smoothies, juices, tea, and soups, as well as some delicious main meals for lunch and lighter options for dinner. All are designed to give your body optimal nourishment and super-charge your energy levels, while allowing it some rest from digesting your usual food, and helping to draw out the toxins naturally.

Stay away from:

# caffeine	# sugar
# alcohol	# wheat and gluten
# dairy products	# processed foods
# meat	

All of the above are extremely acid-forming in the body (and not alkalizing, which is what an alkaline cleanse is all about). To rebalance your body towards a more alkaline state you need to cut these items out of your diet.

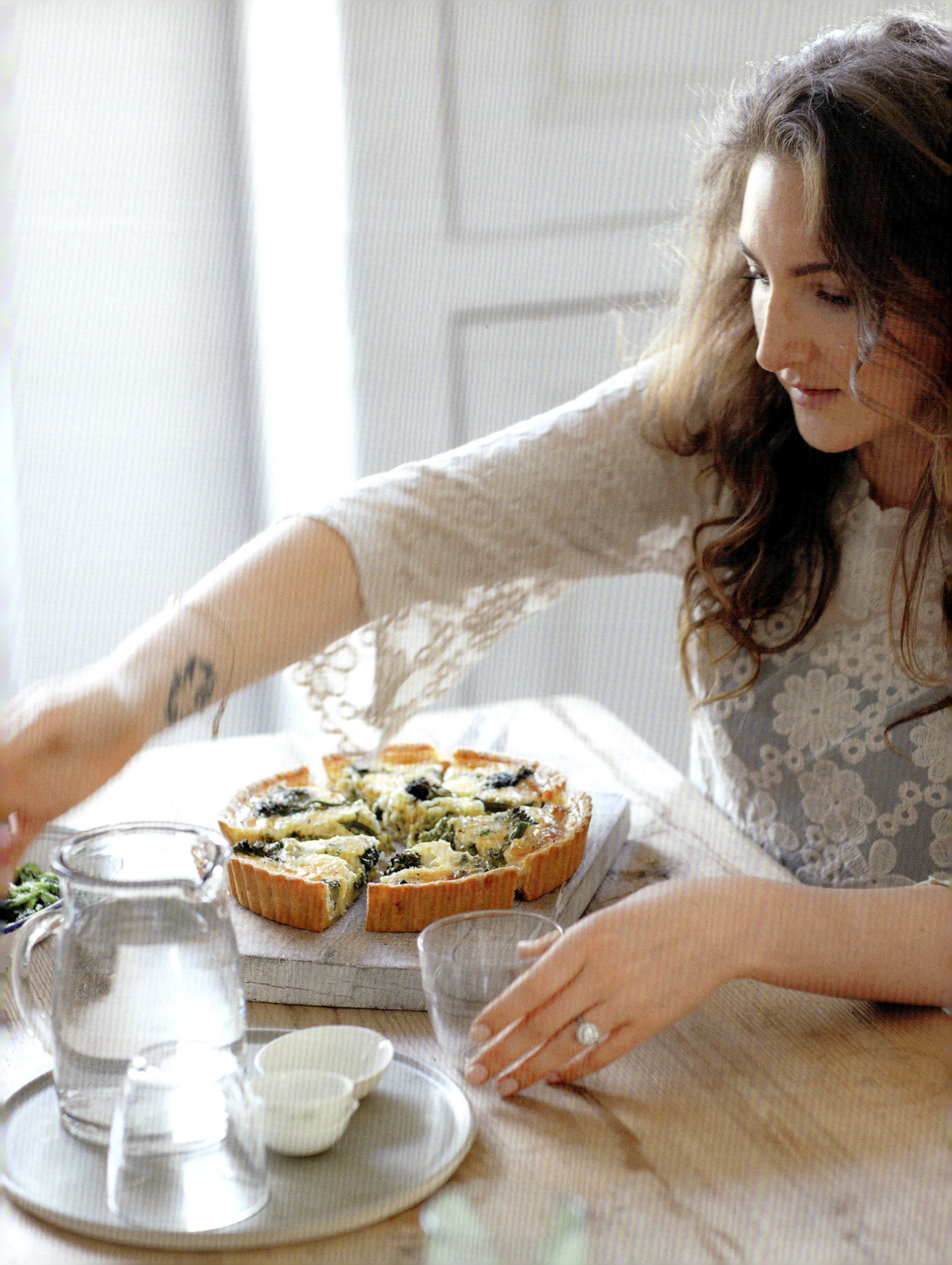

with some tasty snacks, such as the Crunchy chickpeas or the Five-seed protein balls (see pages 146 and 150) Snacks also help keep your blood sugar levels steady, which means you'll be less likely to get tired and irritable – a good thing for you and for the people around you!

On this six-day #highenergy program, you'll start the day with immune-boosting porridges and power smoothies; I suggest that on the days you don't exercise, have the smoothie for breakfast. Have your main protein meal, such as

Spiced tofu balls (page 105) at lunchtime and a lighter option, such as Arame broccoli salad on a bed of celery "noodles" (page 121) for dinner. Eating your main meal in the middle of the day allows your body to rest in the evening and not have to work too hard at digesting your food.

In the past I have found it challenging to have consistency with my exercise as I am an "all or nothing" type of person – however recently I have, thankfully, fallen into a really great routine. I have found that it's about finding something

#highenergy menu planner

If you are on a high intensity workout day (cardio, HIIT, Spinning, cross training) you should make sure you have one meal that is high in protein and have a good breakfast. If you are on a low intensity day (pilates, yoga, walking) you could start with a smoothie – make sure you choose a lighter lunch and dinner and choose more meals from the slimdown phase. If you are doing no exercise in the week make sure you follow either the feelgood or slimdown recipes.

Day 1 high intensity workout day	AM	Immune-boosting porridge (page 88)
	Lunch	Lentil broccoli burger (page 112)
	Bites	Green starter juice (page 30) / Roasted red pepper dip (page 78)
	Dinner	Braised fennel and grapefruit salad (page 205)
Day 2 low intensity workout day	AM	Chlorophyll smoothie (page 31)
	Lunch	Black lentil and salsa verde salad (page 126)
	Bites	Nutmeg matcha latte (page 174) / Beet chips (page 148)
	Dinner	Green cauliflower "rice" risotto (page 76)

that is not going to take too much of your time up and that is sustainable. So telling yourself that you are going to go to the gym 6 days a week might work for the first couple of weeks, but quite often, and that is what I found, you may then stop going at all, as it is all too much. Finding a rhythm with your health and fitness is the best way to stay successful and for exercise to be a part of your life. I find that scheduling exercise sessions is the best way I will stick to it. Organize it as if it was a really important meeting that you cannot cancel for any reason, also working out with friends is a great way to motivate each other.

Day 3
high intensity workout day

AM	Baked eggs in avocado (page 176)
Lunch	Cucumber and tempeh salad (page 65)
Bites	Five-seed protein balls (page 150) / Energizing tea (page 58)
Dinner	Asian noodle soup (page 114)

Day 4
low intensity workout day

AM	Puffed breakfast crispies with milk (page 172)
Lunch	Arame broccoli salad on a bed of celery "noodles" (page 121)
Bites	Kale and oat smoothie (page 56) / Ginger-tamari-dressed edamame (page 224)
Dinner	Lima bean and butternut curry (page 108)

Day 5
high intensity workout day

AM	Chia and teff bread with poached egg or nut butter (page 168)
Lunch	Daikon noodles and grilled ribbon salad (page 218)
Bites	Raw chia and hemp bar (page 228) / Red juice (page 30)
Dinner	Beluga lentil and sweet potato pie (page 137)

Day 6
high intensity workout day

AM	Maca almond milkshake (page 92)
Lunch	Watercress, bean, and hazelnut salad (page 188)
Bites	Green starter juice (page 30) / No grain kale bread (page 152)
Dinner	Coconut-encrusted tofu and black quinoa salad (page 100)

#morning time

Immune-boosting porridge

This hot cereal is bursting with goodness – the cinnamon and baobab fruit serve to boost your immune system, and the oats release their energy slowly, giving you sustained energy levels throughout the day, rather than highs and lows. You may be unfamiliar with baobab fruit powder, but no doubt have heard of the African tree it comes from. The fruit is allowed to dry on the tree, then it is harvested and ground into a powder. This tangy powder is more potent than Vitamin C and helps to keep you well year round. So, here I've included it in a warming cereal, guaranteed to get you started however cold the day.

Put all the ingredients into a saucepan, stir well and let sit for 10 minutes.

Set the pan over low heat and stir the mixture constantly for about 2 minutes until thoroughly heated. If it starts to get too thick, add a little more rice milk to achieve the consistency you like.

Serve hot and garnish with a scattering of pomegranate seeds and a sprinkle of bee pollen, if using, for a perfect winter morning warmer.

serves 2

1 tbsp chia seeds

1⅛ cups (90g) rolled oats

1 small apple, grated

½ inch (2g) piece cinnamon stick

1 star anise

¼ tsp ground cinnamon

1 cup (250ml) rice milk, plus extra if necessary

1 tbsp baobab fruit powder

for the garnish:

4 tbsp pomegranate seeds

bee pollen (optional)

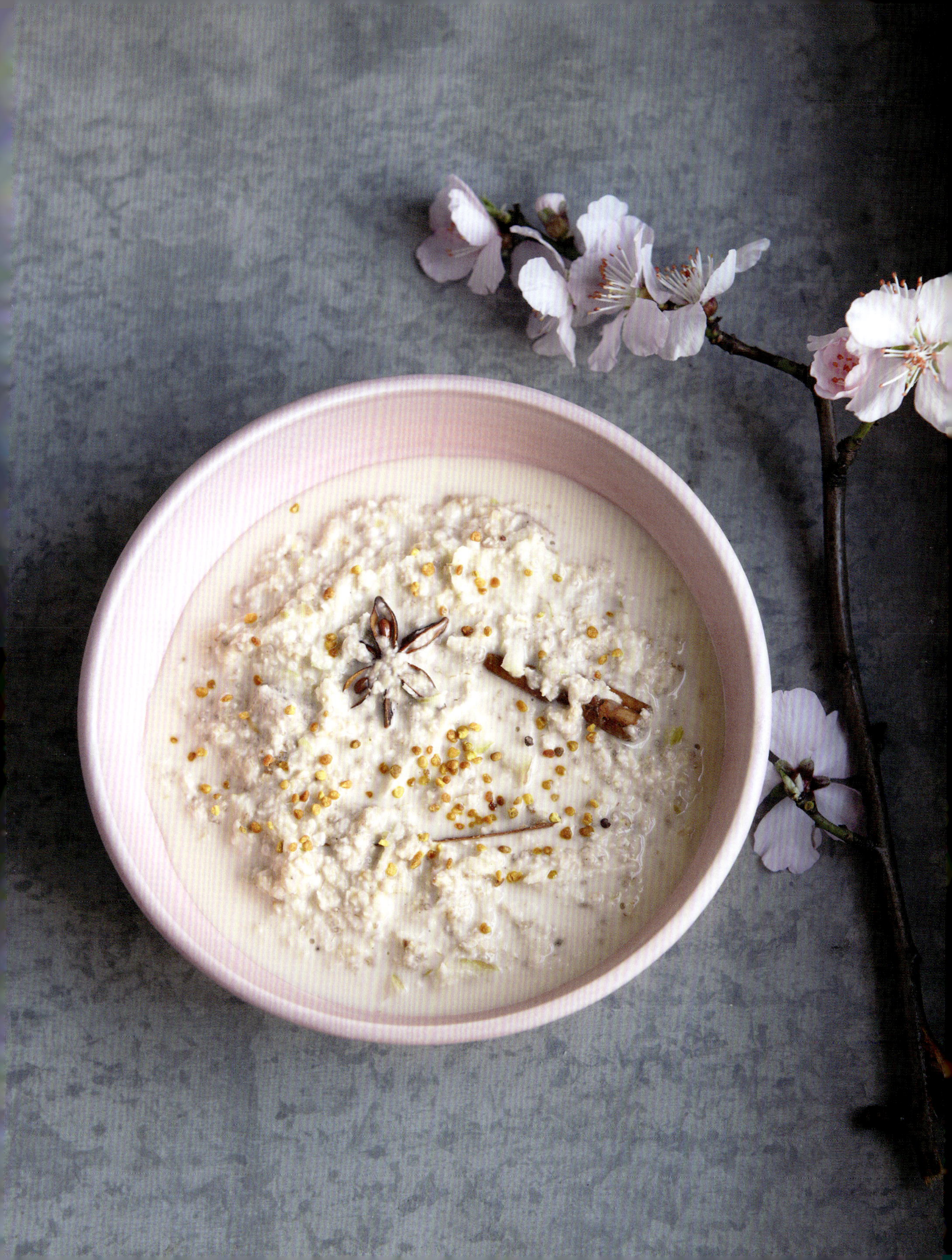

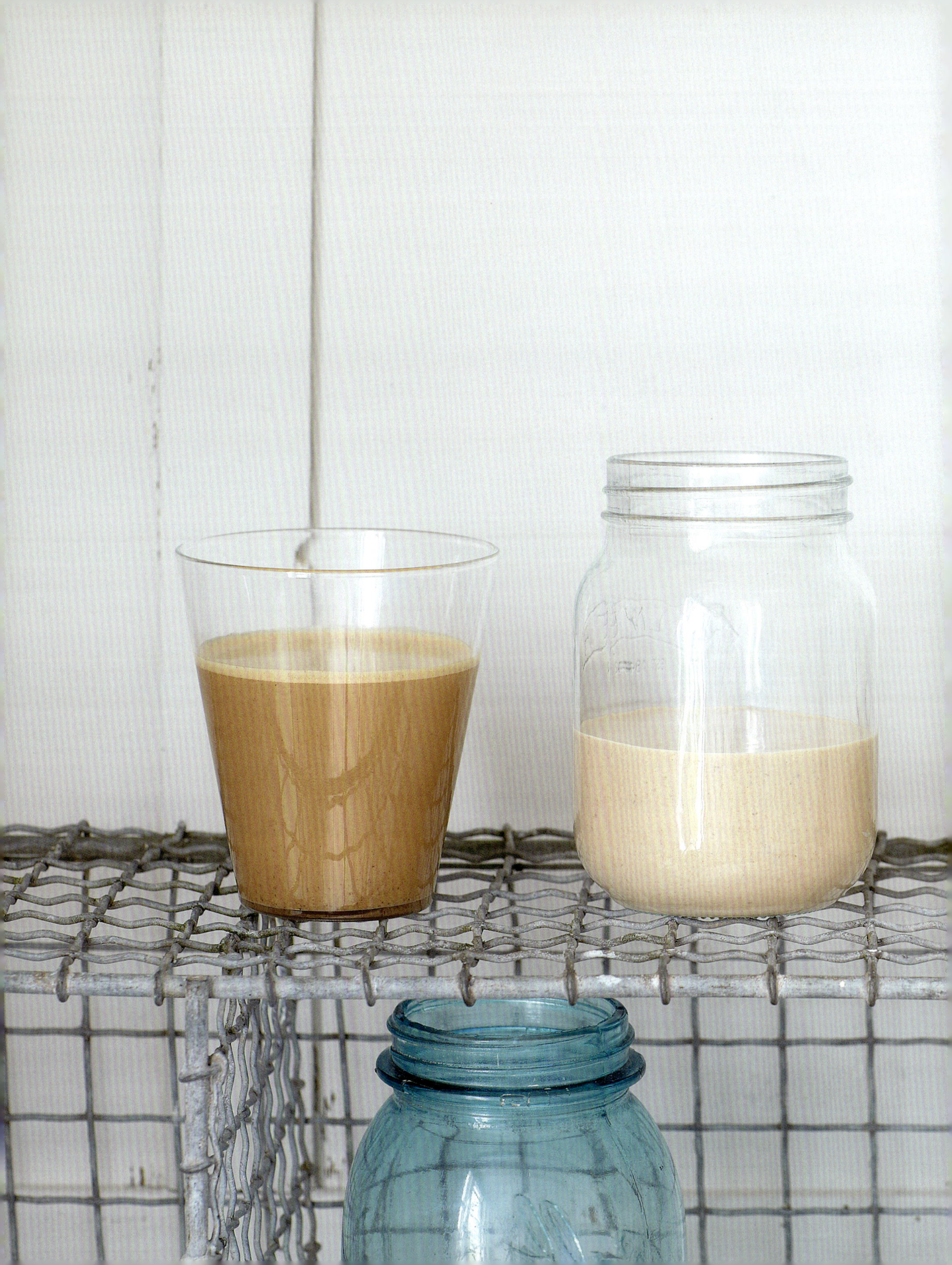

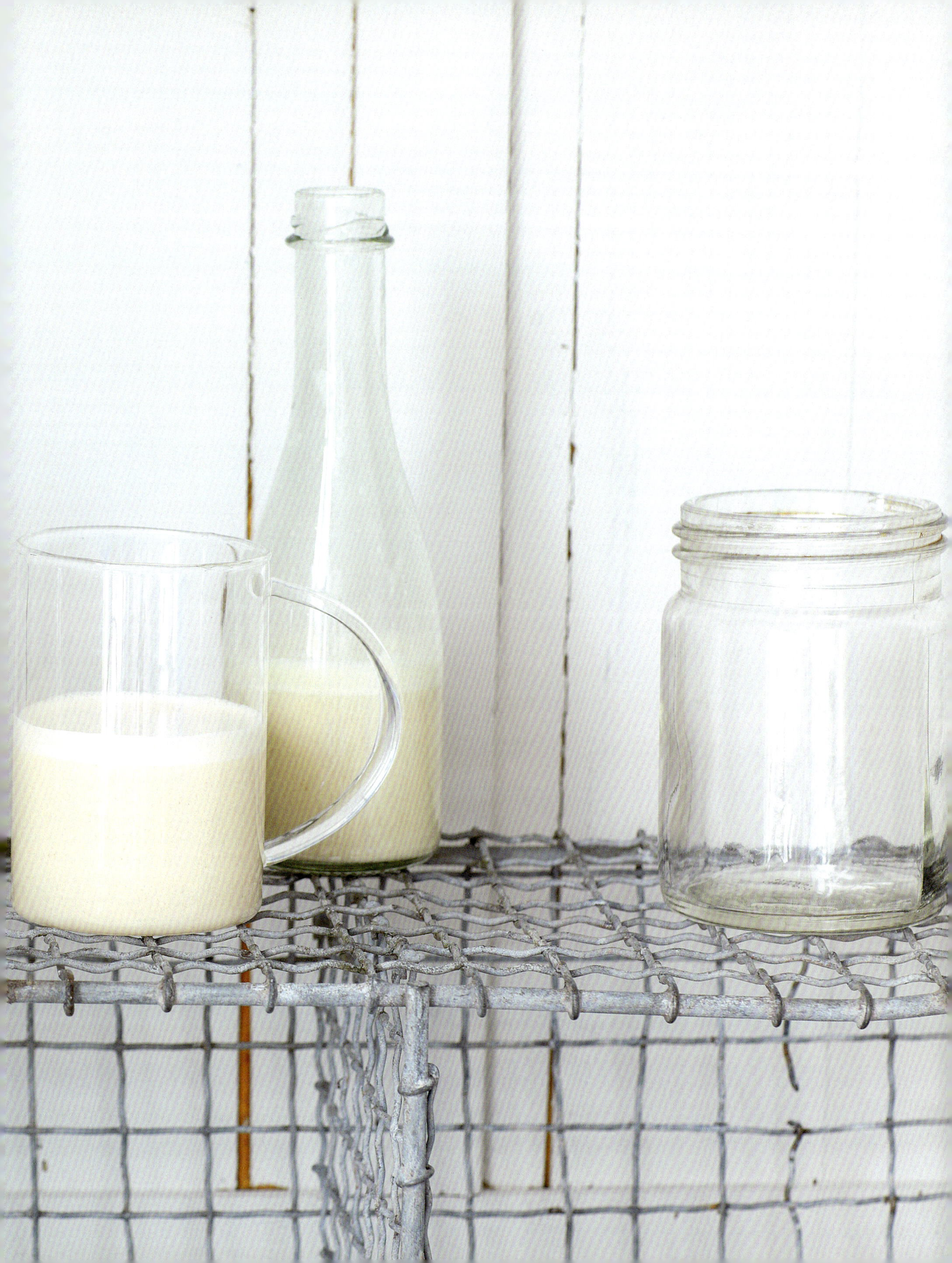

"Coffee" smoothie

Since I don't drink coffee, this smoothie is the ultimate luxury for me. Finding barley coffee was the most exciting thing, as I like the taste of coffee, I just don't like what it does to me – it makes me crazy! This smoothie tastes like a latte, and knowing that it's healthy makes it taste even better. The oats give you an energy boost – a welcome kick some mornings. If it's a hot day, blend this smoothie with some ice and have an iced "coffee" smoothie; on colder days, warm it up for a luxurious café barley latte.

serves 1

2 tsp instant barley coffee or Dandelion coffee

1⅛ cups (270ml) rice milk

2 tbsp almond butter

1 probiotic capsule (optional, but a really good addition)

2 tbsp coconut milk yogurt

1 tbsp rolled oats

optional extras:

½ banana or 1 tbsp lucuma powder

Simply put all the ingredients into a high-speed blender and blend until completely smooth. Enjoy right away.

Photo on previous page (left–right): "Coffee" smoothie, Maca almond milkshake, Lucuma milkshake

Maca almond milkshake

This superfood does exactly what it says on the container … it makes you feel great! It is nutritionally dense, meaning that it is a rich source of minerals and vitamins, including B12, which is especially beneficial for vegetarians. Maca also helps to balance hormones, but it must be used in moderation, if there is breast cancer in your family. It has an amazing nutty and sweet flavor, so is great for bringing this smoothie to life.

serves 2

3 tbsp white almond butter

¼ tsp ground cinnamon

1 cup (240ml) almond milk

½ cup (120ml) coconut water

5 dates

1 tsp maca powder

Simply put all the ingredients into a high-speed blender and blend until completely smooth. The smoothie is best drunk right away, but you can always put it in a jar and take it with you to drink as soon as you can during the day.

Lucuma milkshake

It's great to know that you can add sweetness without reaching for refined sugars. Here I use lucuma powder, which has a low glycemic index, and comes from a delicious fruit grown in South America – it's said to be the "fruit of fertility"! I love this superfood, as it's sweet but is oh-so-good for you; lucuma is full of antioxidants and vitamin B, which is great, as many vegetarians look for something to top up their vitamin B levels. You can enjoy this really indulgent smoothie – it tastes just like a milkshake – safe in the knowledge that it's doing you and your body good at the same time.

serves 1

3½ tbsp almond milk powder

2 tbsp coconut milk yogurt

2 tbsp cashew nut butter

1 banana

1 heaping tbsp lucuma powder

⅔ cup (140ml) water

Simply put all the ingredients into a high-speed blender and blend until completely smooth. For a more refreshing taste add a couple ice cubes before blending. The smoothie tastes best if you drink it right away, but you can always put it in a jar and take it with you to drink as soon as you can during the day.

Milkshakes remind me of my childhood. However they've always been unhealthy, so I had the idea of creating something that tastes creamy and delicious but also supports a high energy cleanse. Enjoy!

Baked Mexican-style eggs

Mixing it up at breakfast is important, especially on the weekend, and if you are a fan of poached eggs on toast, then try this super-tasty egg-based recipe. This take on Mexican eggs has one of my all-time favorite ingredients in it – avocado. If you like, you can add some black beans, too, but I love the stripped-down version below. Serve with a cup of rooibos tea and rice milk and you have a perfect weekend brunch.

Preheat the oven to 325°F/170°C/gas mark 3.

First make the tomato mixture. Heat the coconut oil in a pan. Add the red chili pepper and sauté for 1 minute, then add the tomatoes, red onion, and cumin and cook for 2 minutes over medium heat. Add half the water and simmer for 3 minutes. Add the remaining water, cook for another minute, then take the pan off the heat and set aside.

To make the kale mixture, melt the coconut oil in a separate pan and add the kale, lime juice, and water. Cook for 1 minute until the kale softens.

Take a shallow, 6–8 cup baking dish. Put a layer of the kale in first, then the chili pepper, tomato, and onion mixture, then the avocado. Finally, crack 2 eggs per person over the top.

Bake in a preheated oven for 5–7 minutes until the eggs are cooked. (You could also cook this dish on the stovetop – layer in the same way in a pan, then cover with a lid; it will take about 3–5 minutes, but you won't get the same baked texture on the top.)

Serve immediately with fresh parsley and cracked black pepper sprinkled on top.

serves 2

1 avocado, sliced

4 eggs

3 tbsp (10g) flat leaf parsley, chopped

cracked black pepper

for the tomato mixture:

1 tbsp coconut oil

1 red chili pepper, thinly sliced

3 large vine-ripened tomatoes, diced

½ red onion, sliced

¼ tsp ground cumin

4–6 tbsp water

for the kale mixture:

1 tbsp coconut oil

¾ cup (50g) chopped kale

juice of ½ lime

1 tbsp water

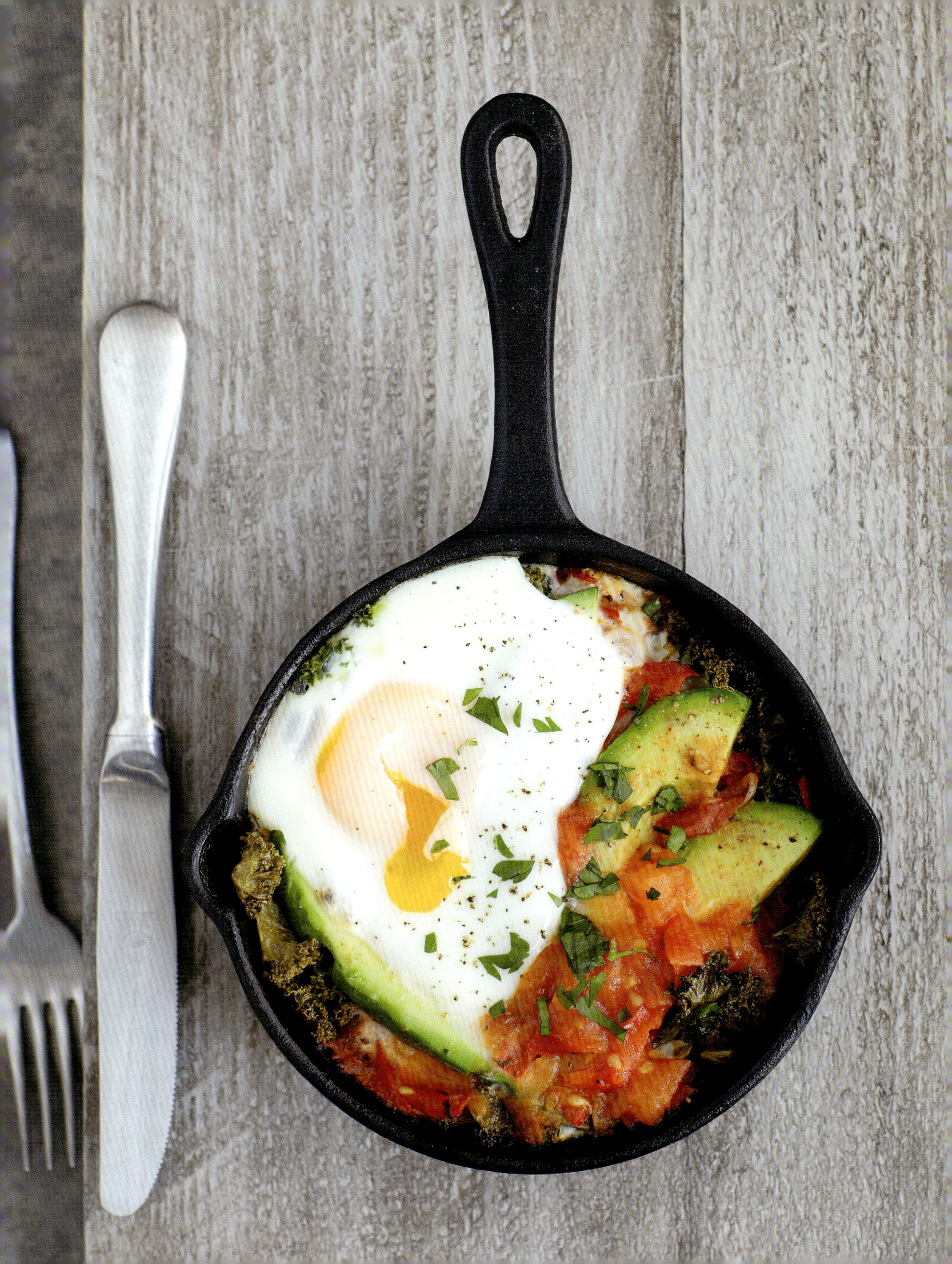

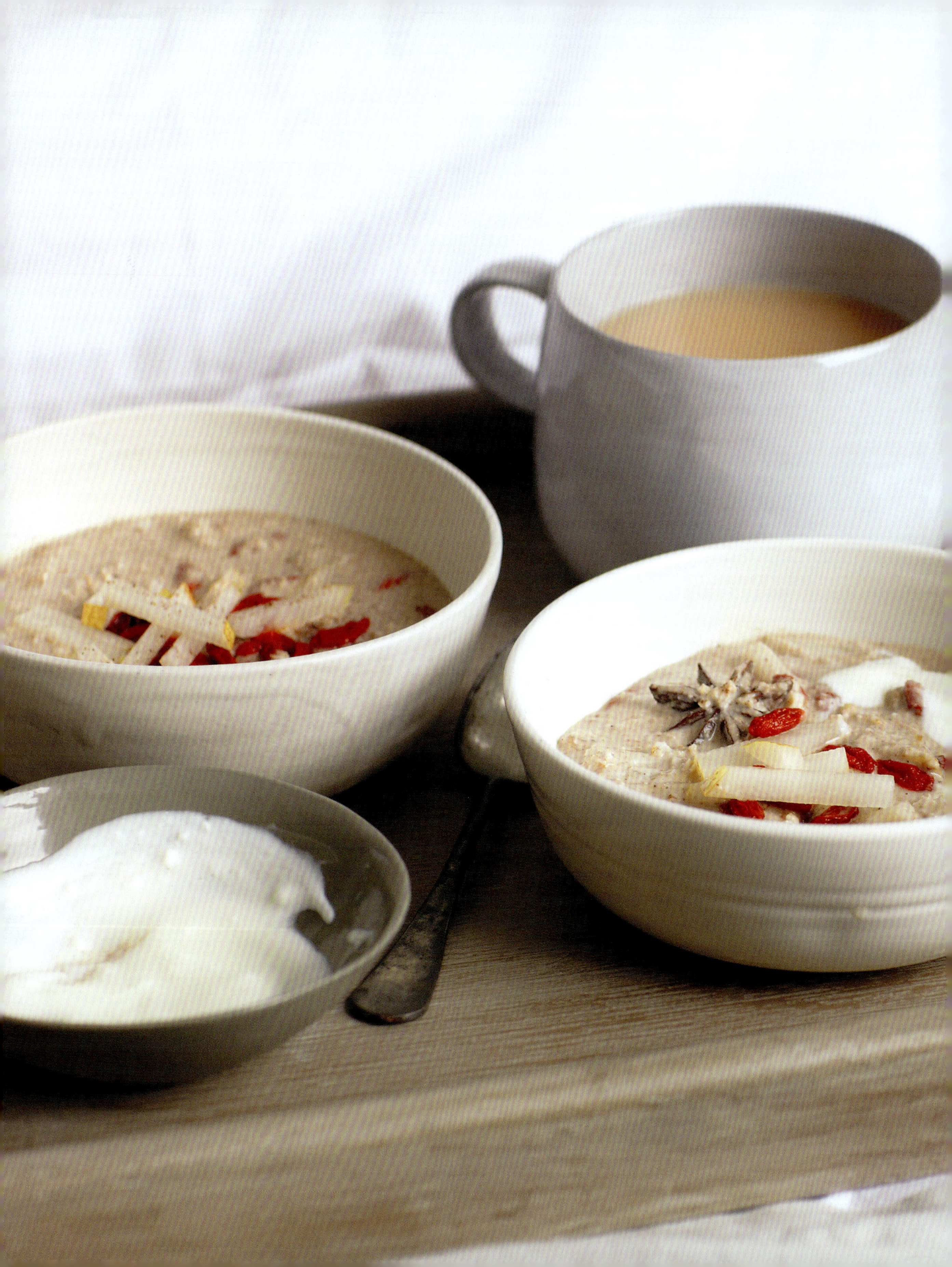

Spiced overnight oats

Have an instant breakfast on hand with this get-ahead dish. If you can't find an Asian pear, just use half an apple and half a regular pear, as that is the taste you are looking for. An oaty breakfast is a great way to start the day, as oats release their energy slowly, balancing your blood sugar levels and making you feel like you have much more energy.

serves 2

½ (60g) Asian pear (see above)

juice of ¼ lemon

1 cup (80g) gluten-free oats

¼ tsp ground allspice

⅛ cup (10g) goji berries

2 star anise

1 cup (200ml) rice milk

1 tbsp coconut oil

Chop the Asian pear into thin slices, about ¾in (2cm) long and squeeze the lemon over them to keep the fruit from turning brown.

Then put the rest of the ingredients into a bowl, finishing off with the chopped pear.

Mix together and leave overnight or for at least 2-3 hours. Divide between 2 bowls, discarding the star anise. If you're eating alone, store the other serving in the fridge, where it will keep for up to 5 days.

#meals

Warm fig and spinach salad

This is a wonderfully alkaline dish – the figs, spinach, parsley, green beans, and apple cider vinegar are all alkaline – and a cleansing one too. It's quick to make and you can play around with the dressing to give it a different taste.

Sauté the onions and green beans in a mixture of sunflower oil and apple cider vinegar for 2 minutes.

Slice the figs in half and put them cut side down in the pan, among the onions and green beans, and cook for 1 minute on each side. After you flip them, add the water and leave for another 1 minute

Serve on a bed of spinach leaves and garnish with the parsley and pistachios.

serves 1

½ red onion, thickly sliced

½ cup (60g) green beans, sliced at an angle

1 tbsp sunflower oil

1 tsp apple cider vinegar

3 figs

2 tbsp water

2⅔ cups (80g) spinach

to garnish:

2 tbsp (5g) flat leaf parsley

¼ cup (30g) pistachios, chopped

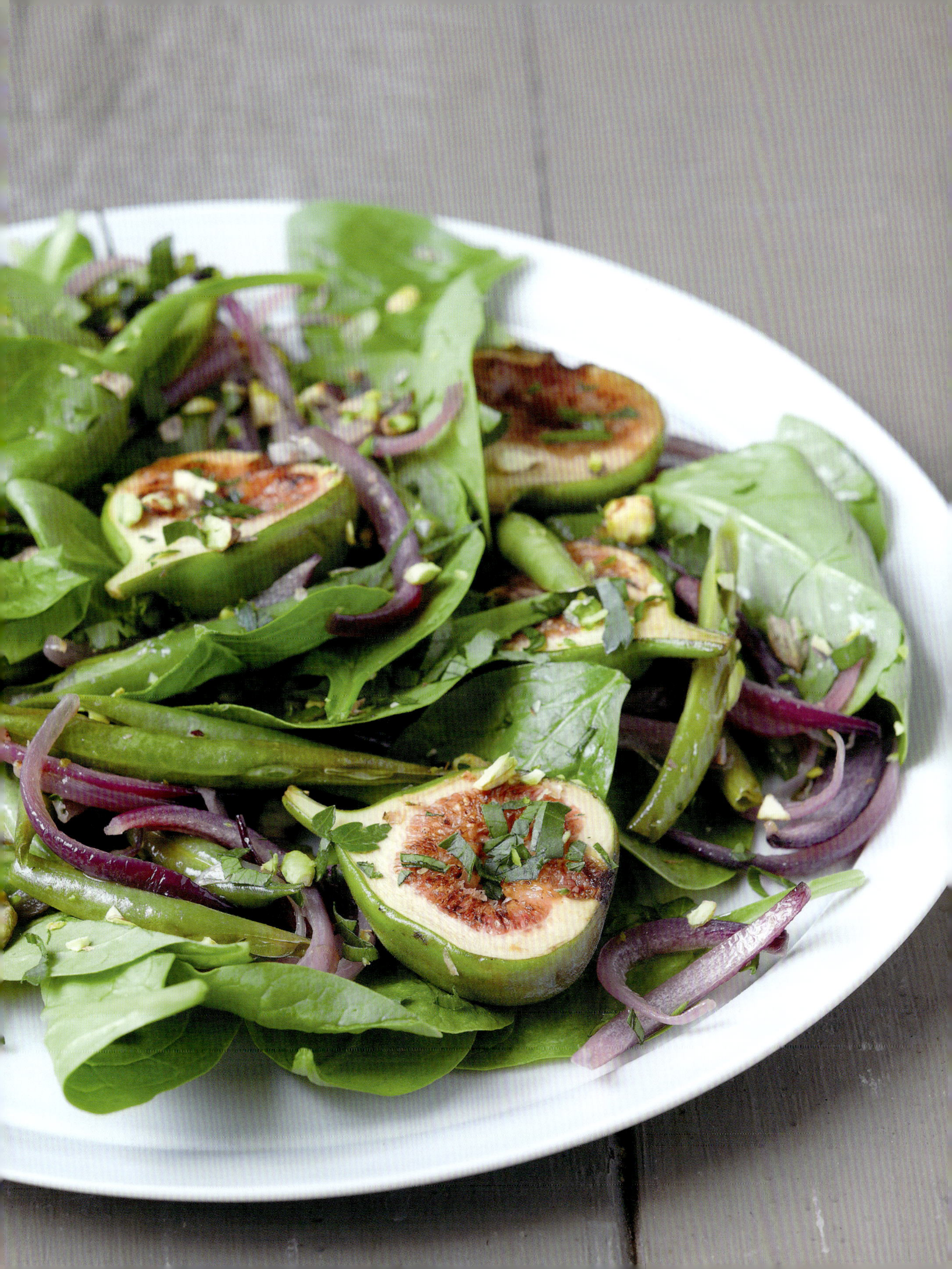

Coconut-encrusted tofu and black quinoa salad

This protein-packed show-stopper of a dish is definitely one to add to your repertoire. I wanted to create a healthy fried tofu dish and found a way to make this nutritious version using coconut flour. Seaweed is a superfood – it adds protein to your diet and complements your body's pH levels, as it's really, really alkaline.

Preheat the oven to 325°F/170°C/gas mark 3, and line a baking sheet with parchment paper.

Cook the quinoa according the instructions on the package – this should take about 20 minutes – then drain and set aside.

Meanwhile, boil a kettle and pour boiling water over the wakame seaweed to cover, leave to expand and set aside.

Cut the tofu into 2cm cubes and put into a bowl. Add the garlic, coconut flour, ground flax seeds, half the olive oil, the salt, and lime zest. Mix thoroughly and press onto the tofu to form the crust.

Put the cubes onto the prepared baking sheet, spacing them well apart, and bake in a preheated oven for 10 minutes to crisp up.

Meanwhile, put the drained quinoa into a clean bowl and add the remaining olive oil, along with the cilantro and lime juice.

Next, drain the wakame, slice off the "stalks," and discard. Mix the seaweed into the quinoa mixture.

To serve, divide the quinoa mixture between 2 plates. Scatter with the grapefruit segments, followed by the crusted tofu.

Make the dressing by mixing all the ingredients together in a cup until fully incorporated. Drizzle over the salad and add whole cilantro leaves to garnish.

serves 2

⅔ cup (100g) black quinoa (white or red work well too)

1¼ cups (25g) wakame seaweed

¾ cup (210g) firm tofu

1 clove garlic, grated

1 tbsp coconut flour

1 tbsp ground flax seeds

2 tbsp olive oil

a pinch of Himalayan pink salt

finely grated zest and juice of 1 lime

1 cup (15g) cilantro, finely chopped, plus extra whole leaves to garnish

1 sweet white grapefruit, segmented

for the dressing:

2 tbsp white miso

1 tbsp brown rice vinegar

2 tsp water

¼ tsp mirin

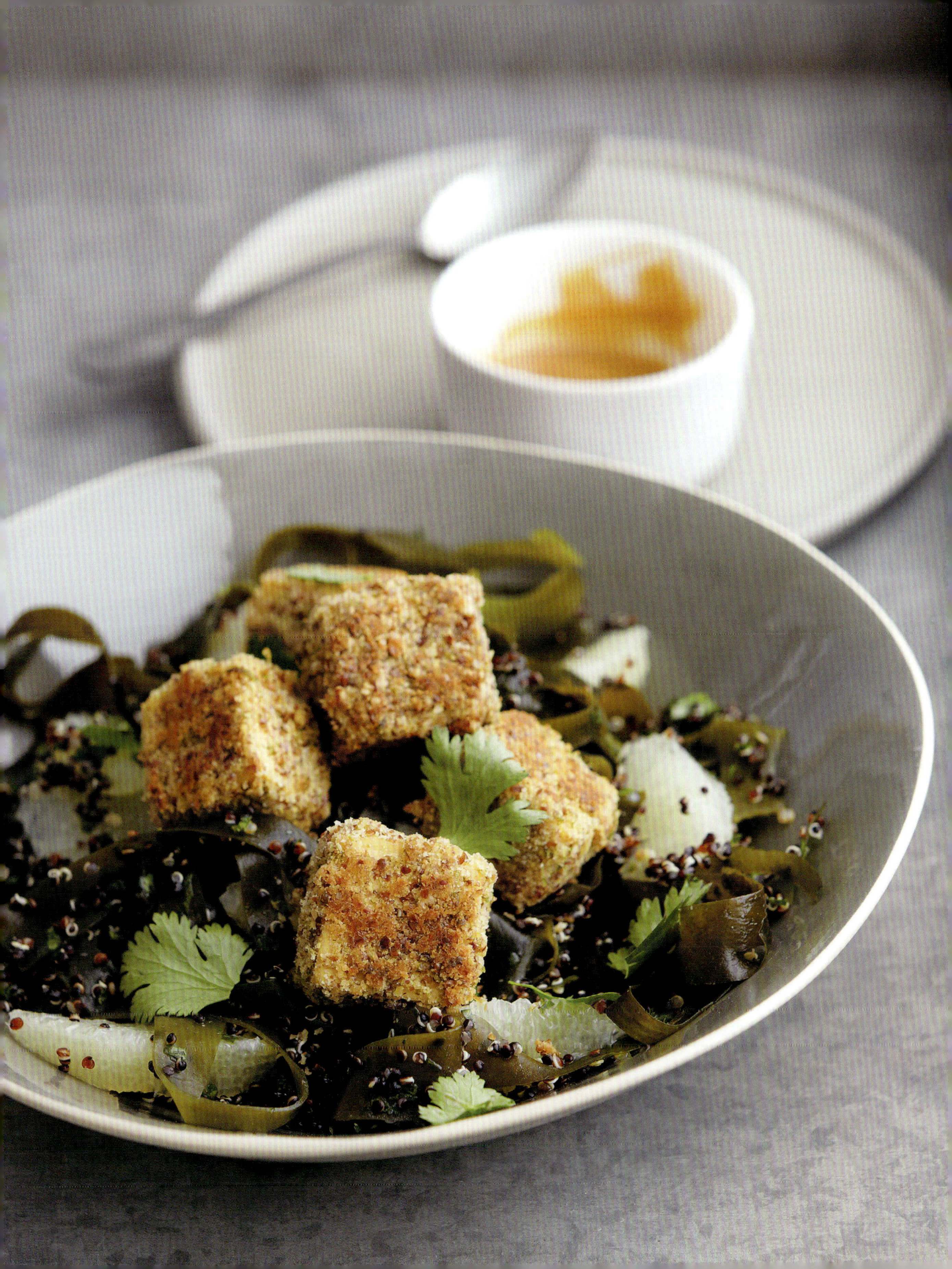

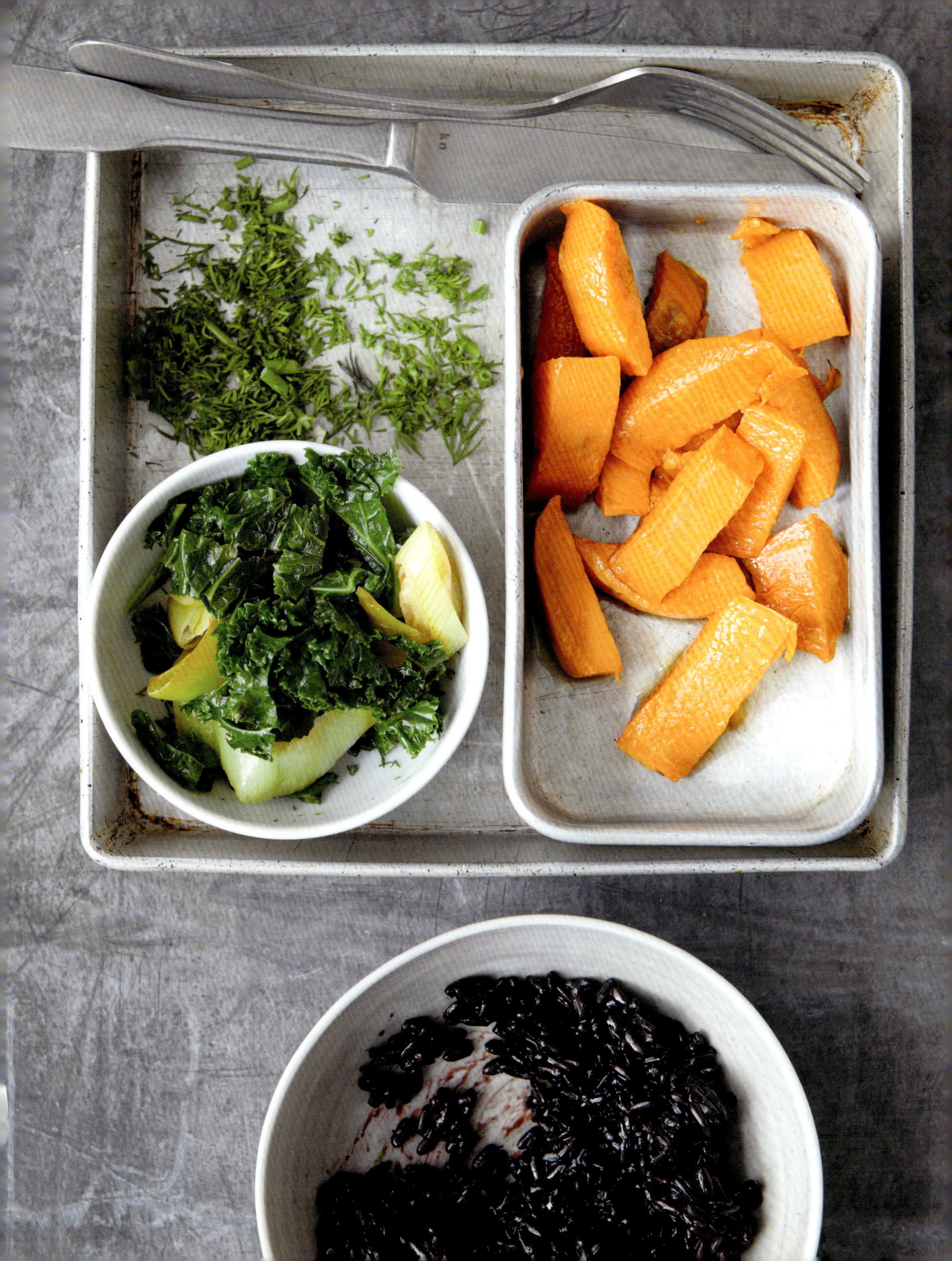

Sweet potato with black rice

This is one of those dishes you can cook while you are otherwise engaged in household chores or bathing the kids, for example. Simply pop the sweet potato in the oven and put the rice on, then forget about it for 40 minutes, until you have to do some quick cooking and assemble the dish (it's a good idea to set the timer, though). Who'd have thought such a simple dish could be as healthy as it is delicious? *Photo on previous page.*

Preheat the oven to 350°F/180°C/gas mark 4.

Cook the black rice according to the instructions on the package and add the bouillon to the cooking water.

Peel and chop the sweet potato into ⅓in- (1cm-) thick half moons, then toss with the sunflower oil. Place on a baking tray and put into a preheated oven for 45 minutes.

Melt the coconut oil in a saucepan and sauté the garlic for 30 seconds. Add the lemon juice and leek and continue to sauté on medium heat, adding the water to cool down the pan. Leave for 1 minute. Stir in the kale and cook for 1 minute until slightly wilted. Remove from the heat.

Once the rice has finished cooking, drain it of any remaining water. Mix in the apple cider vinegar and half of the dill along with some black pepper.

Remove the sweet potato from the oven and get ready to serve.

Make a bed of kale and leeks on each plate, then spoon on the black rice, top with the sweet potato, and sprinkle with the remaining dill.

serves 2–3

1 cup (180g) black rice

3⅓ cups, about 1lb (450g) sweet potato

1 tbsp sunflower oil

2 tsp bouillon powder

1 tbsp coconut oil

1 clove garlic, grated

juice of ½ lemon

1 leek (1⅓ cups/about 120g), chopped into 1in (2.5cm) pieces on the diagonal

1 cup (60g) kale, chopped

3 tbsp water

1 tsp apple cider vinegar

¾ cup (20g) dill sprigs, chopped

freshly ground black pepper

Spiced tofu balls

These delicious alternatives to meatballs are perfect for a meat-free Monday dinner. Throw in some gluten-free spaghetti, if you'd like a traditional Italian dish. And if you don't want the sauce, these balls are great on their own with a lovely, vibrant salad. *Photo overleaf.*

Preheat the oven to 325°F/170°C/gas mark 3.

First make the sauce. Using an ovenproof frying pan, sauté your onions in the sunflower oil for a couple of minutes until translucent. Add the garlic, cumin, and paprika and continue to sauté on low heat for another 2 minutes, when the air will start to smell wonderful.

Add the chili pepper, both types of tomatoes and the water. Turn the heat down to a low simmer and let the sauce reduce and develop a rich flavor – about
20 minutes.

Meanwhile, combine all of the ingredients for the tofu balls in a bowl. Roll the mixture into little balls (you should get about 12 balls) between your hands and set aside. As you shape the balls, squeeze out any excess moisture.

Once the sauce has reduced down, taste and add a pinch of Himalayan salt, if necessary. Add the spinach to the tomato sauce and stir through until completely wilted.

Arrange the tofu balls across the tomato sauce, drizzle with a touch of oil, and bake in the oven for 15–20 minutes, until the tofu balls are golden brown and the tomato sauce is beautifully thick.

serves 4

½ red onion, grated

1¾ cups (200g) zucchini, grated

1¾ cups (200g) carrot, grated

1 tsp ground cumin

1 large clove garlic, finely chopped

1 tsp ground ginger

½ tsp paprika

5¼oz (150g) smoked tofu, grated

2 tbsp brown rice flour

finely grated zest of ½ lime

a pinch of Himalayan pink salt

freshly ground black pepper

for the sauce:

1 white onion, diced

1 tsp sunflower oil, plus extra for drizzling

2 cloves garlic, finely chopped

½ tsp ground cumin

1 tsp paprika

½ red chili pepper, finely chopped

1⅔ cups (400g) canned tomatoes

1¾ cups (200g) cherry tomatoes, halved

½ cup (120ml) water

1 large handful of spinach leaves

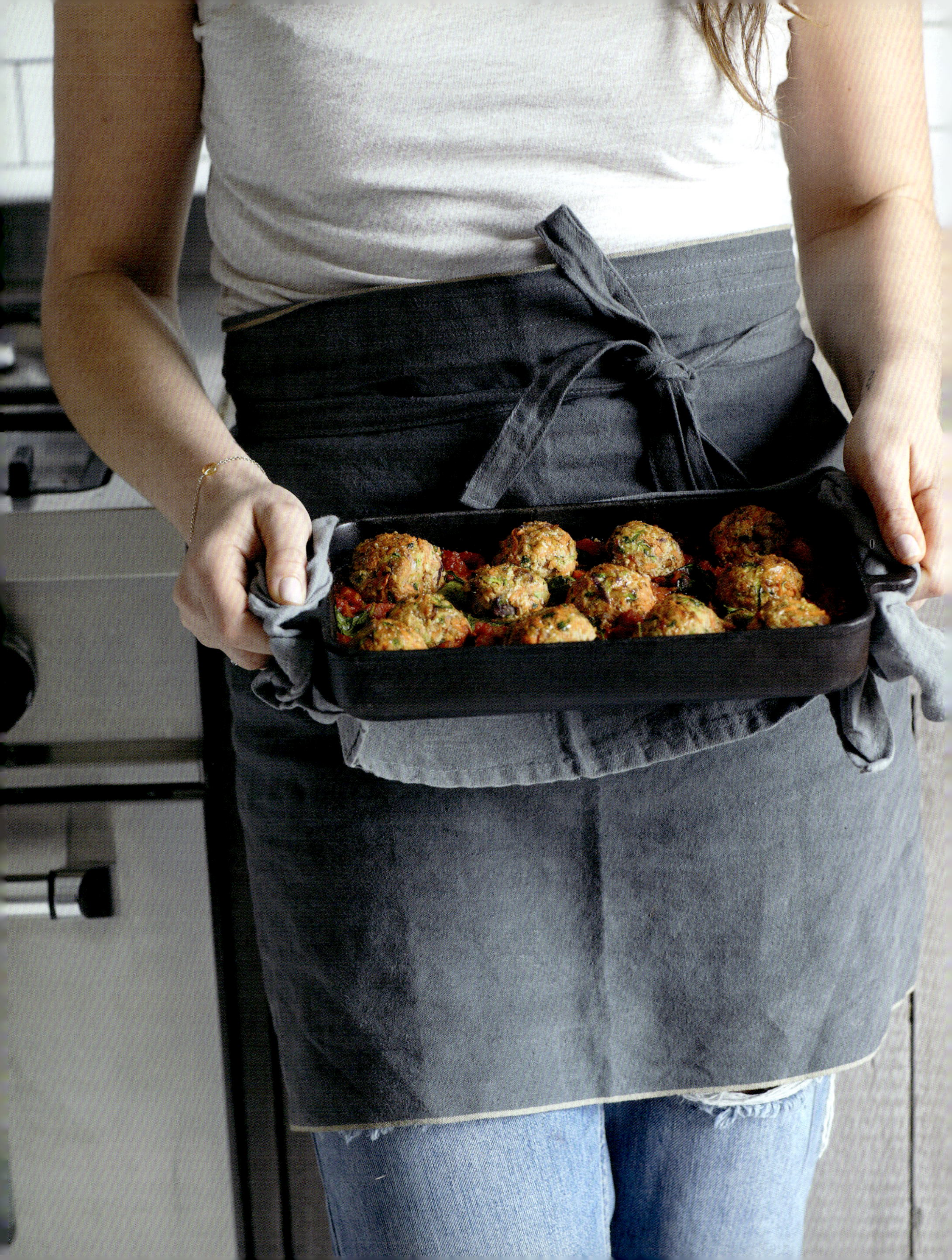

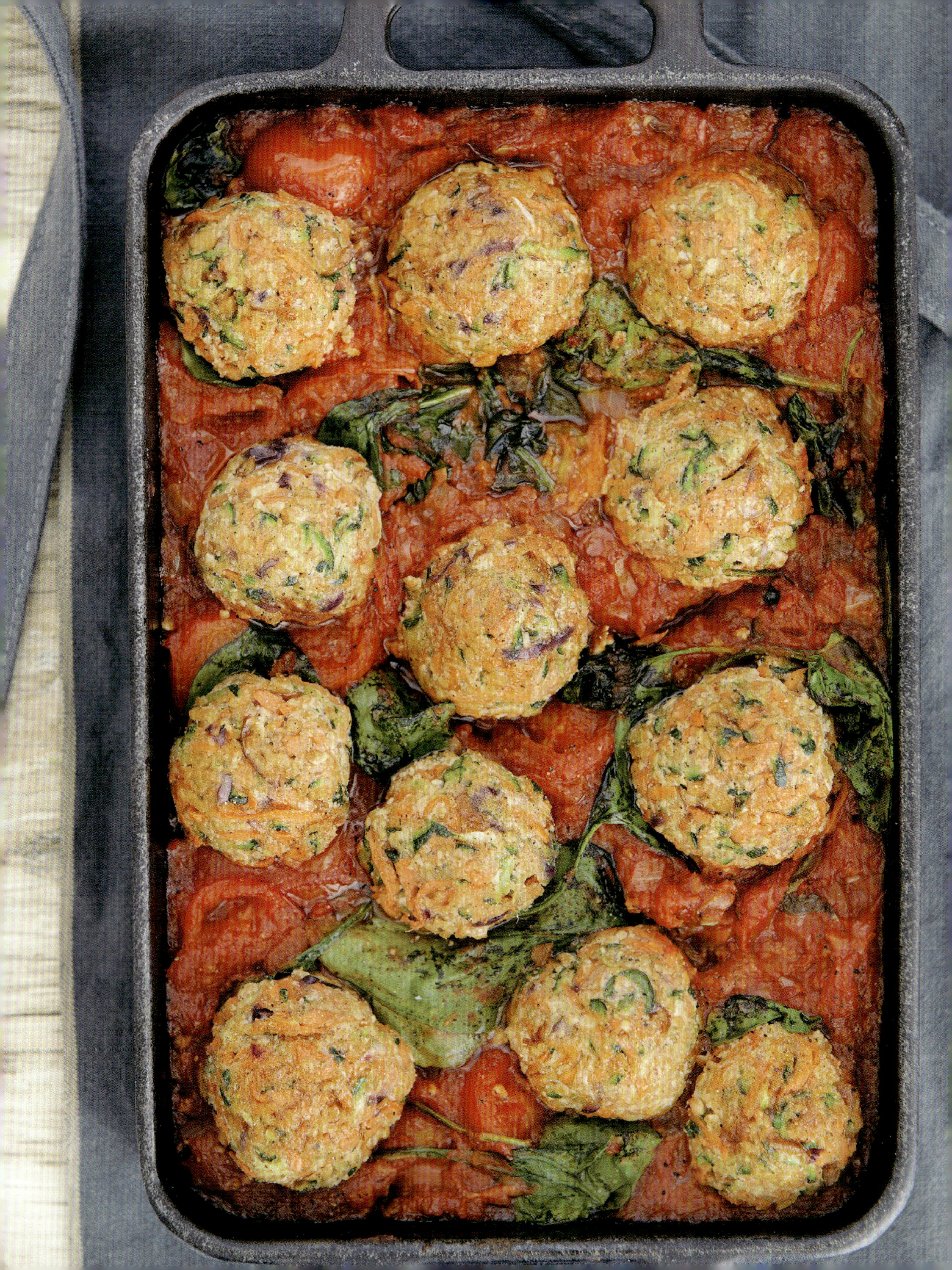

Lima bean and butternut curry

This is one of my new favorite dishes. It's a win-win recipe, quick to make, and a showstopper of a dish, so it's perfect if you're having friends over for dinner. It's now a staple in my house – all you need is some fresh herbs and a butternut squash to transform dried ingredients from your pantry into this delicious meal.

Put all the curry paste ingredients in a small food processor or blender and process until you get a nice chunky paste. Set aside.

Melt the coconut oil in a saucepan and sauté the onion and garlic for 1 minute. Add the curry paste along with the whole lemongrass stalk. Cook the sauce for 2 minutes more, then add another 4 tablespoons of the water.

After another 2 minutes, add the coconut milk and butternut squash, and continue to cook for 5 minutes over medium heat. Finally, stir in the lima beans and half the cilantro leaves and simmer for about 7 minutes. Test to see if the squash is cooked; if not, then simmer for another few minutes until totally tender.

Remove the lemongrass stalk before serving, and sprinkle the curry with the rest of the cilantro. If you'd like your curry with some rice, then use a brown basmati or perhaps some quinoa on the side.

serves 2

1 tsp coconut oil

½ white onion

1 clove garlic, grated

½ lemongrass stalk, crushed with a rolling pin

½ cup (120ml) water

1⅔ cups (400ml) coconut milk

1½ cups (200g) butternut squash, cut into ¾in (2cm) cubes

1⅔ cups (250g) lima beans

¾ cup (20g) cilantro leaves

for the curry paste:

1 tsp cumin seeds

1 tsp fennel seeds

1 tsp ground coriander

1 tsp ground turmeric

¼ tsp paprika

2½in (5cm) piece of ginger

2 tbsp brown rice vinegar

2 × 1in (2.5cm) slices (5g) galangal (optional)

2 tbsp sesame oil

¼ tsp Himalayan pink salt

finely grated zest and juice of 1 lime

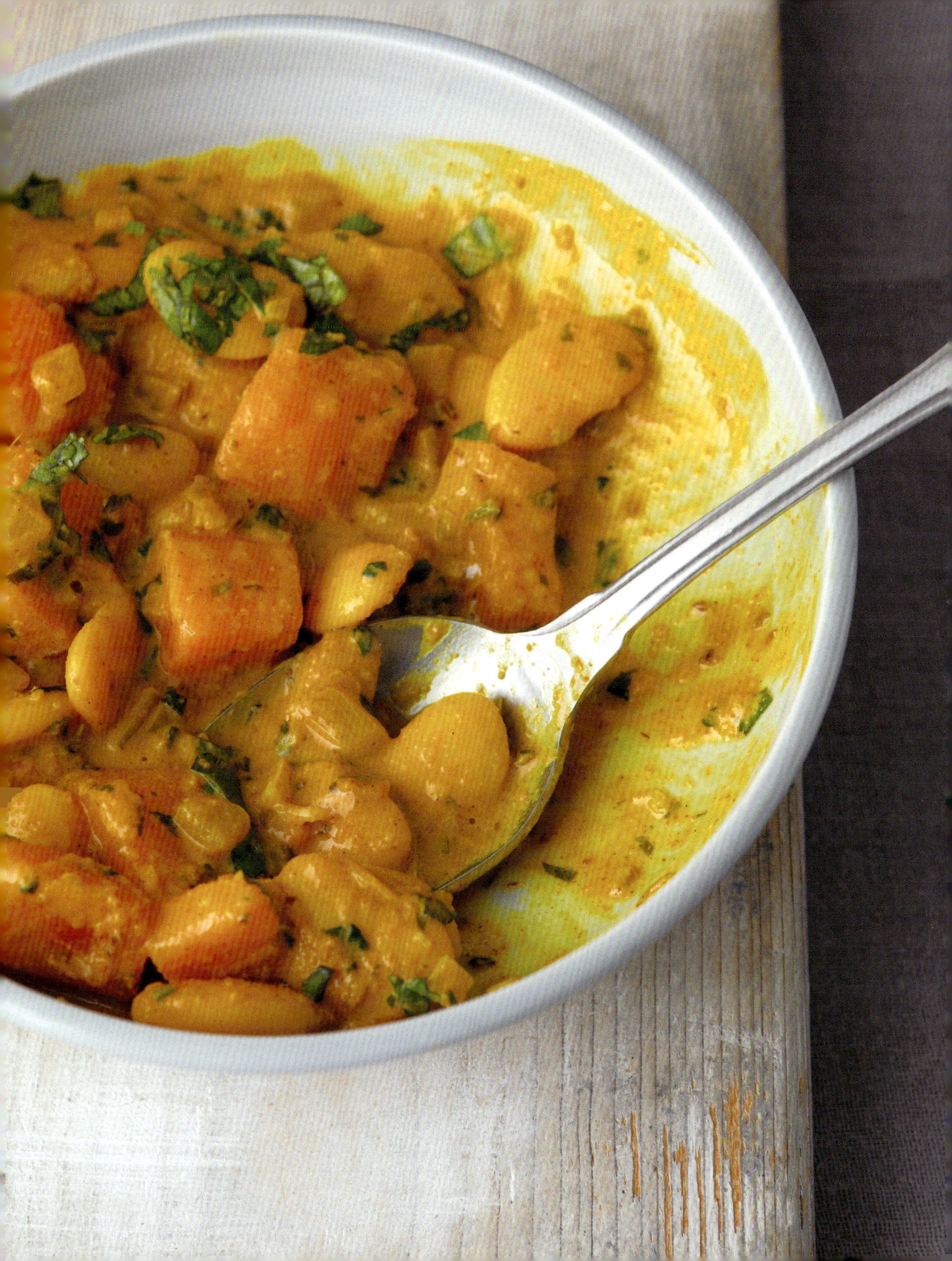

Sweet potato and fennel seed rosti

I love this delicious sweet potato rosti. But don't save this dish for lunch or dinner, this is a perfect breakfast or weekend brunch option! Sweet potato-based dishes are fantastic at getting carbohydrates into your system without making you feel sluggish – you'll have the energy to keep going and going . . .

I find it best to make the rosti in batches, 2 at a time, so you will need to repeat the following process twice.

Put the grated sweet potato into a cloth or dish towel and squeeze all the excess water out: you want the pulp to be as dry as possible. Transfer to a bowl.

Melt half the coconut oil in a non-stick pan and sauté half of the red onion, garlic, and fennel seeds for 1 minute. Add half the sweet potato and stir continuously for 30 seconds, so that the potato absorbs all the other flavors. Transfer to the bowl containing the remaining sweet potato and mix well.

Wipe the frying pan clean and spread half the oil around it with a cloth or paper towel. Place over medium heat.

Divide the rosti mixture into 4 equal pieces and form into patties. Place 2 of them in the hot pan and press down slightly. Cook for about 3–4 minutes on each side or until they are golden. Keep them warm while you cook the remaining patties in the same way.

When finished, set the patties aside while you repeat the process with the remaining mixture.

Serve with the spinach and poached eggs or goat cheese.

serves 2

1¼ cups, about 6oz (160g) sweet potato, grated

½ red onion, finely sliced

2 cloves garlic, crushed

1 tsp fennel seeds

2 tbsp coconut oil

½ tsp sunflower oil

to serve:

1 cup (30g) spinach, wilted

4 eggs poached, or ½ cup (80g) goat cheese, if you prefer

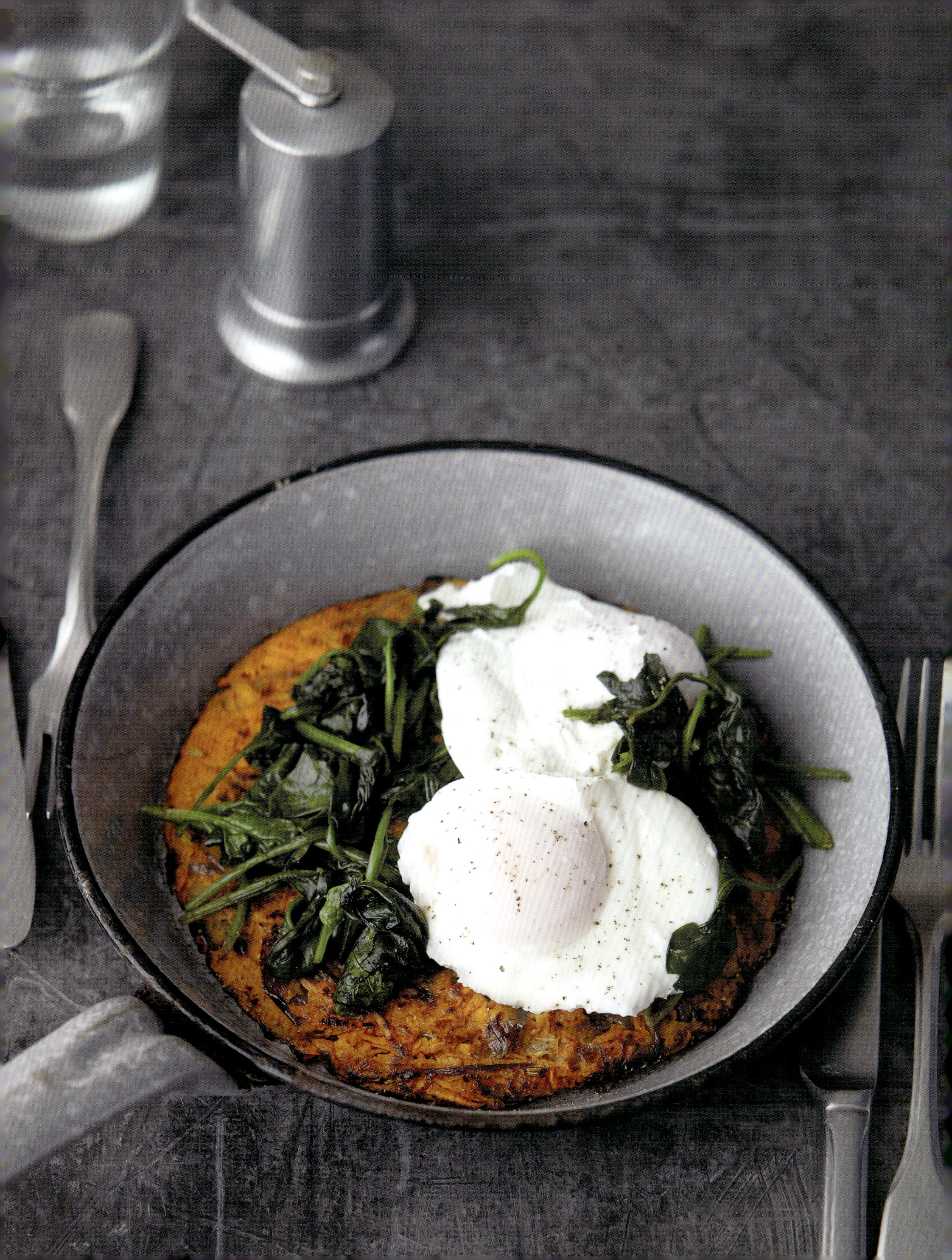

Lentil broccoli burgers

I remember developing these burgers at home after a workout. I was incredibly hungry, but managed to have them on the table within half an hour. Serve with a salad or with some roasted vegetables for the full monty.

Preheat the oven to 325°F/170°C/gas mark 3.

Blend the broccoli florets in a food processor or blender until the mixture looks like a bit like rice. Alternatively, chop the ingredients by hand as finely as possible.

Add three-quarters of the lentils to the food processor or blender while it's running. (Again, if you don't have a processor, you can do this manually with a bowl and wooden spoon, adding the lentils in small batches and crushing them.) When combined, transfer the broccoli and lentil mixture to a bowl and add the rest of the lentils, plus the tahini, salt, garlic, and ginger, and mix well. Form the mixture into 4 patties.

Heat the coconut oil and tamari in an ovenproof frying pan until hot. Add the patties and sear each side for 2 minutes until they turn a slightly darker color.

Transfer the pan to a preheated oven for 15 minutes or until the burgers are warmed all the way through.

Meanwhile, blend all the dressing ingredients together.

Serve 1 or 2 burgers per person, adding a swirl of delicious tahini dressing alongside some mixed salad greens, with broccoli and radish sprouts.

makes 4

½ head of broccoli, broken into florets

⅔ cup (130g) cooked Puy lentils

1 tsp black tahini (white tahini works too)

a pinch of Himalayan pink salt

1 clove garlic, grated

⅓in (1cm) piece of ginger, grated

2 tsp coconut oil

1 tsp tamari

mixed salad greens with broccoli and radish sprouts to serve

for the dressing:

3-4 tbsp tahini

6 tbsp water

juice of ½ lemon

a pinch of Himalayan pink salt

Asian noodle soup

If you need a fix of Asian flavors, then this delicious and aromatic dish will hit the spot; it's both warming and cleansing. Here, the cinnamon and star anise provide the mouthwatering base flavors as well as their nurturing and antiviral properties. The soup is amazing for your immune system and tastes wonderful, too.

Heat the coconut oil in a frying pan and add the onion, garlic, ginger, cinnamon, star anise, and coriander seeds. Sauté over medium heat for 2 minutes.

Add the cold water (not the measured boiling water) and the tamari, and simmer for another minute. Stir in the Chinese celery and sweet basil.

Add the boiling water to the pan along with the bouillon, stir, and leave until the liquid has reached boiling point again.

Meanwhile, chop the snow peas on the diagonal and slice the root off the bok choy so that the leaves are released. Add to the pan along with the shiitake and half of the chopped cilantro. After 1 minute add the rice noodles and cook for another 3–4 minutes until they are done.

Finish off by squeezing the lime juice over the top and stir through with the tempeh, the remaining cilantro, and the sliced chili if you want some extra heat.

serves 2

1 tbsp coconut oil

½ white onion, finely chopped

1 clove garlic, grated

2 × 1in (2.5cm) slices (5cm) piece of ginger, sliced

¾in (3g) cinnamon stick

1 star anise

1 tsp coriander seeds

6 tbsp cold water

1 tbsp tamari

⅛ cup (10g) Chinese celery, roughly chopped

1 heaping tbsp (3g) sweet Thai basil

3 cups (720ml) boiling water

1 tbsp bouillon powder

¾ cup (50g) snow peas

1½ cups (100g) bok choy

¾ cup (60g) shiitake mushrooms, sliced

⅓ cup (5g) fresh cilantro, roughly chopped

⅓ cup (50g) rice noodles

juice of 1 lime

⅓ cup (50g) tempeh, cut into strips, to garnish

6 thin slices of red chili pepper, sliced at an angle (optional)

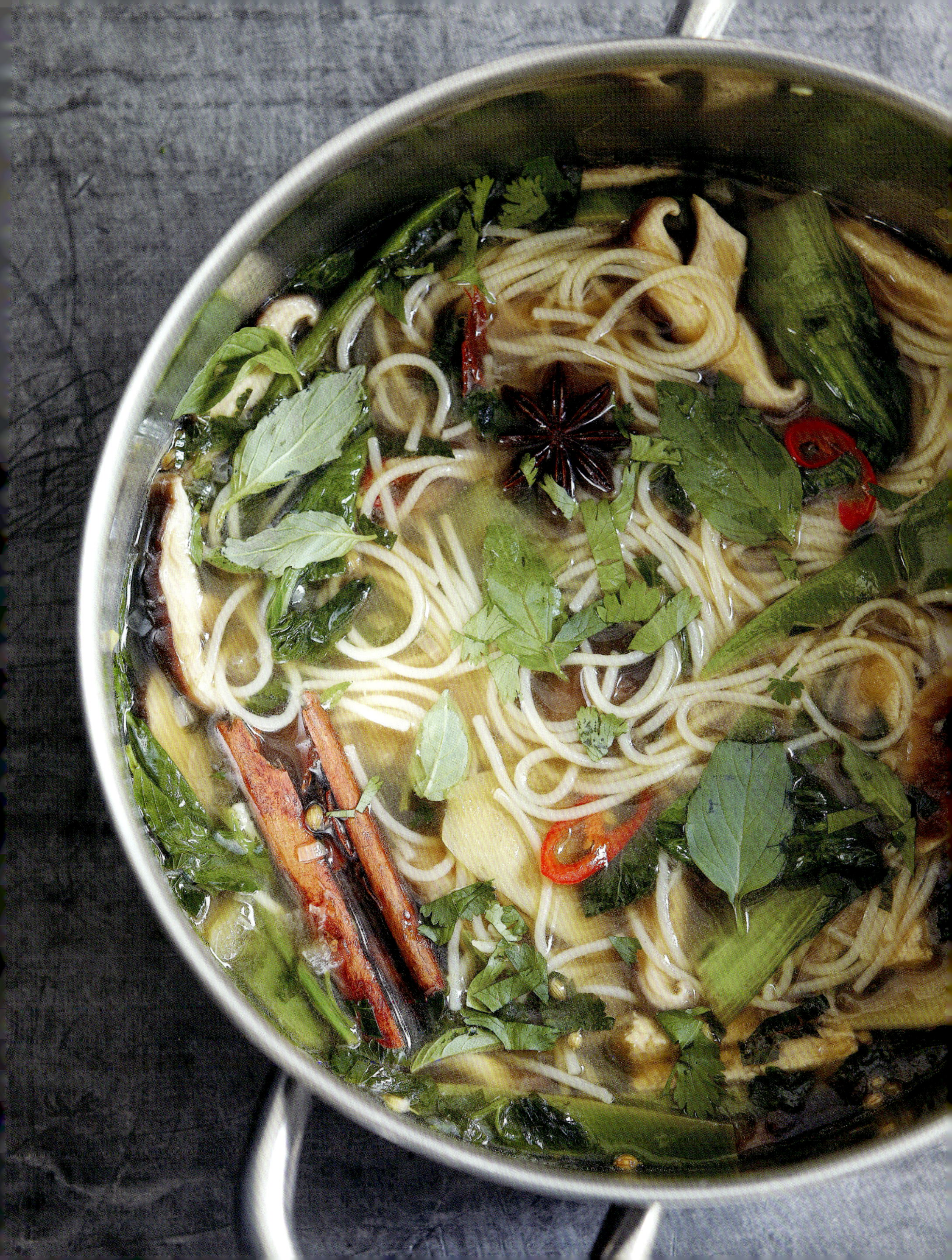

Black rice and celeriac risotto

This warming risotto is perfect on a cold day – it'll warm you up and nourish you at the same time. If you can't get hold of black rice, you could also use brown or red rice as alternatives, though the cooking times will be about 20 minutes longer. In the finished risotto, the black rice will still have some bite to it; it won't be gooey and soft like white rice.

Add the bouillon powder to the boiling water to make a vegetable stock and stir until all the powder has dissolved. Set aside.

Place the black rice into a wide-bottomed saucepan with half of the stock and simmer gently over medium heat for about 30 minutes, adding more stock if it dries up.

Meanwhile, heat the sunflower oil in a frying pan and sauté the onions and garlic until the onions become translucent. Then, add the celeriac and leeks and continue to sauté for about 5 minutes until the celeriac begins to soften. Add a splash of water (about 1 tablespoon) if the pan gets too hot and dry; this splash will help to steam the vegetables.

After the rice has been cooking for 30 minutes, stir through the sautéed vegetables. Then, gradually add in a ladleful of the remaining stock and stir gently. Once the rice has absorbed the stock, repeat with another ladleful and continue in this way until the rice has softened, being sure to stir as much as you can. This may take another 50 minutes depending on your pan.

Once the rice is almost cooked, add the broccolini and stir through the last of the stock. Continue to cook for 2–3 minutes more until the broccoli softens.

Finally, stir through the tarragon and parsley, and season with salt and pepper.

I like to serve this risotto with a sprinkling of feta and some of the fresh herbs.

1 tbsp bouillon powder

1 litre boiling water

1⅛ cups (200g) black rice

1 tbsp sunflower oil

1 red onion, diced

1 large clove garlic, chopped

1⅛ cups (175g) celeriac (also known as celery root), cut into ¼in (5mm) cubes

1¼ cups (100g) leeks, finely chopped

3–4 pieces broccolini, chopped into tiny florets

1 tbsp finely chopped tarragon, plus extra to serve

1 tbsp finely chopped flat leaf parsley, plus extra to serve

a pinch of Himalayan pink salt

freshly ground black pepper

⅓ cup (50g) feta cheese, crumbled or 2 tbsp nutritional yeast, to serve (optional)

Arame broccoli salad on a bed of celery "noodles"

This gorgeously cleansing salad is high in fiber and high in protein. How, I might hear you ask? Well, seaweed is high in protein; in fact, it has a higher percentage than a steak. And with the brown rice miso you get your ultimate fix of fermented foods, as well as fresh green vegetables. It's an all-round perfect meal, I think.

Bring a pan of salted water to a rolling boil. Drop in the beans and broccoli and blanch for 3 minutes. Using a slotted spoon, transfer the vegetables to a colander and refresh under very cold water. Set aside.

Soak the arame in the hot vegetable water for 15 minutes, then drain.

Meanwhile, make the "noodles" by paring each celery stick with a potato peeler. Slice each length in half with a knife.

Blend all the dressing ingredients in a blender until smooth.

Put the beans, broccoli, cucumber, cilantro, and drained arame in a bowl and mix together.

On each plate, create a nest with the celery "noodles." Arrange the arame mixed salad greens in the middle, drizzle the dressing over the top and, finally, garnish with the lime zest, pickled ginger, and an extra sprinkling of cilantro.

serves 2–3

¼ tbsp Himalayan pink salt

1 cup (100g) green beans, topped and tailed

1⅓ cups (160g) purple sprouting broccoli (regular broccoli works too)

1¾oz (50g) arame seaweed

4–6 sticks celery (I use 2 per person)

⅔ cup (120g) cucumber, diced

⅔ cup (10g) cilantro, chopped, plus extra to garnish

for the dressing:

2½ tbsp (40g) brown rice miso

2 tbsp water

1 tbsp toasted sesame oil

juice of 1 lime

to garnish:

finely grated zest of 1 lime

3 tbsp (40g) pickled ginger

Unlike other seaweeds, you buy packages of arame seaweed as small short strings; you can use it dried if you want a crunch and, however you use it, it has a mild taste.

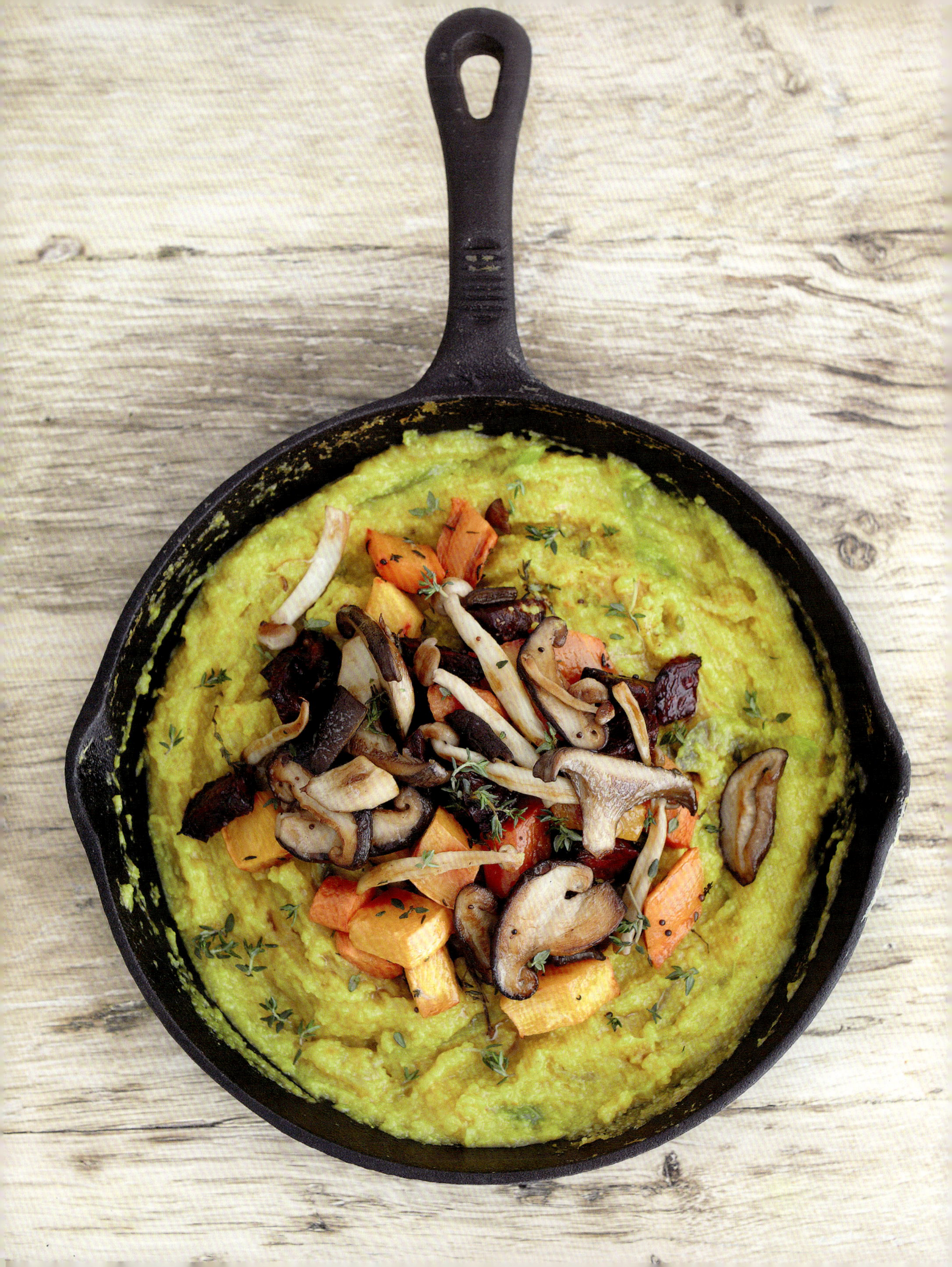

Polenta with roasted root vegetables

This dish is perfect for a winter's evening and a cosy night in.
Polenta is quick to make, it just needs a little love in the flavor
department! You could add some smoked tofu on the top if you
want to give yourself an extra protein kick before or after a
work-out session.

Preheat the oven to 350°F/180°C/gas mark 4.

Put the rutabaga, beets, and carrots into a baking tray along with the
sunflower oil, mustard seeds, and fresh thyme. Mix together so all are well
coated and roast for 40 minutes in a preheated oven.

Meanwhile, put half the vegan butter or coconut oil in a frying pan and
sauté the red onion, turmeric, garlic, and fennel seeds over medium heat
for 1 minute. Add 2 tablespoons cold water to cool the pan and add
moisture, then add the celery and lemon zest. Sauté again and add another
4 tablespoons cold water and leave for 1 minute for it to be absorbed.

Next, add about 1 cup (230ml) of the hot water, along with the polenta, and
stir constantly, for about a minute, until it starts to thicken. Add the
remaining hot water, still stirring, and turn the heat under the pan down to
low, as the polenta will start to bubble and spit at you. Then add the lemon
juice and umeboshi paste. Just before serving, stir in the nutritional yeast.

Once the roasted vegetables are nearly done, put the remaining butter or
oil in a clean frying pan and sauté the mushrooms until soft.

To serve, scoop the polenta into a bowl, top with the roasted vegetables
and sautéed mushrooms, followed by a garnish of fresh thyme.

serves 2-3

*1 cup (140g) rutabaga,
cut into ¾in (2cm)
cubes*

*2 × 2in (145g) beets,
sliced into half-moons
about ¼in (5mm) thick*

*2 carrots (about ⅔
cup/200g total), cut
into matchsticks*

*¼ tsp black mustard
seeds*

*1½ tbsp (4g) thyme
leaves, plus extra to
garnish*

1 tbsp sunflower oil

*2 tbsp vegan butter or
coconut oil*

*½ red onion, finely
sliced (I use a
mandoline)*

*2 tsp (4g) fresh
turmeric, grated*

*1 clove garlic, finely
grated*

¼ tsp fennel seeds

*6 tbsp water, for
cooling the pan*

*1 stick celery, sliced at
an angle*

*finely grated zest and
juice of ½ lemon*

*2⅓ cups (560ml) hot
water*

½ cup (70g) polenta

½ tsp umeboshi paste

¼ tbsp ground cumin

*2 heaping tbsp
nutritional yeast*

*2½ cups (200g) mixed
mushrooms*

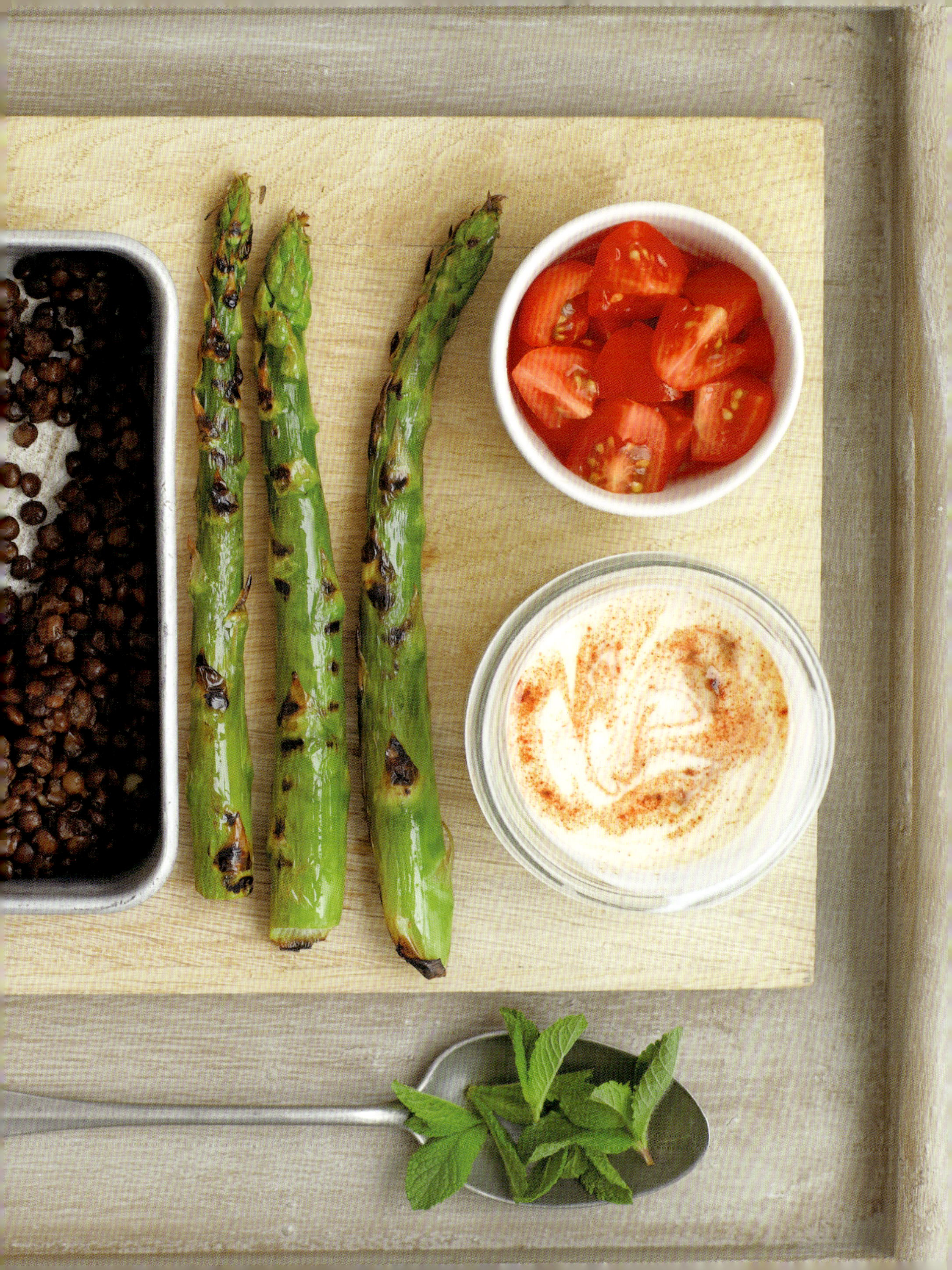

Black lentil and salsa verde salad

This simply beautiful and tasty salad is high in protein, so it's perfect for a high-energy day after a workout. If you're pressed for time, you can buy pre-cooked lentils; but you might need slightly less than the amount listed below.

Cook the lentils according to the instructions on the package. When cooked, stir in the rice wine vinegar and set aside.

Next, make the salsa verde. Put the sorrel leaves, mint, cilantro, olive oil, and lime juice into a food processor or blender and pulse until you get a chunky texture. Alternatively, chop and combine them by hand.

Transfer the salsa verde to a bowl and stir in the chopped tomatoes.

Add a splash of sesame oil to a grill pan over high heat and grill the asparagus on each side until soft and striped with lovely, dark charcoal lines.

Put the lentils on a serving platter and season with salt. Then, pile the salsa verde–tomato mixture and asparagus on top, with a final garnish of lime zest. If you'd like to have this salad with the minty yogurt, simply mix all the ingredients together in a separate bowl and serve alongside.

serves 2

½ cup (100g) Puy lentils

1 tsp rice wine vinegar

3 tbsp chopped (20g) sorrel leaves

⅔ cup (10g) mint leaves

⅔ cup (10g) cilantro

¼ cup (65ml) olive oil

finely grated zest and juice of 1 lime

1½ cups (200g) cherry tomatoes, chopped

sesame oil, for griddling

2 cups chopped (250g) asparagus

Himalayan pink salt

for the mint yogurt (optional):

½ cup (120ml) goat milk yogurt or coconut milk yogurt

⅔ cup (10g) mint leaves

¼ tsp smoked paprika

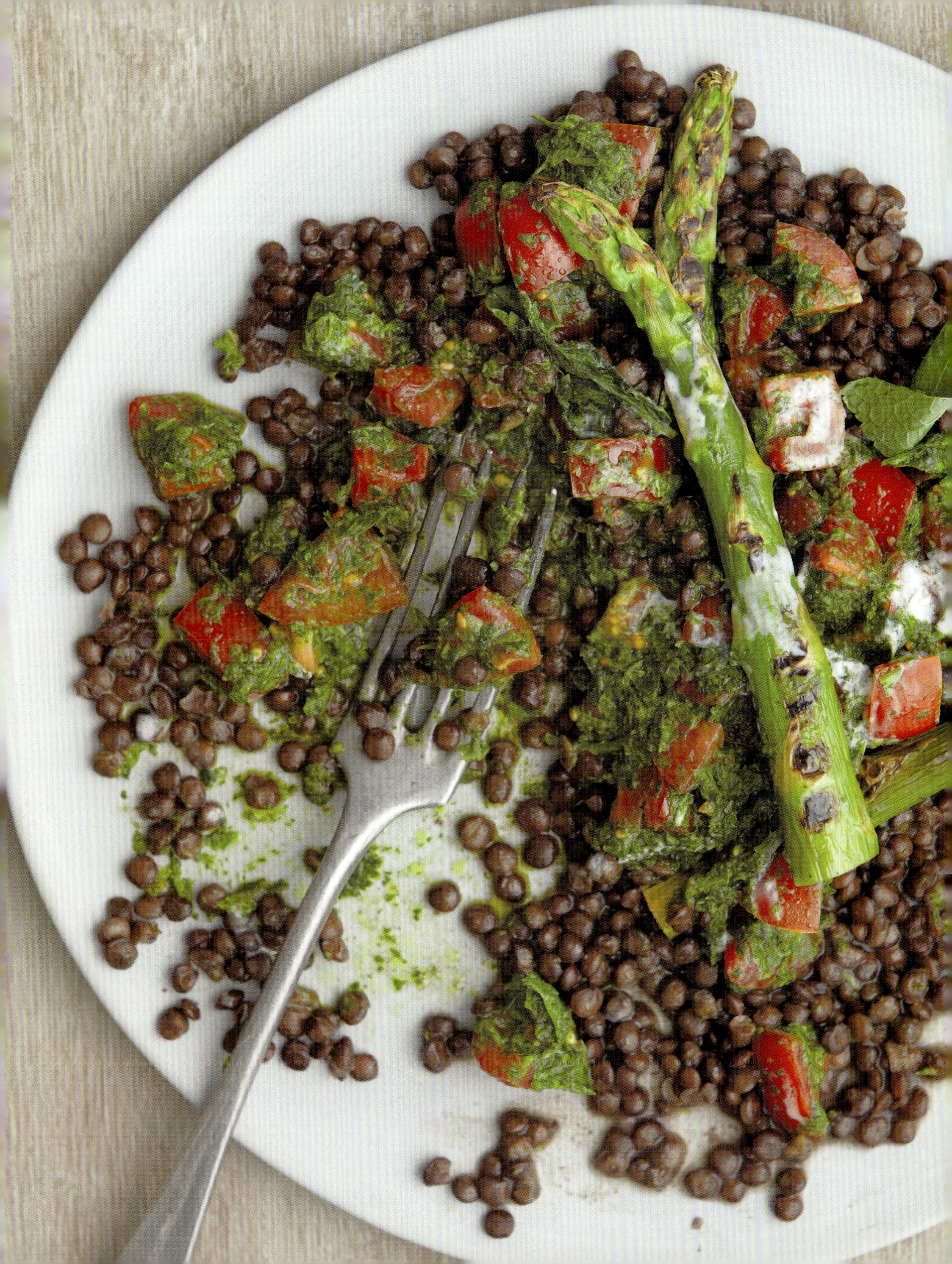

Chickpea tofu aka "chifu"

Soy products offer vegetarians a great source of protein, though do be sure to choose non-GM varieties. But I really don't like to eat too much soy on a daily basis. So, I devised a healthy alternative using chickpea flour. The texture of my "chifu" is more buttery than tofu, and the flavor is unbelievably delicious. What's more, it's incredibly easy to make and keeps for up to four days in an airtight container in the fridge.

makes 16 "steaks"

6 cups (1.4 litres) water

3 cups (280g) chickpea flour

1 tbsp olive oil

¼ tsp cumin seeds

¼ tsp fennel seeds

a pinch of Himalayan pink salt

1 tsp dried rosemary

Bring 4 cups (960ml) of the water to a boil in a shallow pan and line a baking tray with parchment paper.

Sift the chickpea flour gradually into a bowl and whisk in the remaining measured water, so it combines and makes a thick glossy mixture without any lumps.

Put the olive oil, cumin, and fennel seeds, salt, and rosemary in a pestle and mortar and mash together to combine. Then, stir this into the chickpea mixture.

Once the water has come to a boil, slowly pour in the spiced chickpea mixture, stirring all the time to avoid any lumps. Once everything is completely incorporated, the "chifu" will become glossy and thick.

Remove from heat and pour the mixture into the prepared tray. Transfer to the fridge for 4 hours or until solid.

Cut into the desired shape for your soy-free tofu.

I've used "chifu" in the great salad overleaf.

Roasted cauliflower and saffron quinoa chifu salad

This is an amazing main meal that is also impressive enough to serve to guests at a dinner party. The saffron is not essential, but gives the quinoa a lovely aroma as well as a gorgeous orange color. If you don't have the time to make the chifu, you can always use regular tofu instead.

Preheat the oven to 325°F/170°C/gas mark 3.

Put the cauliflower into a baking dish with the sunflower oil and salt and roast for 10 minutes.

Next, add the celery to the mix and roast for 15 minutes more, until the cauliflower starts to brown.

Meanwhile, cook the quinoa according to the instructions on the package and add the saffron and lemon zest to the water.

Combine all the marinade ingredients in a pan, add the chifu steaks to marinate, and set aside. When the quinoa and vegetables are ready, set them aside.

Take the steaks out of the marinade and heat up the liquid until it starts to sizzle slightly, and then reduce.

Either warm the chifu steaks in the hot marinade or cook them, as I like to, on a hot grill pan to get charred lines across them.

To serve, pile up the quinoa in 2 bowls, add the chopped dill and parsley, then drizzle with half the marinade. Arrange the cauliflower and celery on top, followed by the chifu, then drizzle with the remaining marinade.

serves 2

2 cups (200g) cauliflower, broken into florets

1 tbsp sunflower oil

a pinch of Himalayan pink salt

1¼ long stalks (80g) celery, torn and sliced lengthways

1 cup (150g) quinoa

a pinch of saffron strands

2 pieces of lemon zest, cut with a potato peeler

10oz (280g) chifu (see page 129), cut into 4 "steaks"

1½ tbsp (5g) dill, chopped

3 tbsp (10g) flat leaf parsley, chopped

for the marinade:

8 tbsp apple cider vinegar

4 tbsp sesame oil

4 tsp rice vinegar

1 tsp fennel seeds

juice of ½ lemon

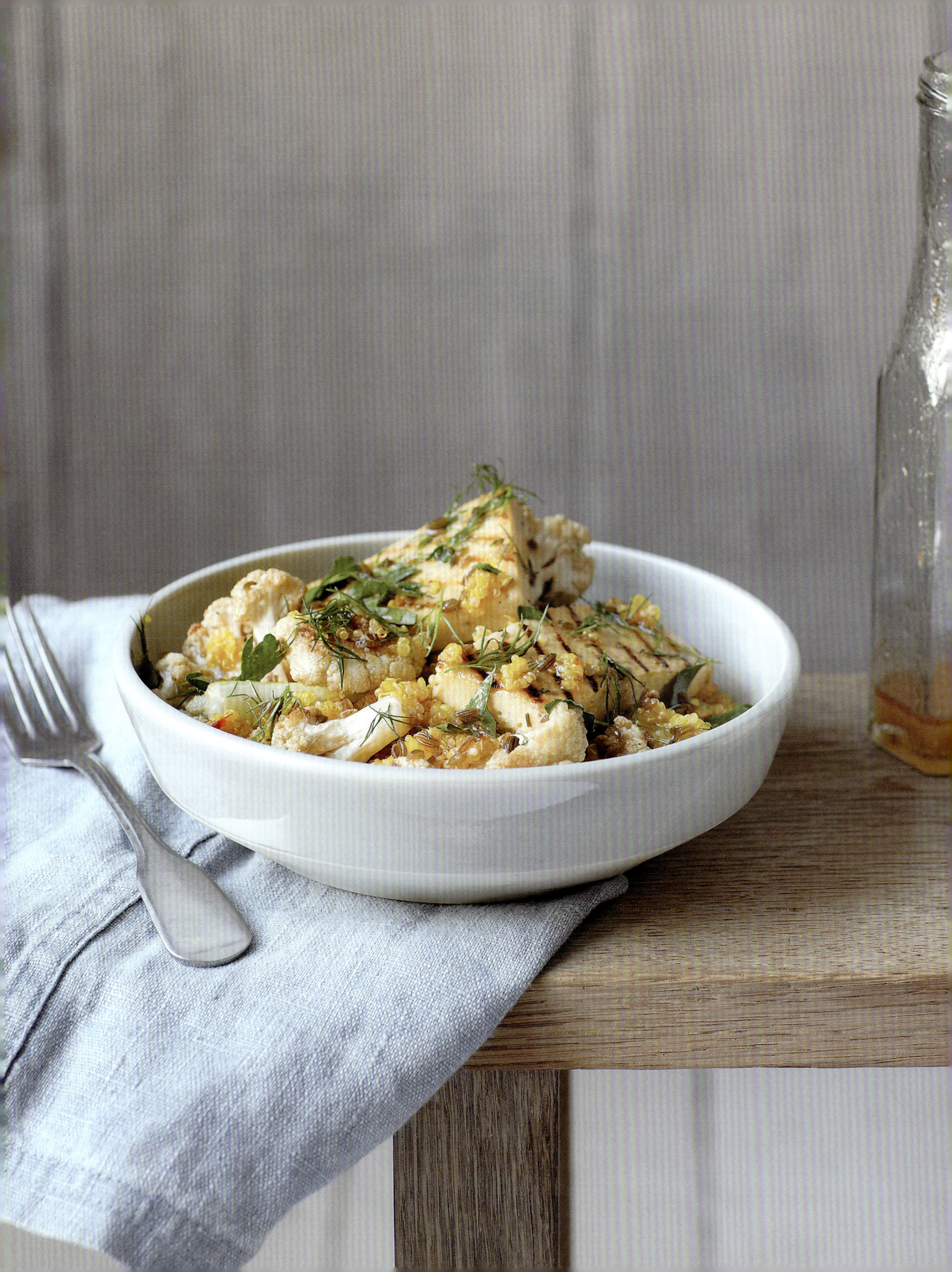

Little gem and wakame salad

I think the thing I love the most about this salad is the mouthwatering dressing. But be warned, if you are not as much of a garlic fan as I am, simply reduce the amount from one clove to half. This is a super-cleansing dish – it's really alkaline and has an extra protein hit from the tahini dressing.

First make the dressing: simply blend all the ingredients in a blender until smooth. If it comes out a little thick for your liking, then add a little more water; if it's too thin, then add some more tahini.

Soak the wakame in hot water for 15 minutes.

Meanwhile, prepare the salad vegetables and put into a bowl with the sesame seeds and mix together.

Drain the wakame, slice off the stalks, cut into strips (about 1cm wide), and add to the bowl. Pour over the dressing and mix together well.

Serve with a scattering of the radish sprouts for a beautiful and peppery garnish.

serves 2–3

1 cup (20g) wakame seaweed

2½ cups (140g) Little Gem lettuce or hearts of romaine (iceberg works well, too), chopped

¼ cup (30g) radishes, sliced

1 cup (130g) cucumber, sliced and quartered

2 tbsp (15g) sesame seeds

½ cup (15g) radish sprouts, to garnish

for the dressing:

4 tbsp tahini

1 cup (240ml) water

juice of ½ lemon

1 clove garlic

¼ tsp Himalayan pink salt

Wakame becomes really alkaline in the body; it also acts as a diuretic, so it counters water retention and bloating, and is a fabulous source of calcium and magnesium, thereby promoting strong bones. What's more, the pigment in wakame has been shown to improve insulin resistance, helping your body to become better at balancing blood sugar.

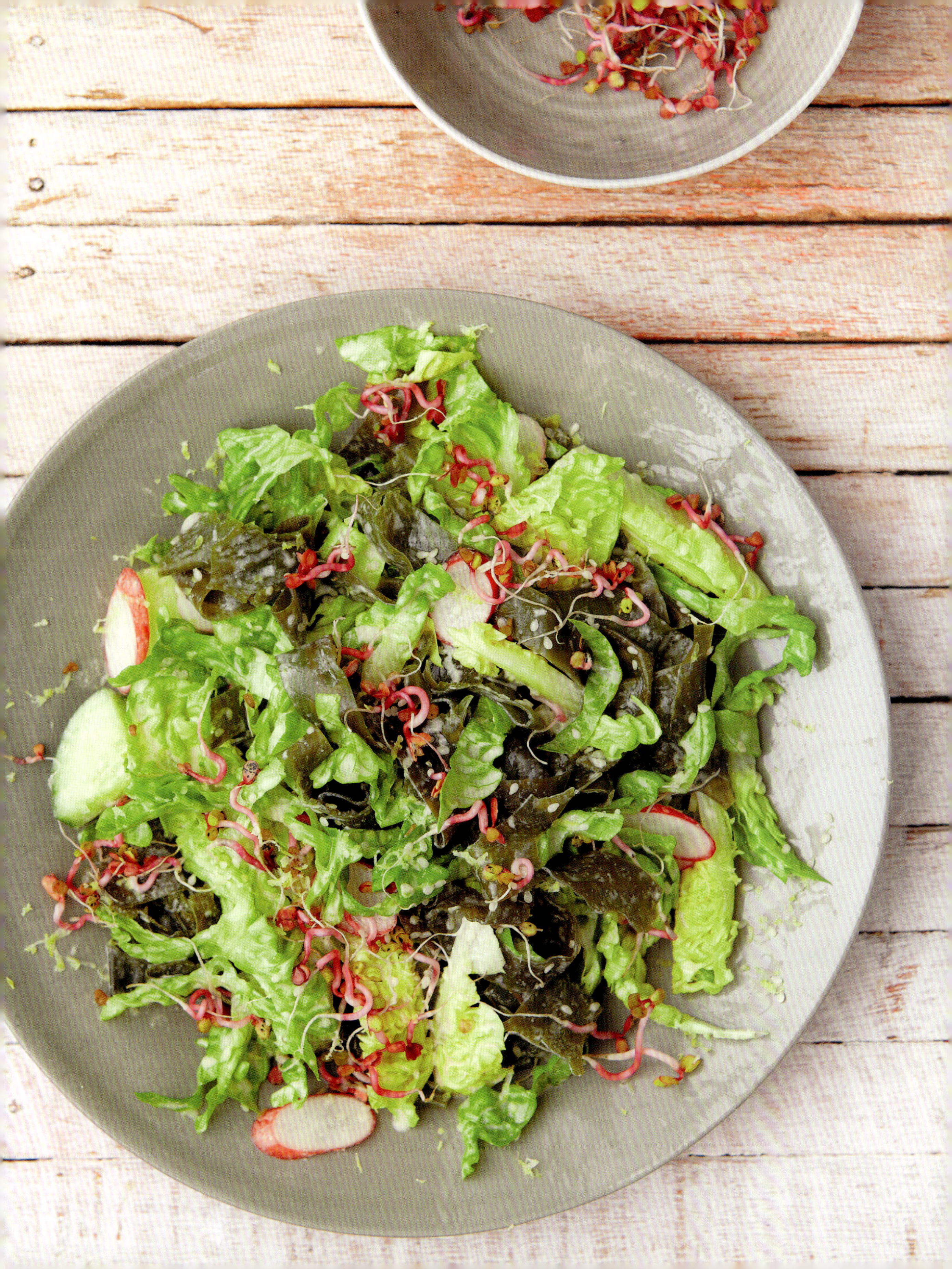

Fluffy eggs and asparagus with a fresh dill dressing

If I want a change from scrambled eggs, then this is the breakfast I go for. Expect a zingy dish full of flavor and one that is very filling. If asparagus is out of season, why not substitute broccoli or kale?

Bring a pot of water to a boil and put the eggs in for 10 minutes. Then, remove the eggs from the pan and run them under cold water until they are cool to the touch.

Put a little oil in a grill pan and cook the asparagus until they are soft and lightly charred – about 3 minutes on each side.

Make the dressing by putting the olive oil, dill, salt, and lemon juice into a blender and process until just combined. (I like a bit of texture in my dressing.)

Peel the eggs, place them in a bowl and mash them up with the capers. Drizzle in a quarter of the dressing and mix in.

To serve, arrange a bed of asparagus on each of two plates and top with the egg and capers followed by a drizzle of the remaining dressing over the top; add cracked black pepper to taste and garnish with any extra dill sprigs.

serves 2

4 eggs

12 asparagus spears

scant ½ cup (95g) capers, drained

cracked black pepper

for the dressing:

5 tbsp olive oil, plus extra for grill pan

1 cup chopped (25g) dill sprigs

¼ tsp Himalayan pink salt

juice of ½ lemon

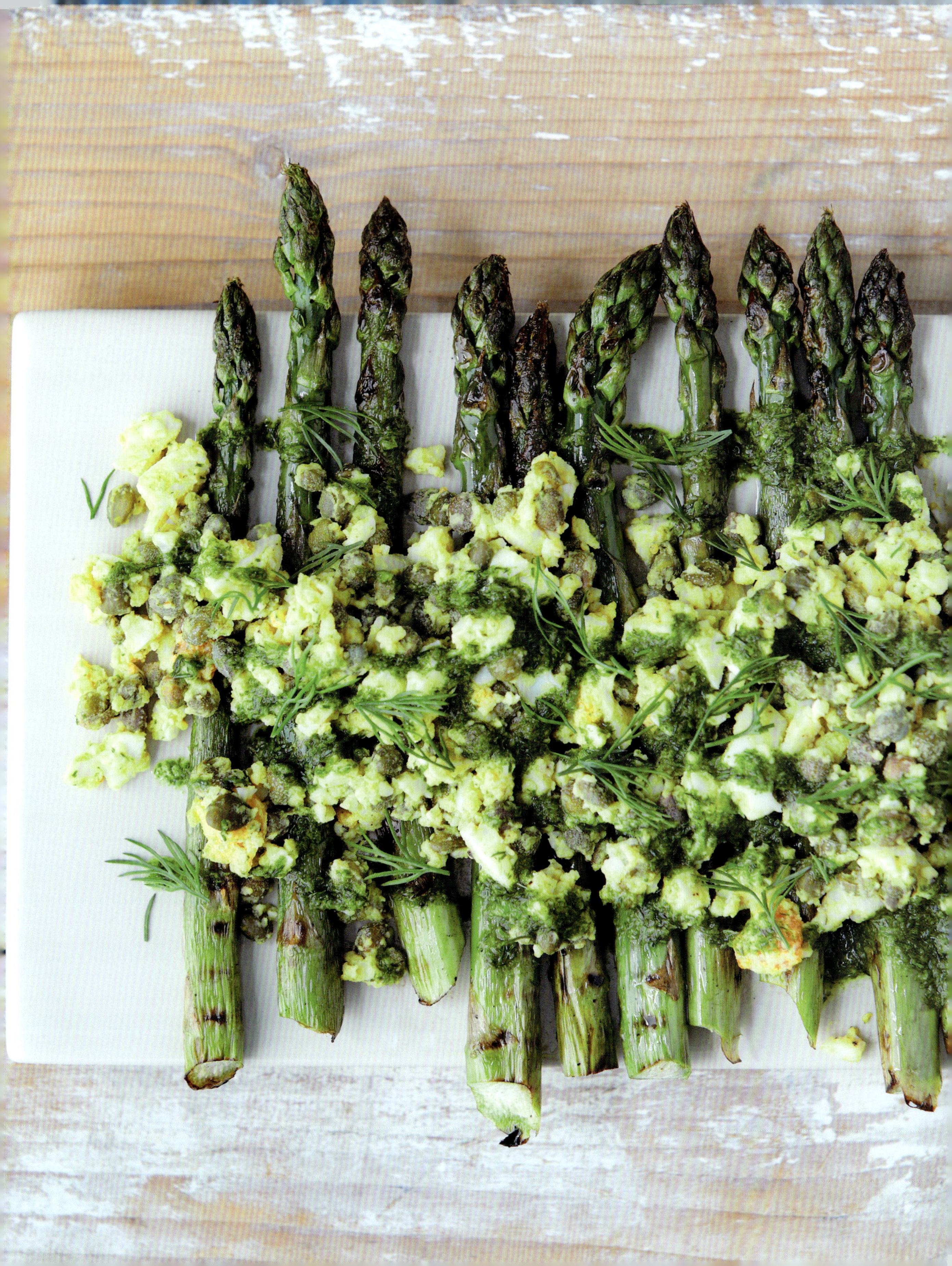

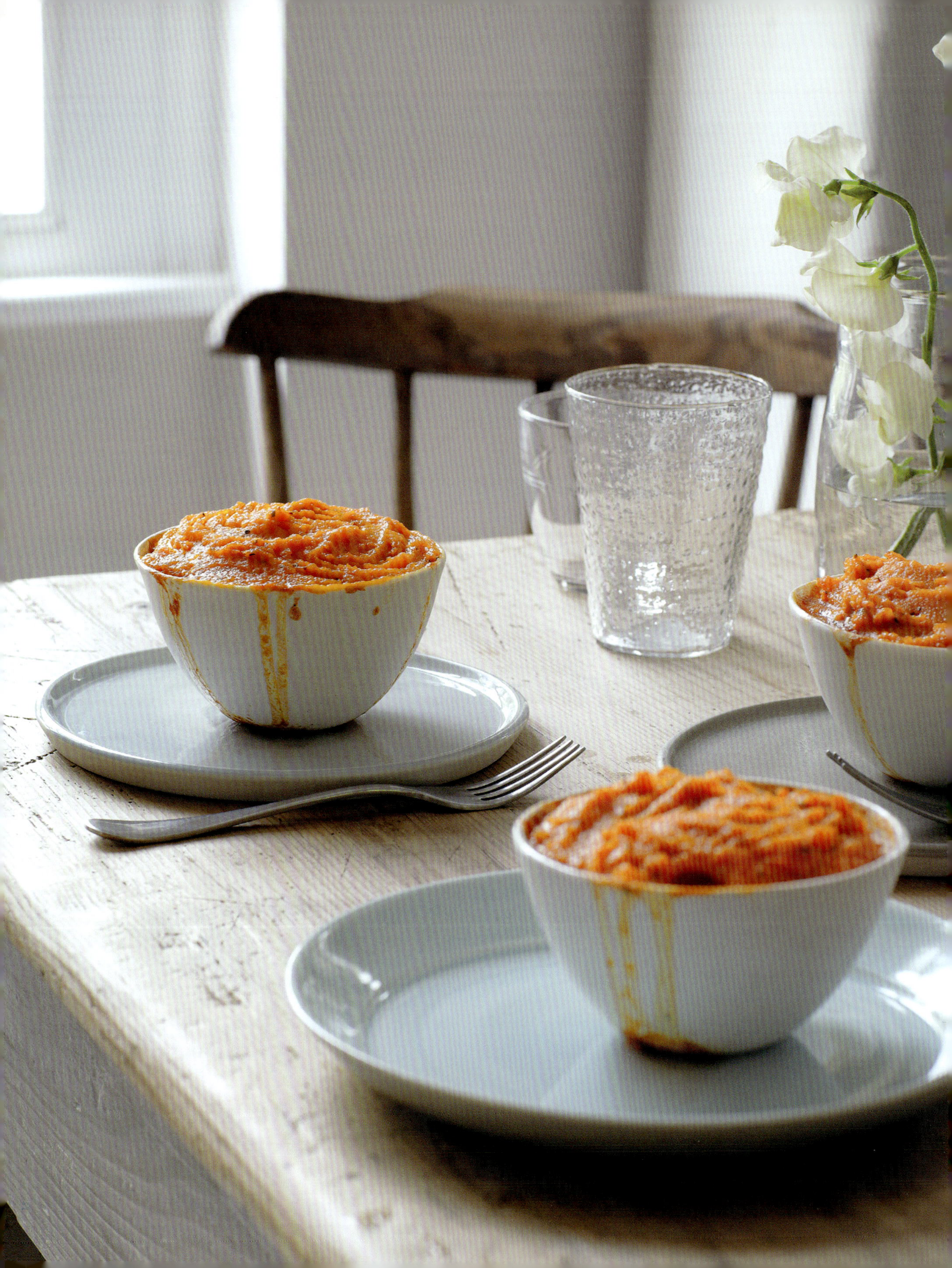

Beluga lentil and sweet potato pie

This vegetarian version of a shepherd's pie is the dish to turn to when you need a fix of comfort food. Here, I use kombu seaweed when cooking the lentils; this seaweed has the right enzyme to help break down the sugars in the lentils, thereby easing their digestion and causing less gas in the process. You can use a piece of kombu when cooking all beans and lentils.

Cook the sweet potatoes in a pot of boiling water for 15 minutes until soft to the touch with a knife.

In a pan (I like to use a wok for this) melt the coconut oil with the garlic, onion, cumin seeds, and fennel seeds, and sauté for 2 minutes.

Add the tomatoes, followed by the bay leaves, half the chopped rosemary, and ½ cup (120ml) of the measured water, and cook over high heat for 2 minutes.

Next, add the beluga lentils, 2 cups (480ml) of the water, the kombu, and the celery, and simmer over medium heat for 15 minutes.

Meanwhile, drain the sweet potatoes, return them to the pan, and add the rice milk, salt, and remaining rosemary. You'll want this mash super-smooth, so use a blender or food processor if possible. Alternatively, mash by hand.

Preheat the oven to 350°F/180°C/gas mark 4.

After 15 minutes of the lentils cooking, add the remaining water and simmer for another 15 minutes. Just before you take the pan off the stove, toss in the kale so that it wilts in the warmth of the lentils. Remove the bay leaves and kombu from the lentils.

Pour the lentil mix into a large ovenproof dish and spread the sweet potato mash over the top. I like to bake them in small sharing dishes, so you can divide it into two if you decide to do this.

Pop the dish into a preheated oven and bake for 10 minutes. If you want to set it aside for the next day, reheat at the same temperature for 20–30 minutes until piping hot all the way through.

serves 4–6

4⅓ cups chopped (650g) sweet potatoes

1 tbsp coconut oil

1 clove garlic, sliced

1 small white onion, sliced

¼ tbsp cumin seeds

¼ tbsp fennel seeds

4 large vine-ripened tomatoes (about 1lb/400g in total), diced

2 bay leaves

2 sprigs rosemary, chopped

3½ cups (840ml) water

1 cup (200g) black Beluga lentils (Puy lentils also work well)

1 strip of kombu seaweed

2 sticks celery, sliced at an angle

4 tbsp rice milk

a pinch of Himalayan pink salt

⅓ cup (40g) lacinato or dinosaur kale, finely chopped

This dish is a great one to make up the night before a dinner party, so you don't have to run around cooking all night.

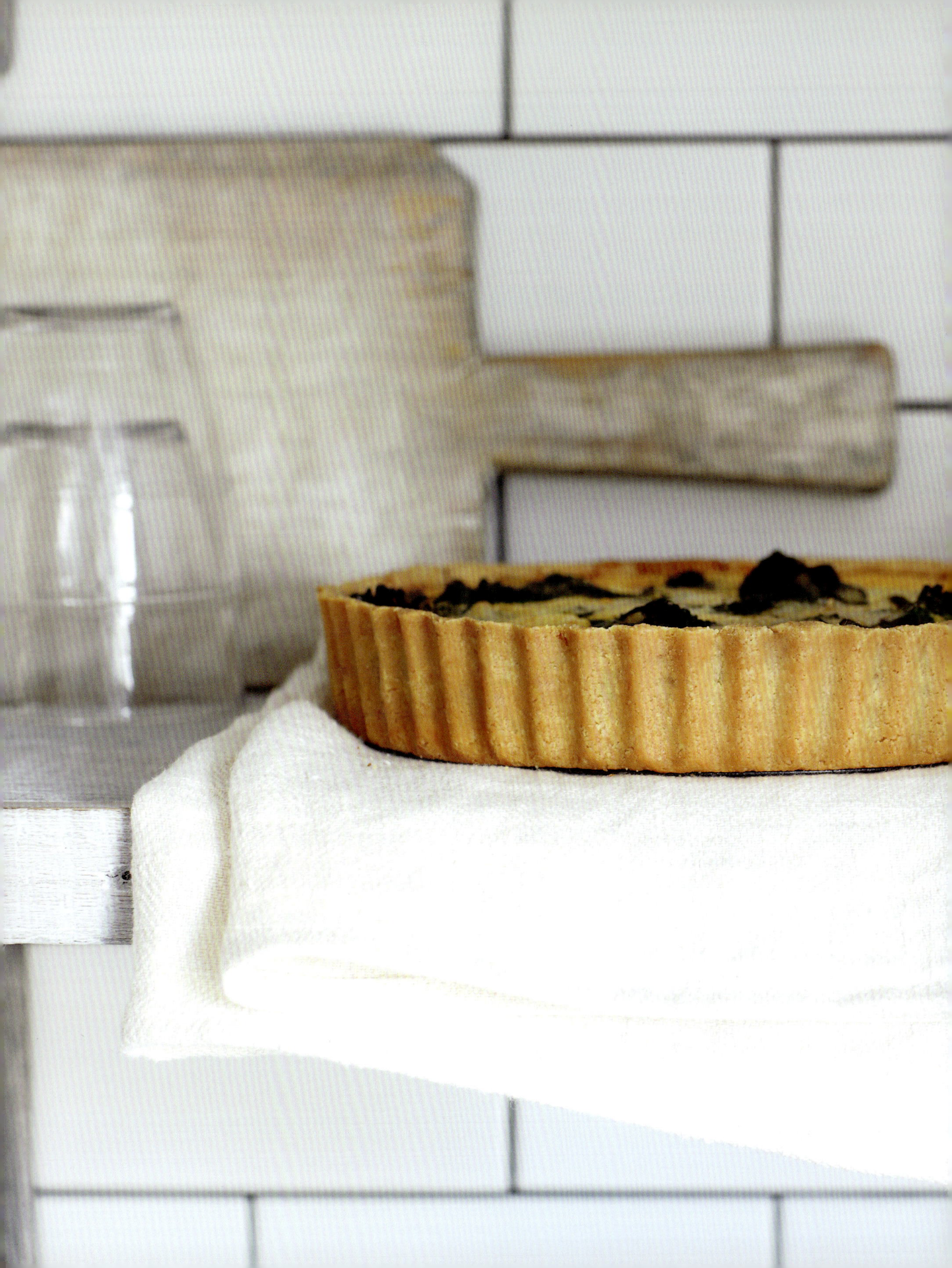

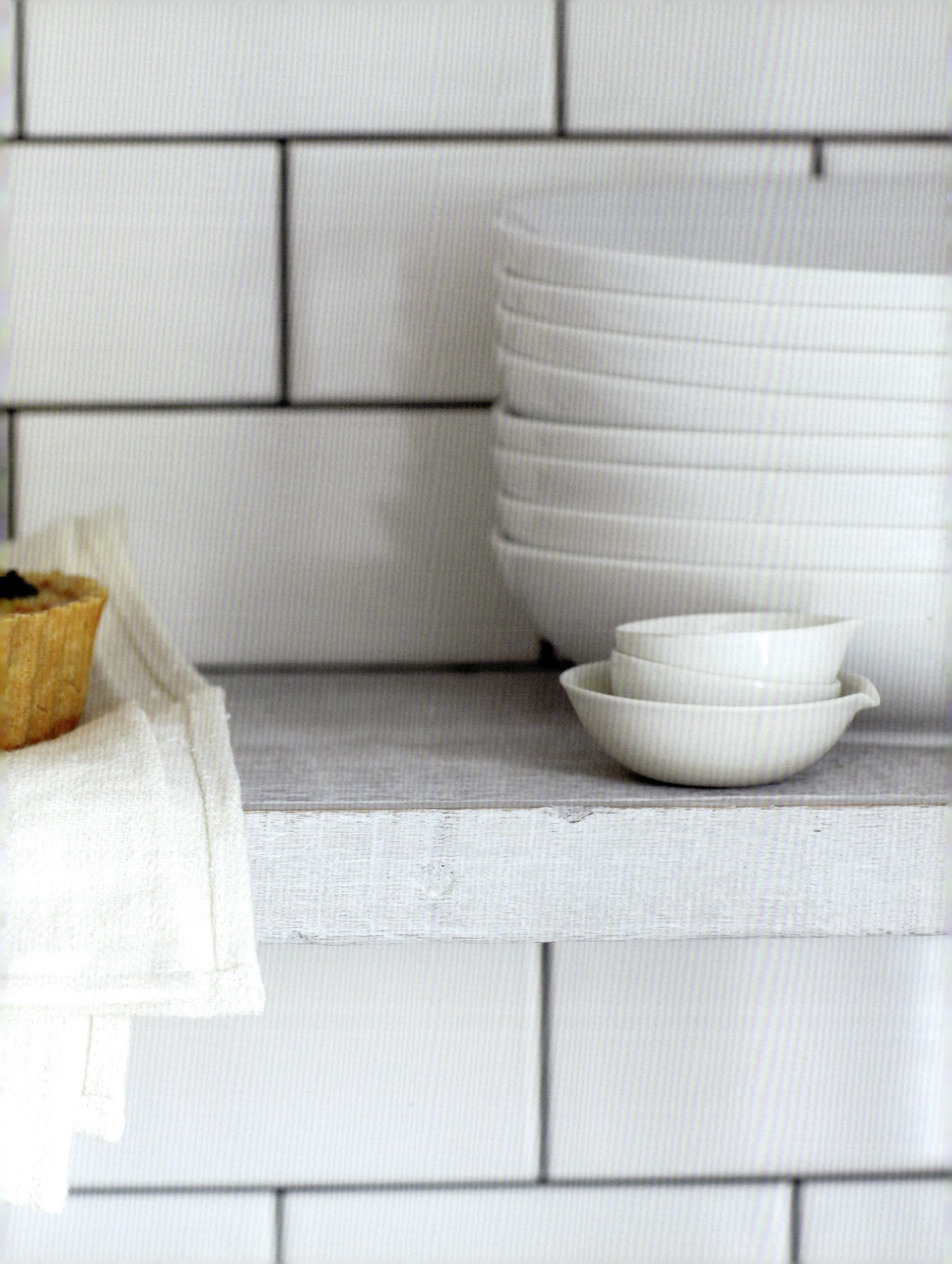

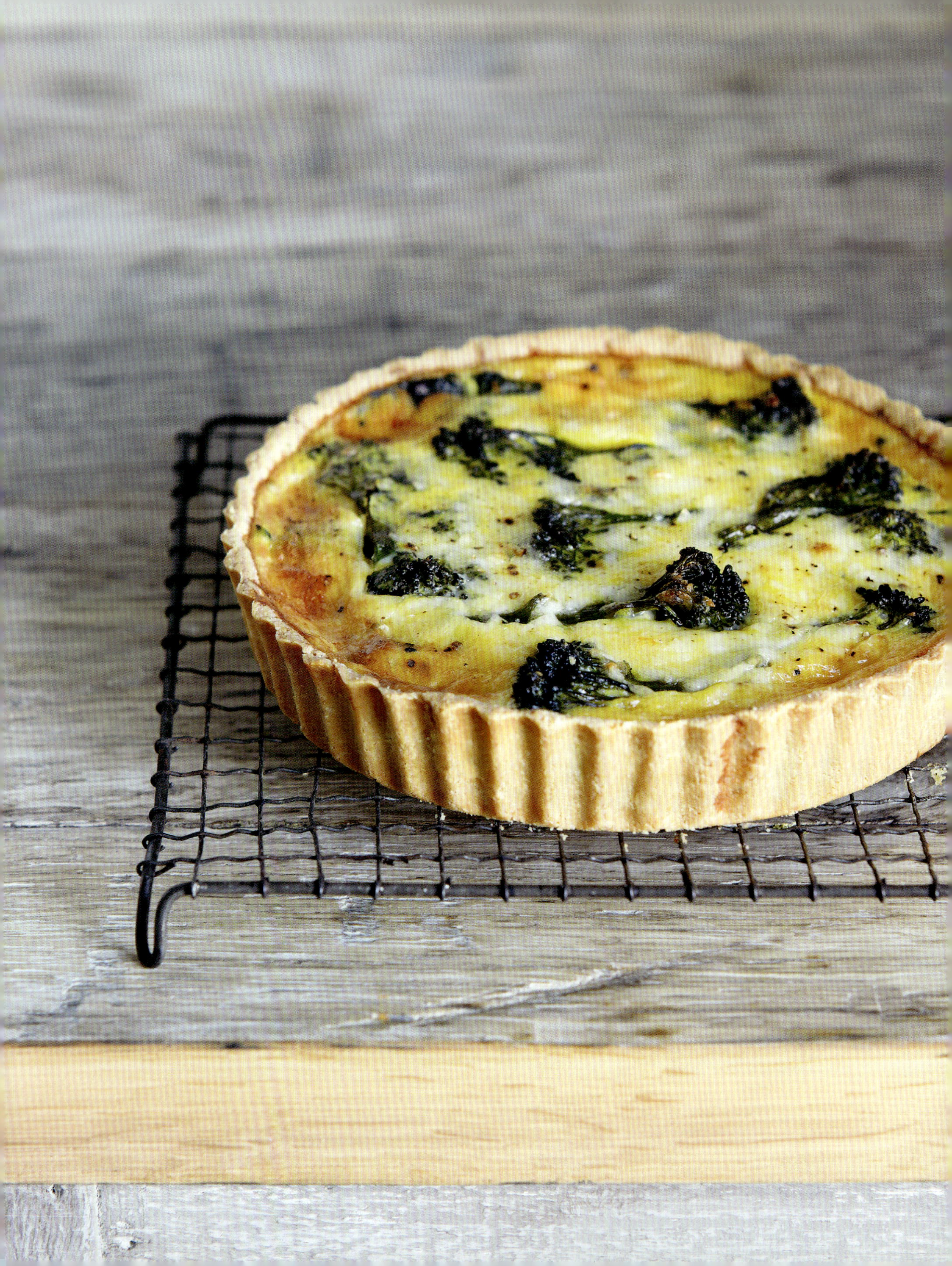

Egg tart

When you are exercising hard or training for a particular event, what better thank you for all your hard work than this high-protein treat? It even tastes great the next day, so it's a good one to take to work with you for lunch with a gorgeous leafy salad.

Preheat the oven to 350°F/180°C/gas mark 4. Grease a 6-cup (20cm) tart pan with coconut oil and line it with parchment paper.

First, make the pastry. Mix the ground almonds and egg together in a bowl until well mixed. Press this mixture into the prepared tart pan, being sure to press it up the sides, too. Bake in a preheated oven for 10-12 minutes until it just starts to color. (Don't bake for longer as it will end up overbaked.) Remove from the oven and set aside.

Meanwhile, melt the coconut oil in a pan and sauté the onion and garlic with the sesame seeds for 1 minute. Add half of the water and the broccolini - it'll start to cook in the steam. After about 1 minute, add the rest of the water and cook for another 2-3 minutes until the broccolini starts to soften. Next, add the spinach and turn the heat off and let it cook in the residual heat.

Now, make the filling. Grate the goat cheese into a bowl and mix in the eggs, almond milk, and salt.

Put the sautéed broccolini and spinach mixture into the base of the tart and pour the cheesy mixture over the top.

Bake in a preheated oven for 25-30 minutes until golden on the top.

serves 4-6

1 tbsp coconut oil, plus extra for greasing

1 small white onion, chopped

1 clove garlic, grated

¼ tsp black sesame seeds

4 tbsp water

½ bunch (100g) broccolini

1 cup (30g) spinach leaves, chopped

1¼ cups shredded (140g) hard goat or sheep cheese

2 eggs

¾ cup (200ml) almond milk

¼ tsp Himalayan pink salt

for the pastry:

1¾ cups (250g) ground almonds

1 egg, beaten

#bites

Broccoli pesto

Pestos are wonderful things and can be used for so many different dishes. I love to use one as an extra layer of flavor in Portobello burgers (see page 184), and you could also use it in risottos or pasta – in fact it gives a healthy alkaline kick to any dish.

To make the pesto, put all the ingredients into a high-speed blender or food processor and pulse until you get a wonderfully thick texture. Alternatively, use a pestle and mortar to pound the ingredients.

Pop the pesto into a clean glass jar and store it in the fridge, where it keeps for up to 1 week.

makes about 1 cup (150g)

1⅔ cups (120g) broccoli

1¼ cups (30g) basil leaves

¼ cup (40g) pumpkin seeds

1 small clove garlic

4 tbsp olive oil

juice of ½ lemon

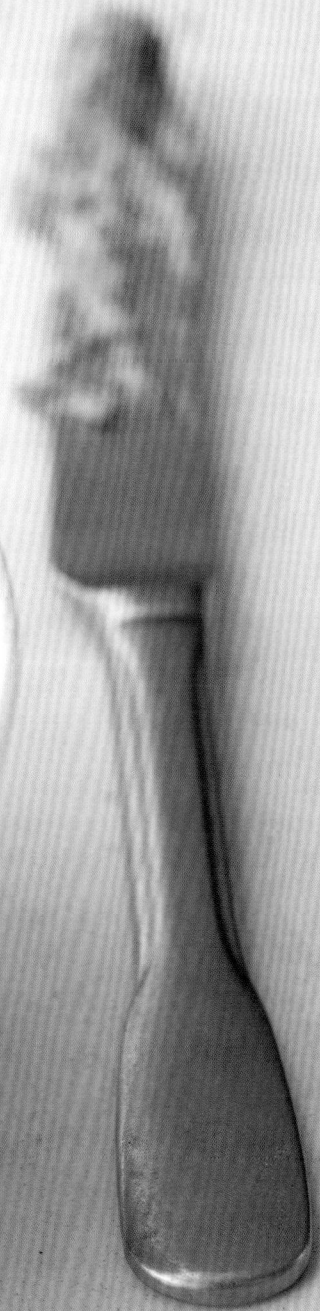

Edamame and avocado temaki

For many people, sushi conjures up the classic images of sliced raw fish or California rolls, but I love these temaki or "hand rolls." All you need to do is slice a few vegetables (whatever you have on hand or whatever's in season) and herbs, whip together the edamame dip, and you're ready to roll. If you're making these for an al fresco lunch, simply take the dip in one container, the vegetables and herbs in another, and the nori in its package. Then friends can choose their own fillings, roll them up on a plate, and eat right away.

Pop the avocado flesh into a blender and squeeze the lime over the top. Add the edamame and cilantro and blend until the consistency of a textured dip.

To make the temaki, first put a nori sheet on your work surface followed by a spinach leaf. Spread about 2–3 tablespoons of the edamame dip on the top and then layer with some sliced vegetables and fresh herbs.

Roll the nori around the filling to make a cone. Dip your finger into some water and skim along the edge of the nori sheet, press lightly together to seal the nori cone. Your tamaki is now ready to eat.

makes 4

1 avocado

juice of 1 lime

¾ cup (150g) shelled edamame beans (defrosted if frozen)

⅓ cup (5g) cilantro leaves

4 nori sheets

⅔ cup (20g) spinach leaves

my favorite additions:

radish # cilantro # mint # zucchini cucumber # daikon radish # carrots # red pepper

Crunchy chickpeas

If you need an alternative to popcorn or wasabi peas, then try out these crunchy delights. But be warned: this high-protein snack is incredibly addictive! If you cook the chickpeas for less time (25 minutes), they won't be as crunchy, but will be equally delicious, more like the texture of a macadamia nut.

Preheat the oven to 350°F/170°C/gas mark 3, and line a baking tray with parchment paper.

Mix all of the ingredients together and transfer to the prepared baking tray. Bake in a preheated oven for 45 minutes or until crunchy.

Remove from the oven and allow to cool. This crunchy snack will keep for 1 week in an airtight container.

serves 2-3 as a snack

1 cup (240g) can of chickpeas, drained

½ tsp smoked paprika

¼ tsp Himalayan pink salt

1 tbsp sunflower oil

4 gratings of fresh nutmeg

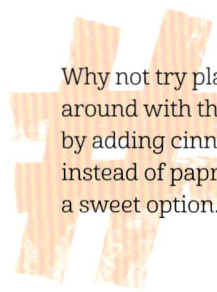

Why not try playing around with the flavors by adding cinnamon instead of paprika for a sweet option.

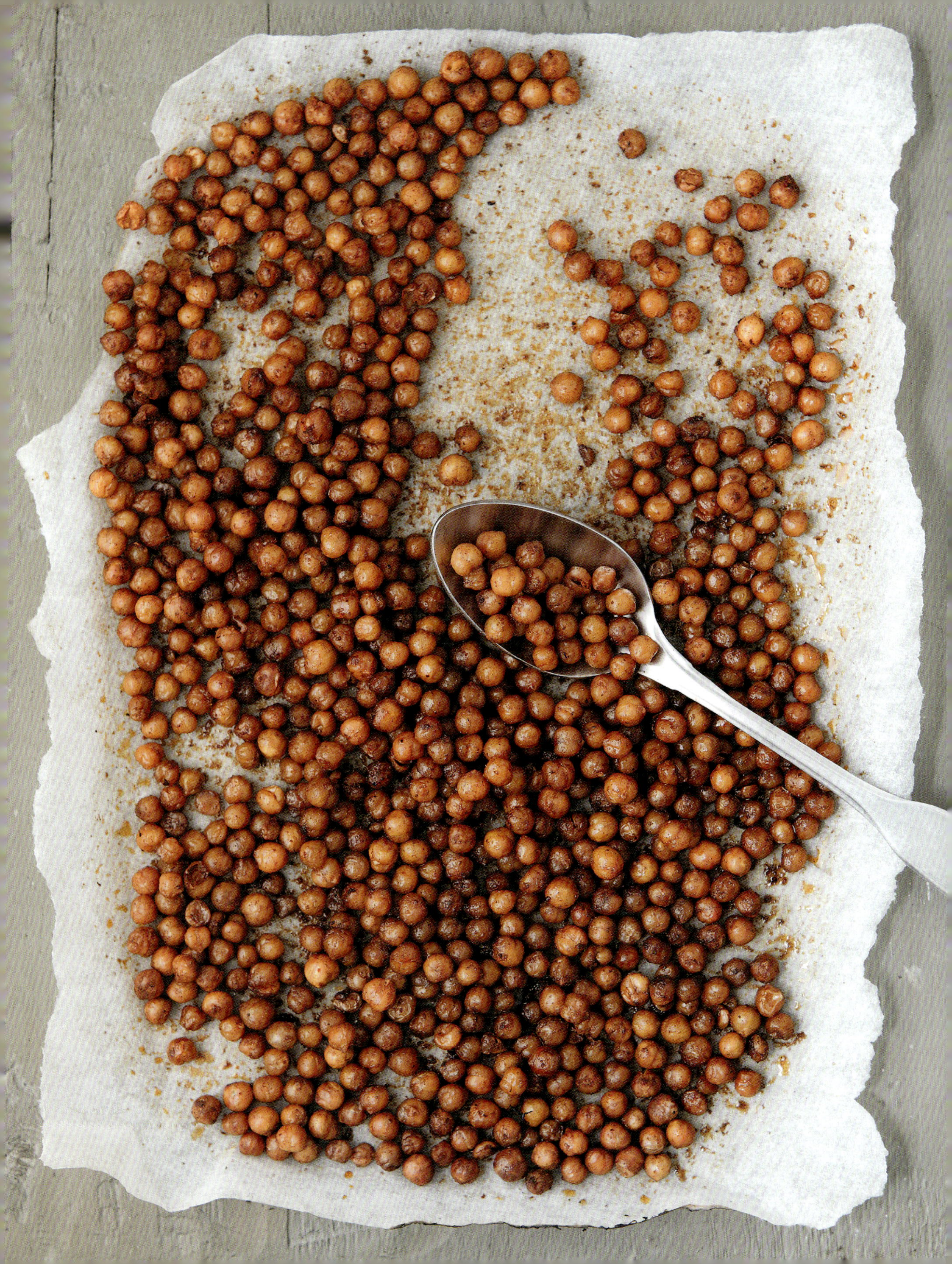

Beet chips, two ways

Everyone gets a craving for chips now and again, and this recipe is the perfect way of satisfying it. I love the two different flavor combinations offered below, but you can always just try simple salt and cracked black pepper, as well.

Preheat the oven to 325°F/170°C/gas mark 3. Line a baking tray with parchment paper and have several sheets of parchment on hand.

Slice the beets, preferably with a mandoline to get them evenly thin. Divide between 2 bowls and drizzle half the sunflower oil into each bowl.

If you'd like to try both options, simply add flavor 1 ingredients to one bowl and flavor 2 to the other bowl. Make sure all the ingredients are mixed together well and the beet slices are perfectly covered. (If you'd prefer just one type of beet chip, then double the quantity of the option you're doing or halve the beet and oil quantities.)

Arrange a single layer of beets on the prepared tray, cover with a sheet of parchment paper, and arrange another layer of slices on top. Repeat until all the beet slices are used.

Put the tray into a preheated oven and bake for 25–30 minutes. About halfway through, take the baking tray out of the oven, uncover and rotate the sheets of parchment paper so that all the chips are baked evenly. Once the edges start to crisp up they are done. Some will cook faster than others, so you can take individual ones out, as they start to cook faster, and put them onto a wire rack.

The chips will crisp up further, as they start to dry and cool on the rack. Store them in an airtight container, where they'll keep up to 3 days.

2 beets (about 400g in total)

1 tbsp sunflower oil

for flavor 1:

¼ tsp ground cinnamon

¼ tsp Himalayan pink salt

for flavor 2:

¼ tsp fennel seeds

¼ tsp Himalayan pink salt

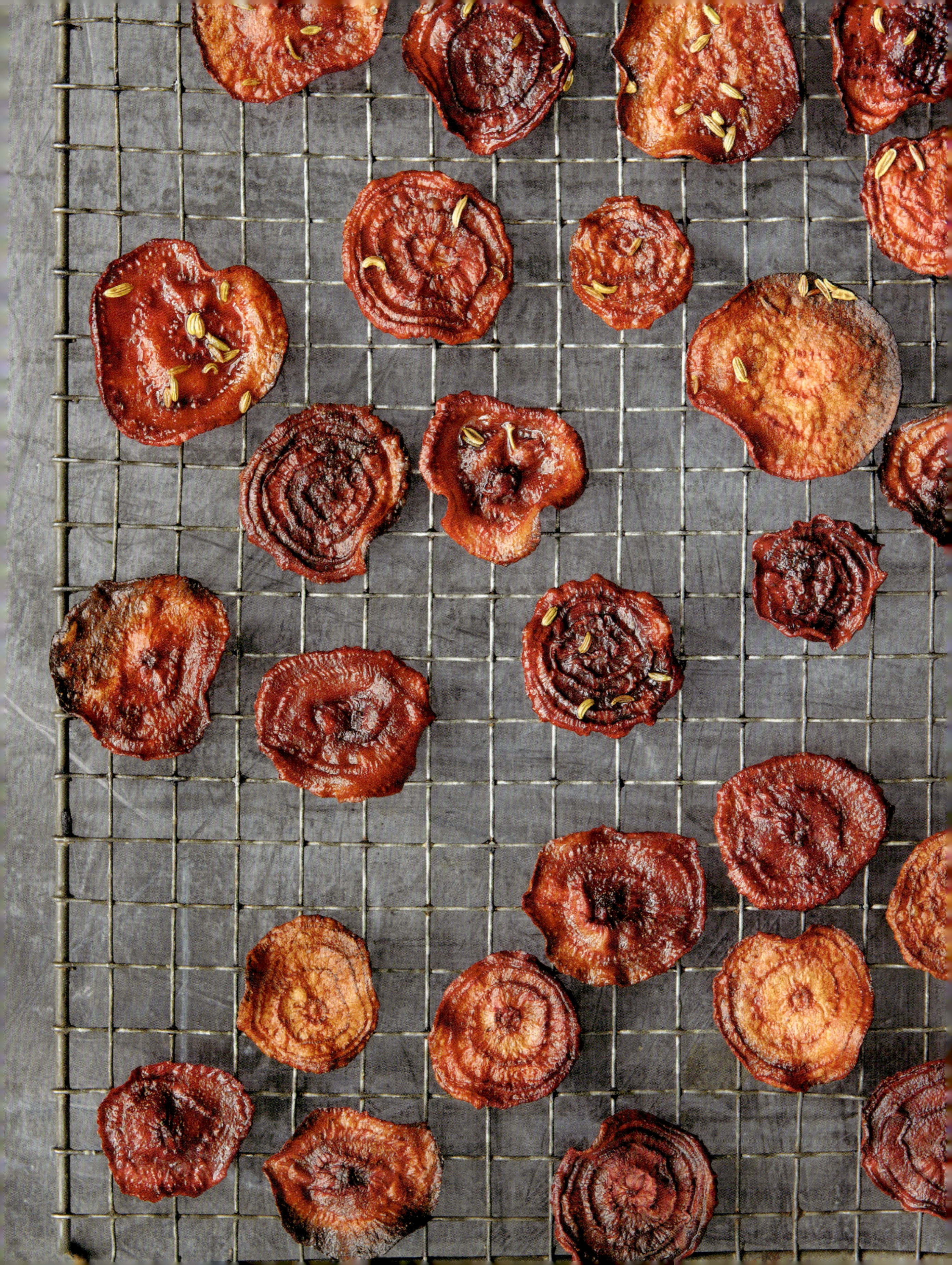

Five-seed protein balls

These tasty balls of goodness make a great pre- or post-workout snack. They're packed with protein and are utterly delicious. If you find it tricky to source quinoa flakes, you can use gluten-free oats instead.

Put the quinoa flakes, hemp seeds, sunflower seeds, and coconut oil in a food processor or blender and pulse until you get a coarse paste. Alternatively, pound them by hand in a pestle and mortar.

Transfer the contents to a largish bowl. Add the tahini, sesame seeds, poppy seeds, cashew butter, cinnamon, and rice syrup to the seed mixture and stir until well combined.

Form the mixture into about 14 balls (they should be about the size of a ping-pong ball) and put into the fridge to set (about 1–2 hours).

Roll the chilled balls in the sesame seeds. Store in an airtight container.

makes 14

1¼ cups (130g) quinoa flakes

3 tbsp hemp seeds

3 tbsp sunflower seeds

5 tbsp melted coconut oil

3 tbsp tahini

2 tbsp sesame seeds, plus extra for rolling

2 tbsp poppy seeds

¼ cup (60g) cashew nut butter

¼ tsp ground cinnamon

2 tbsp brown rice syrup

If you are in need of a sweeter treat, you could try adding dates to the processor, which will make these protein balls really soft and sweet!

No-grain kale bread

This wonderfully tasty bread is very rich, so you will only need one or two slices at a time. Try slicing it when it's fresh and freezing it as slices, so that you can enjoy a piece toasted straight from the freezer.

Place the coconut oil in a cup with the water and brown rice syrup.

Sauté the kale in a saucepan over medium heat with 1 teaspoon of coconut oil for 2-3 minutes until softened. Transfer the kale to a mixing bowl. Add all the remaining ingredients and mix well.

Pour the contents of the cup into the bowl and mix to form a thick dough.

Grease a 9 × 5 × 3in (1kg) loaf pan with melted coconut oil and pack the dough into it. Set aside for 1-2 hours.

Preheat the oven to 325°F/170°C/gas mark 3. Bake the loaf for about 50 minutes.

Remove from the pan and return it to the oven for another 15-20 minutes until golden brown all over.

Cool on a wire rack before slicing.

makes 1 loaf

4 tbsp melted coconut oil, plus 1 tsp for wilting and extra for greasing

1½ cups (350ml) water

1 tbsp brown rice syrup

1½ cups (100g) kale, finely chopped

⅓ cup (45g) sunflower seeds

½ cup (85g) flaxseed

¾ cup (125g) almonds, toasted and roughly chopped

1 cup (100g) quinoa flakes

2 tbsp (25g) chia seeds

3 tbsp psyllium husk powder

½ tsp salt

½ cup (70g) pumpkin seeds

1 tbsp coconut flour

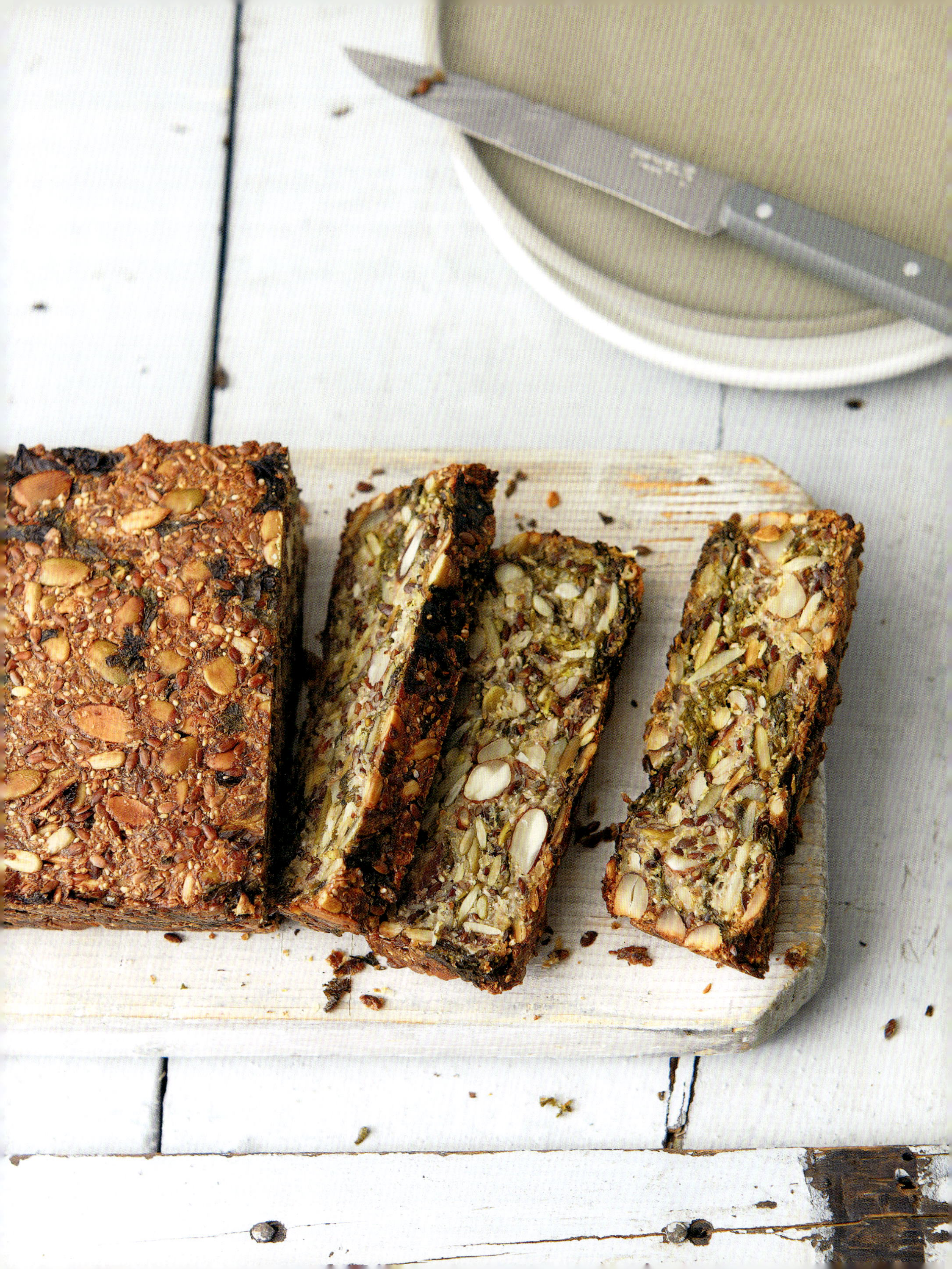

Quinoa, teff, and almond one-layer cake

Quite often I find that the best recipes arrive by mistake; this recipe is one of those. I decided to experiment with teff flour, expecting to create a more biscuit-like texture, but in fact ended up with a super-fluffy result, so this recipe became a great one-layer cake. The recipe can also be used for making muffins – perfect to put into your bag for a post-workout treat or an afternoon pick-me-up. They are also ridiculously healthy – with whole grains as well as omega fatty acids in the chia seeds – so your health halo can shine when you make these at home.

Preheat the oven to 350°F/180°C/gas mark 4. Line a baking dish with parchment paper, or use a 12-hole muffin pan with baking cups if you prefer.

Cook the quinoa according to the instructions on the package. Drain and leave to cool in a bowl.

Soak the ground chia seeds in the measured cold water for 10 minutes until you get a thick gooey texture.

Put the warm water, coconut oil, almond butter, syrup, soaked chia seeds, vanilla, and cooked quinoa into a blender and blend until fully mixed.

Sift the teff flour and the baking soda into a largish bowl and add the zest and cacao nibs.

Now, stir in the wet mixture (from the blender) – it will be thick.

Scoop the mixture into the prepared baking dish, keeping it about 1½in (3cm) thick. Pop the tray into a preheated oven and bake for 12–15 minutes. The cake will be ready when a sharp knife inserted into the middle comes out clean.

Lift the cake out of the dish, using the parchment paper to help you, and transfer to a wire rack. Sprinkle with the crushed nuts (if using) and drizzle with orange-flower water. Set aside to cool.

½ cup (80g) quinoa

2 tbsp ground chia seeds

6 tbsp cold water

½ cup (130ml) warm water

2 tbsp coconut oil

⅔ cup (150g) almond butter

¼ cup (100g) coconut blossom syrup or agave nectar

1 tsp vanilla extract

1 cup (150g) teff flour

1 heaping tsp baking soda

finely grated zest of 1 orange

3 tbsp (30g) cacao nibs

1 tsp orange-flower water

raw walnuts and almonds, roughly chopped, for the topping (optional)

Cashew cookies

These sweet treats take literally 5 minutes to mix and 10 minutes to bake, so if you're in need of a sweet fix, you can make these now. If you don't have cashew butter, use almond or macadamia butter instead. Here I use coconut blossom syrup as a sweetener because it has a low glycaemic index and keeps blood sugar levels balanced. If you can't find it anywhere, just substitute it with agave nectar.

Preheat the oven to 325°F/170°C/gas mark 3, and line a baking sheet with parchment paper.

Put the flour, baking soda and baking powder into a bowl.

In a separate bowl, mix together the melted coconut oil, coconut blossom syrup, and cashew butter. Add this sticky mix to the other bowl of dry ingredients and mix together until it's a doughy ball.

Pinch off pieces of dough about the size of a ping-pong ball and roll them between your hands. Arrange the balls on the prepared baking sheet and, as you do so, press them so you flatten them slightly – you want them to be about ¾in (1–2cm) thick. Next, push your thumb into the center of each one, and place a halved cashew in the dent.

Bake in a preheated oven for 10 minutes or until golden brown.

Remove from the oven and transfer to a wire rack to cool. Enjoy with a cup of tea.

makes 10

1 cup (130g) gluten-free, all-purpose flour

¼ tsp baking soda

1 tsp baking powder

3 tbsp melted coconut oil

¼ cup (70g) coconut blossom syrup (or coconut nectar)

⅓ cup (80g) cashew nut butter

10 raw cashew halves

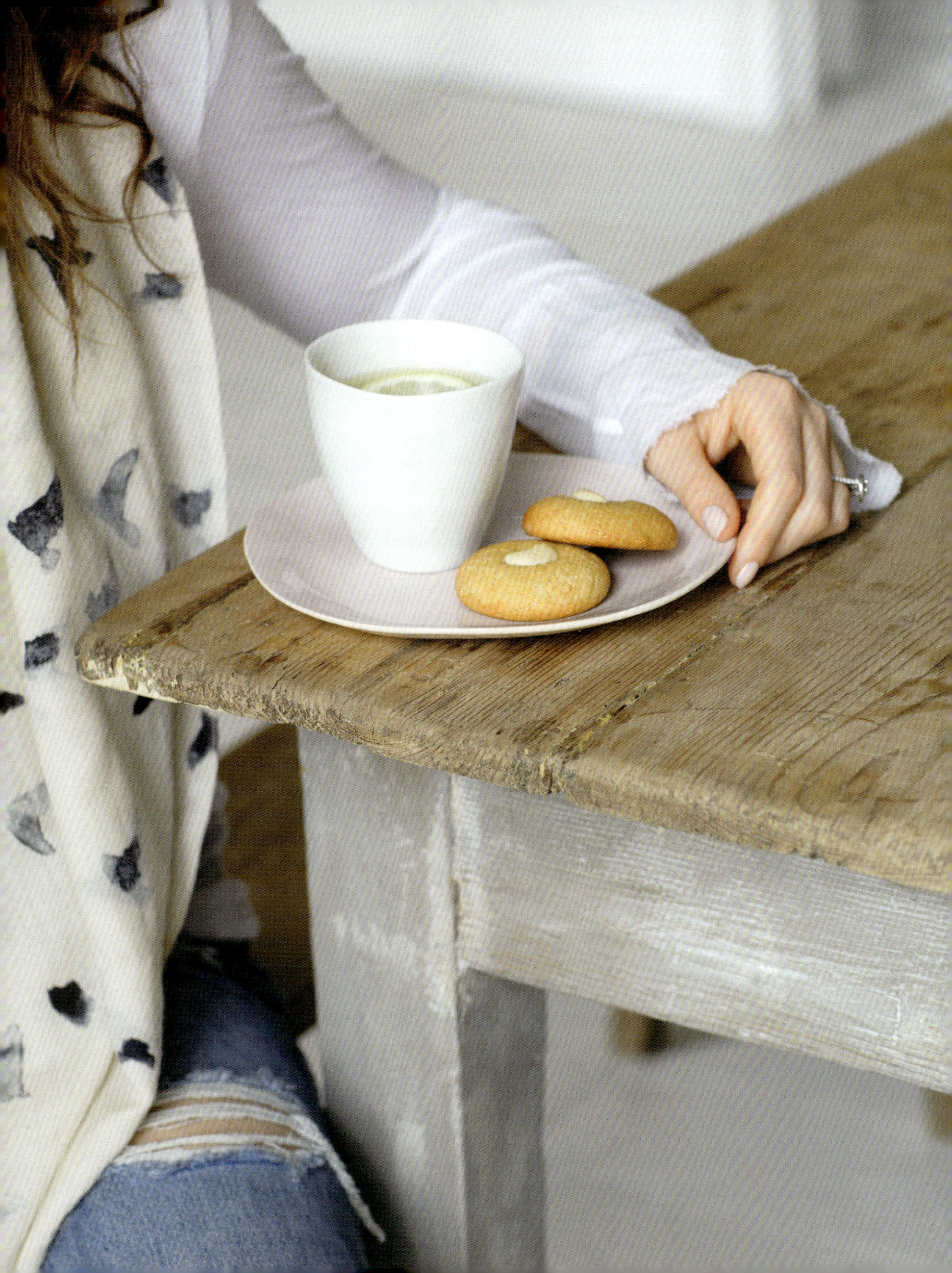

#lifechanging

Nutritious food for everyday life

30 days of tasty meals, rejuvenating salads
and healthy sweet treats

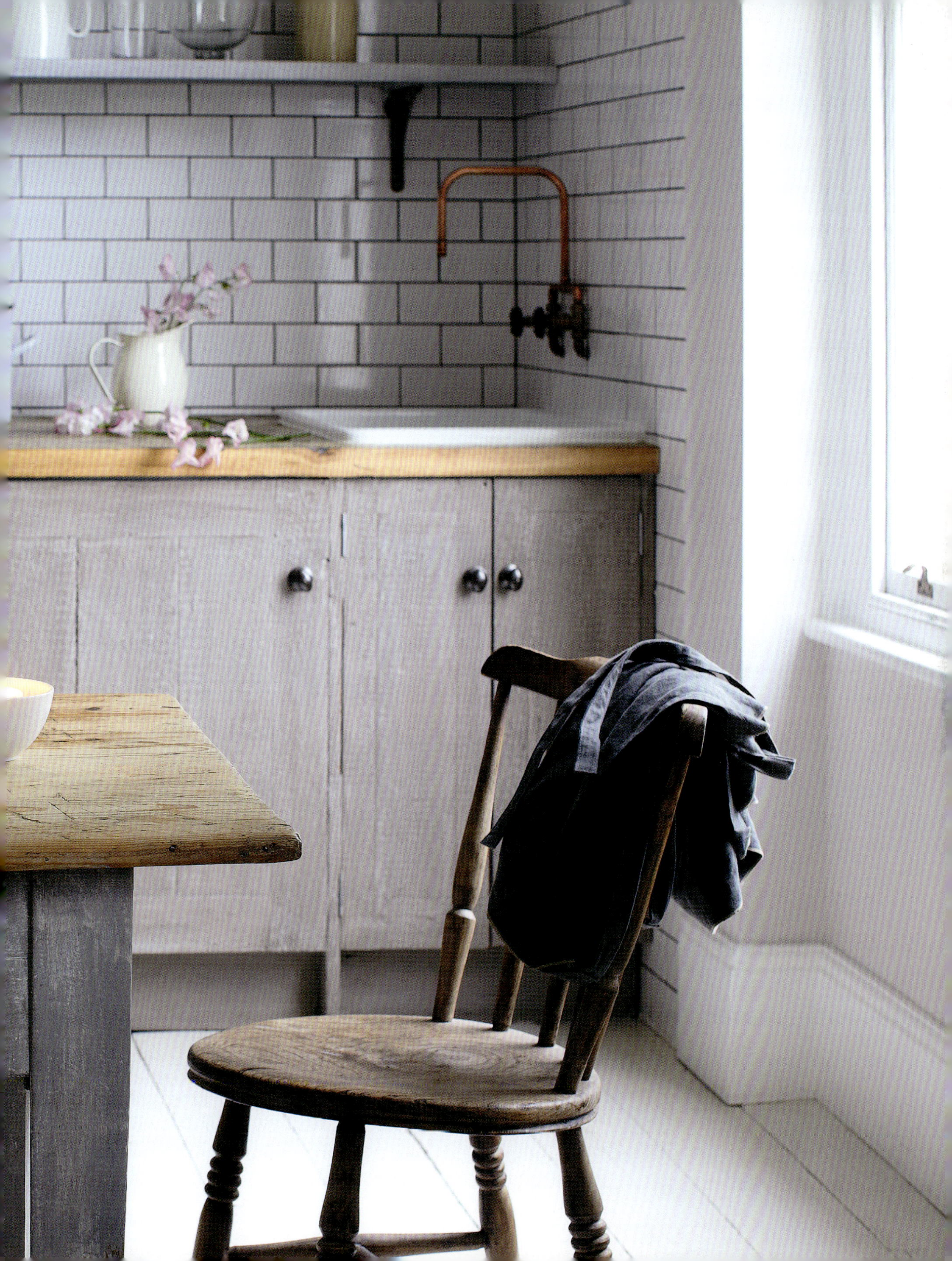

I am asked quite often what my lifestyle plan is, and this #lifechanging cleanse is it. So I wanted to share with you these 40 delicious recipes that are sure to become your lifestyle plan, too. This 30-day cleanse is a stepping stone to a new, healthier you – no more quick fixes will be needed once you're following this plan, and you'll be "red carpet ready" all the time. I am convinced that once you've achieved the first 30 days on this #lifechanging plan there will be no turning back – you will make definite lifestyle changes for the better, as you'll feel so energized and full of life.

The key to any success in finding a new and sustainable way for you to cook and eat is to find a program that works for you on every level. So in the next 30 days you will be cooking up a nutritious storm that is both satisfying and cleansing to your body – and you'll have a wide selection of recipes to ease you through the transition.

Two things to keep in mind when heading off on this lifechanging journey are: balance and moderation. There's no denying yourself sweet treats or dishes from cuisines you've deemed fattening on the #lifechanging plan. The moment you deny yourself something, the more you want it. I, for one, have never been satisfied with someone telling me that I can't have a certain dish, so I'm not going to tell you that either. Instead, I've discovered and created nutritious and cleansing versions of everyday foods –

You will need # a gym membership or home workout program – try our high-intensity interval training as part of the downloadable 30-day slimdown on the Honestly Healthy website for a six-day home workout # ingredients for your recipes # food processor or a blender

What to expect . . .

What can I say? The next 30 days are the start of a new, healthier you – you are going to be feeling fantastic! This #lifechanging cleanse is exactly that – you will be changing your life for the better. And you'll still have plenty of energy for working out frequently.

Start your work days with smoothies, Puffed breakfast crispies (see page 172) or Baked eggs in avocado (see page 176), and on the weekend indulge in a healthy portion of Lemon teff pancakes (see page 166).

As for lunch and dinner, simply alternate between a light option and a heartier option. And don't forget to congratulate yourself on day 7 of each week and enjoy a sweet treat to say well done!

Stay away from:

- # caffeine
- # alcohol
- # dairy products
- # meat
- # sugar
- # wheat and gluten
- # processed foods

All of the above are extremely acid-forming in the body (and not alkalizing, which is what the alkaline cleanse is all about). To rebalance your body to achieve a more alkaline state, you need to cut these items out of your diet.

from pizzas and Indian dishes to burgers and fries. You'll see, too, that I've created a host of gorgeous sweet things – from Crimson crumble and Lemon yogurt cake to Gooey chocolate pots (see pages 239, 247 and 249) – these aren't everyday treats, but they are every week treats. Every seven days, choose a new treat to try out and share with friends – they'll never guess this indulgent dessert is actually healthy too!

If you've tried either the #feelgood or #slimdown cleanses earlier in the book, then you can just go straight into this #lifechanging cleanse. If you do, stick to the salads in this section for the first week of the program to ease your body back into digesting some of the heavier protein dishes, such as Chickpea dumplings and the pizzas (see pages 182, 198 and 211).

#lifechanging menu planner

This plan is very much designed for you to live out your healthy lifestyle all the time and taking your knowledge from the other cleanses. If you are exercising, make sure you pick a high protein recipe to have during the day and start the day with a substantial breakfast. However, if you are not exercising, pick recipes that can be eaten in the slimdown or feelgood sections – also remember that the treats are still in your 30%, so enjoy in moderation. Having a healthy piece of cake is much better for you than buying one from a store.

Day 1		
	AM	Avocado smoothie (page 57)
	Lunch	Pea, fava bean, and pine nut salad (page 220)
	Bites	Raw chia and hemp bar (page 228) / Energizing tea (page 58)
	Dinner	Winter greek salad in a bag (page 181)

Day 2		
an ideal plan to follow if you are having an active day or feeling low in energy	AM	Nutmeg matcha latte (page 174) with Chia and teff bread (page 154) and Raspberry chia jam (page 170)
	Lunch	Roasted butternut squash with balsamic onions (page 212)
	Bites	Broccoli pesto and crudité (page 142) / Green starter juice (page 30)
	Dinner	Chickpea dumplings (page 182)
	Sweet treat	Gooey vegan brownies (page 233)

Day 3

AM	Fennel seed and vanilla millet "porridge" (page 164)
Lunch	Fluffy eggs and asparagus (page 134)
Bites	Cashew cookies (page 156) / A cleansing and calming tea (page 36)
Dinner	Pumpkin soup (page 68)

Day 4

AM	Cacao, cinnamon, pear, and fennel smoothie (page 57) with No-grain kale bread (page 152)
Lunch	Beet wraps (page 200)
Bites	Ginger-tamari-dressed edamame (page 224) / Green starter juice (page 30)
Dinner	Baked and stuffed eggplant with salad (page 196)

Day 5

AM	Baked Mexican-style eggs (page 94)
Lunch	Kale salad (page 178)
Bites	Roasted red pepper dip and crudité (page 78) / Energizing tea (page 58)
Dinner	Almond-crust pizza (page 211)

Day 6

AM	Lemon teff pancakes (page 166)
Lunch	Lime sprouted salad (page 74)
Bites	Tamar-toasted seeds (page 78) / Carrot and turmeric smoothie (page 31)
Dinner	Green cauliflower "rice" risotto (page 76)
Sweet treat	Crimson crumble (page 239)

Day 7

AM	Rooibos and blueberry chia porridge (page 52)
Lunch	Warm fig and spinach salad (page 98)
Bites	Pea and mint pesto (page 226) and red raw crackers (page 32) / Red juice (page 30)
Dinner	Spiced tofu balls (page 105)

#morning time

Fennel seed and vanilla millet "porridge"

I love porridge, especially when it's cold outside or if I am working out a lot at the gym. But rather than give all my morning love to oats, I wanted to find another grain to use. Millet works really well, as you can take it off the heat before it gets too soft – great for those of us who like a bit of a crunch to our porridge.

Put everything but the blueberries into a saucepan over medium-high heat and cook for 10–12 minutes.

Just before you take the pan off the heat, drop in the blueberries and cook for 1 minute until they soften and start to burst.

Serve this "porridge" warm with a drizzle of almond milk to loosen it up.

serves 2

1½ cups (80g) millet

1 cup (240ml) almond milk, plus extra to serve

1 cup (240ml) water

¼ tsp ground cinnamon

¼ tsp fennel seeds

¼ tsp vanilla extract

⅓ cup (50g) blueberries

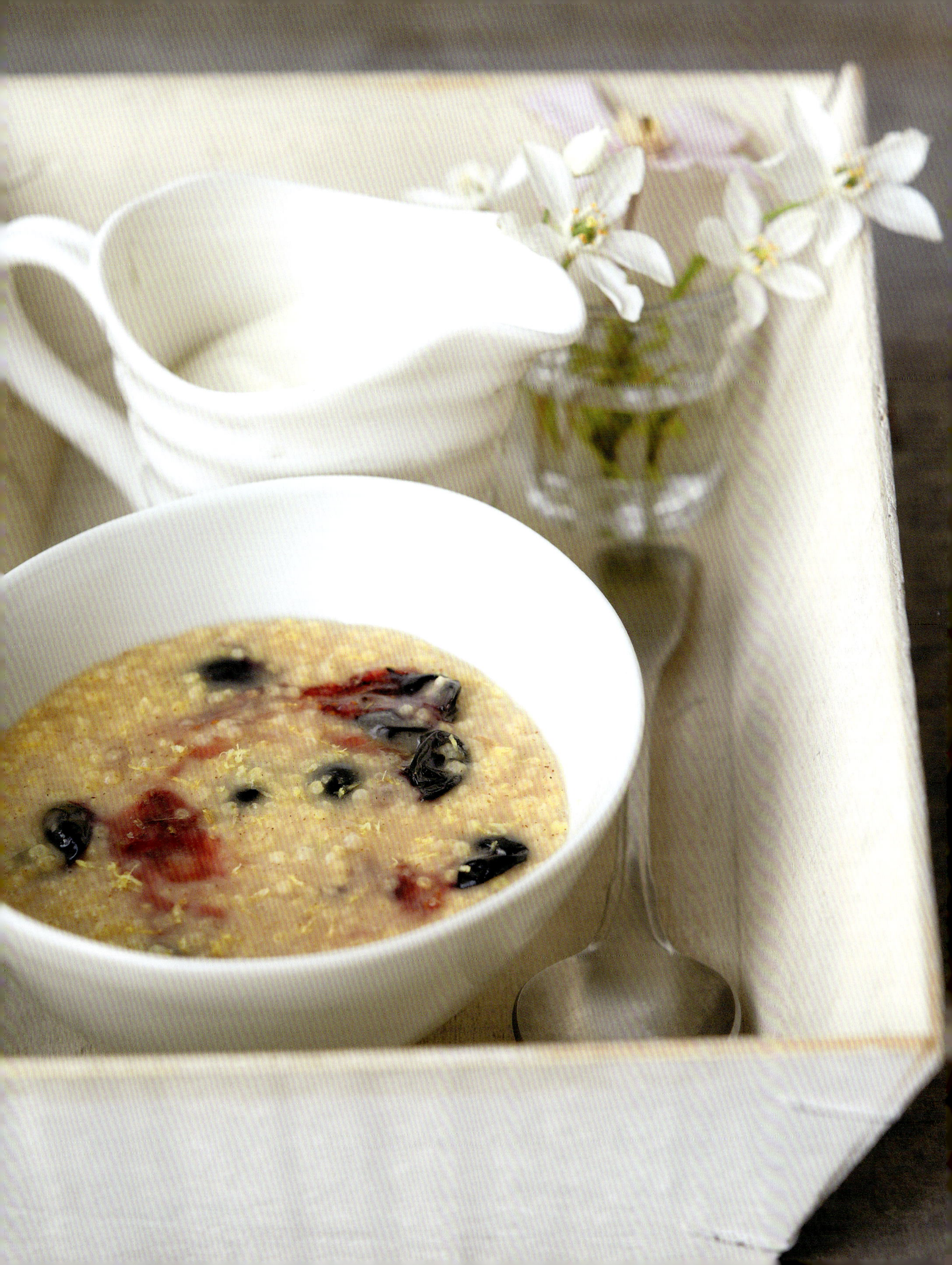

Lemon teff pancakes

My ideal breakfast would, of course, have pancakes on the menu. And the fact that they're so full of nutritious qualities will brighten up your weekend to no end. You can vary the flavors to suit your taste (swap lemon for orange, for instance) or whatever fruit happens to be in season (raspberries, for example).

Sift the teff and buckwheat flours into a bowl.

In a separate bowl, whisk the egg with the agave nectar, rice milk, vanilla and lemon zest.

Pour the wet ingredients into the dry, and mix until well incorporated.

Get a non-stick frying pan piping hot (I find the hotter the better for pancakes). Put a teaspoon of sunflower oil or coconut oil into the pan and wipe it around with a paper towel; repeat this wiping between pancakes.

Pour a ladle of the pancake batter into the hot pan and drop a few blueberries on top. Tilt the pan around to spread the mixture out as far as it will go. Leave for about 30 seconds until bubbles start to appear on the surface. Gently look underneath the pancake to see if it's turned golden, then either be brave and toss the pancake or use a spatula to flip it. Push the blueberries down into the pan with the back of the spatula, so that the whole side of the pancake browns. Leave for about 1 minute and then transfer to a warm plate and set aside.

Repeat this for all the mixture. Serve 2 pancakes per person with some lemon juice and a little extra agave nectar, to taste.

makes 4

⅛ cup (20g) teff flour

½ cup (60g) buckwheat flour

1 egg or chia replacer (1 tbsp ground seeds mixed with 3 tbsp water)

2 tbsp agave nectar, plus extra to serve

½ cup (130ml) rice milk

1 tsp vanilla extract

finely grated zest of 1 lemon

⅓ cup (60g) blueberries

sunflower oil, for frying

juice of 1 lemon, to serve

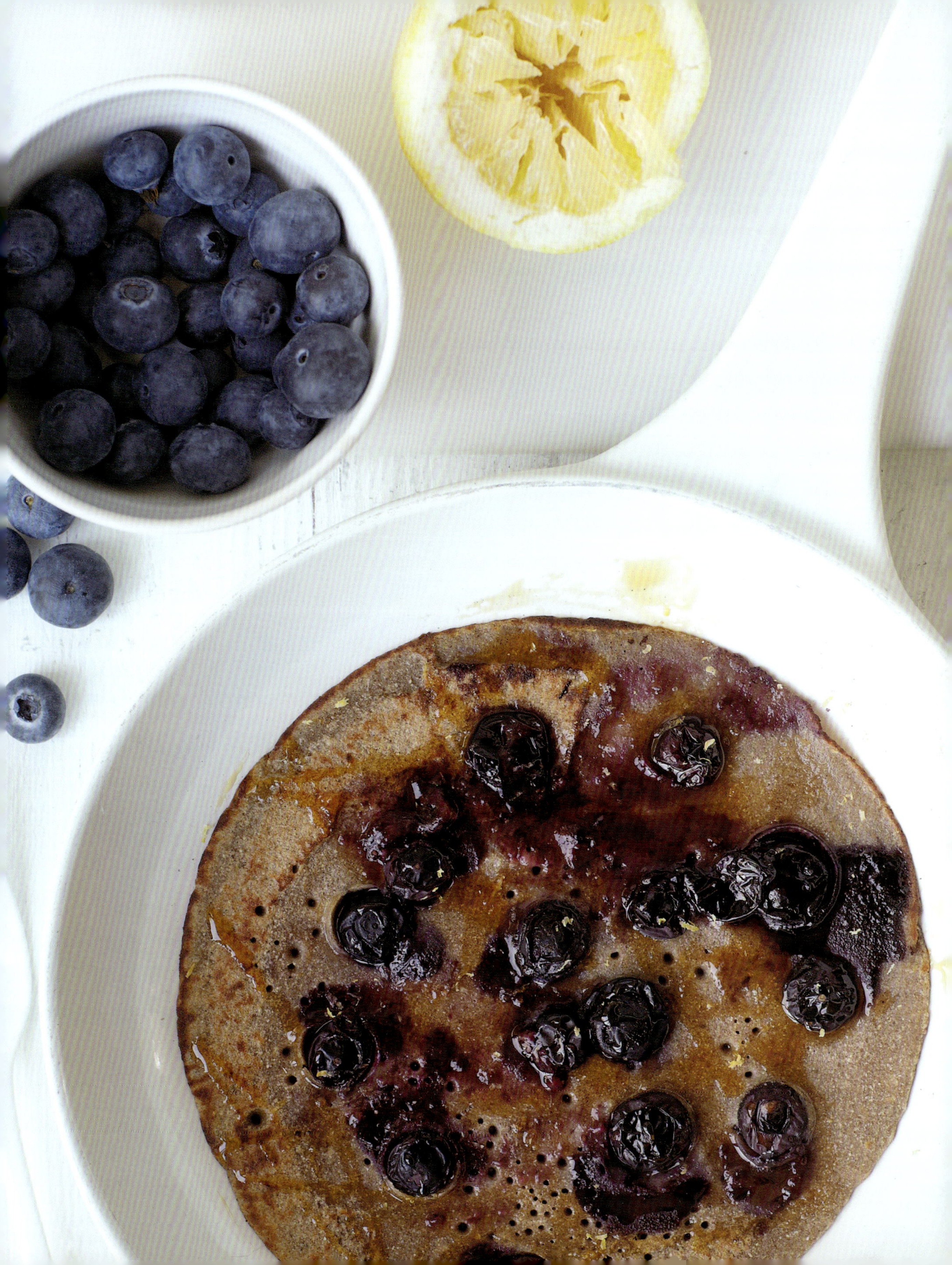

Chia and teff bread

This bread is a gorgeous brown color due to the teff – an amazing grain that gives this bread a fluffy texture. It's also really simple to make. I'd say this bread is definitely best when toasted and spread with a delicious nut butter or topped with a poached egg.

To activate the yeast, mix the boiling water and sugar together in a bowl, then add ½ cup (125ml) cold water and the yeast, and stir well. Move to a warm area with a dish towel over the top of the bowl for 15 minutes, until the mixture becomes frothy.

Meanwhile, soak the ground chia seeds and psyllium husks in the remaining cold water, and mix together until they become gooey.

Once the yeast is ready, stir the chia seed mixture into it until smooth, then add the chia oil and mix again.

Combine the flours, xanthan gum, salt, baking powder, and seeds in a bowl. Slowly stir in the yeast mixture until a dough forms.

Dust a clean work surface with a little buckwheat flour and knead the dough for about 4–5 minutes.

Form the dough into a round shape and place on a baking tray lined with parchment paper. Cover the dough and allow to rise for 3–4 hours in a warm place (the warmer the better).

Punch the dough to knock out the air and knead again for about 2 minutes. Cover and allow to rise again for 30 minutes.

Preheat the oven to 350°F/180°C/gas mark 4.

Bake the loaf for 50 minutes, then transfer it to a wire rack to cool. Once cool, slice and enjoy!

makes 1 loaf

¼ cup (60ml) boiling water

1 tbsp coconut palm sugar

1 cup (245ml) cold water

1 tbsp active dry yeast

⅓ cup (30g) ground chia seeds

¼ cup (20g) psyllium husks

1 tbsp chia oil

⅔ cup (100g) teff flour

½ cup (70g) buckwheat flour, plus extra for dusting

¼ cup (30g) quinoa flour

¾ cup (100g) tapioca flour

1½ cups (160g) almond flour

⅛ cup (20g) potato flour

1 tsp xanthan gum

1 tsp Himalayan pink salt

1 tbsp baking powder

2 tbsp sesame seeds

3 tbsp whole chia seeds

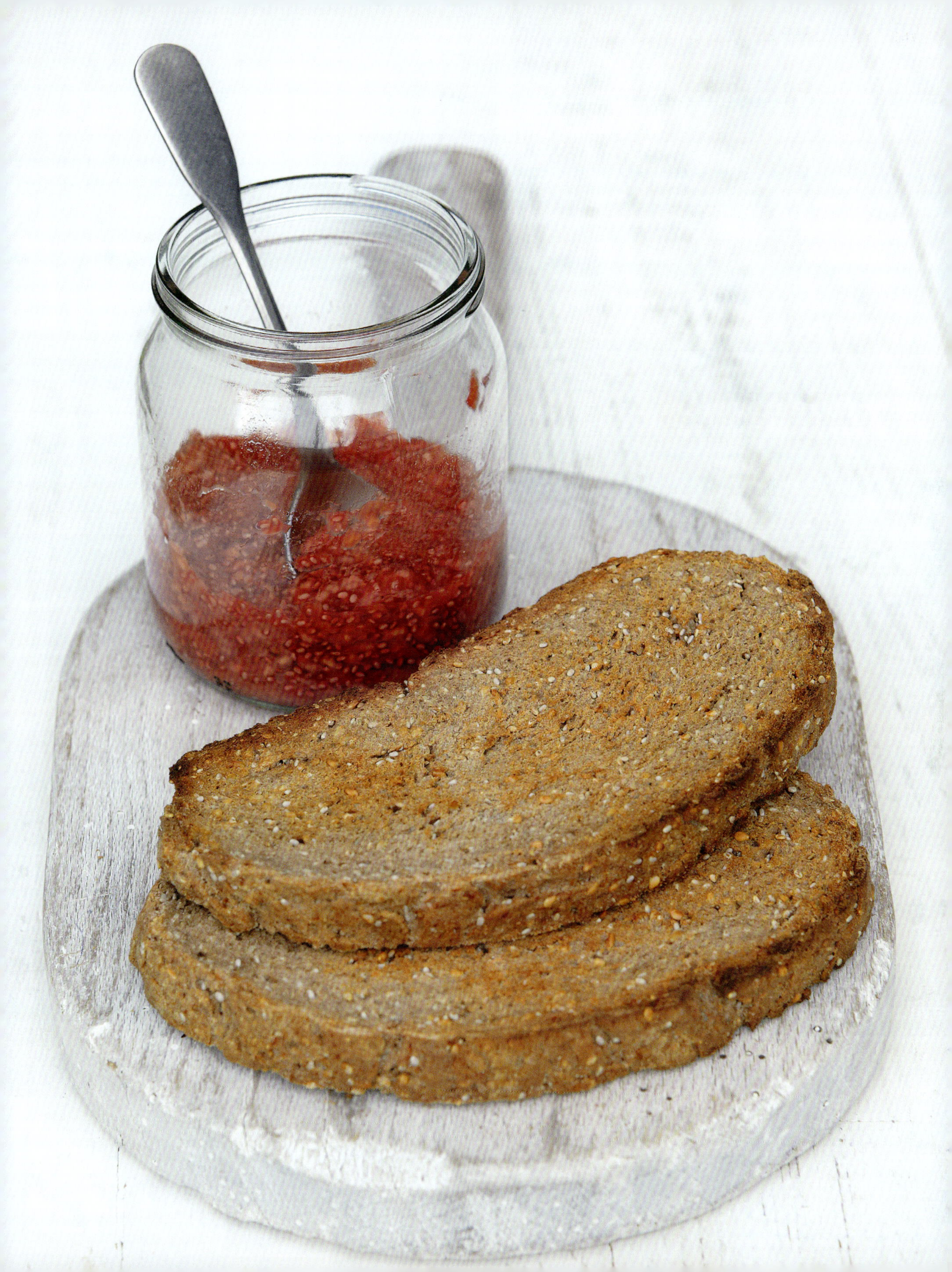

Raspberry chia jam

They say the best things come in small packages, and this luscious jam certainly does. Since the sugar content is much lower than in commercial jams, which have lots of added sugar, this version won't keep as long. That's why it's best to make it in small batches for whenever you want it—on a slice of gluten-free toast, for example.

Soak the chia seeds in ½ cup (100ml) of the water and set aside.

Place half the raspberries in a saucepan with the remaining water and the agave, and simmer over medium heat until the raspberries start to break down. At that point, crush them further with the back of a wooden spoon.

Add the soaked chia seeds and stir until incorporated – you may need to use a whisk to break down any clumps. Add the lime zest, if using.

Finally, add the remaining raspberries and continue to simmer for about 2 minutes until the larger raspberries break down a little – not too much, though, as they add a nice texture.

Transfer the mixture to a clean glass jar and place in the fridge to set for about 1 hour.

fills a small (8oz) canning jar

4 tbsp chia seeds

¾ cup (175ml) water

1⅔ cups (200g) raspberries

1 tbsp agave nectar

finely grated zest of ¼ lime (optional)

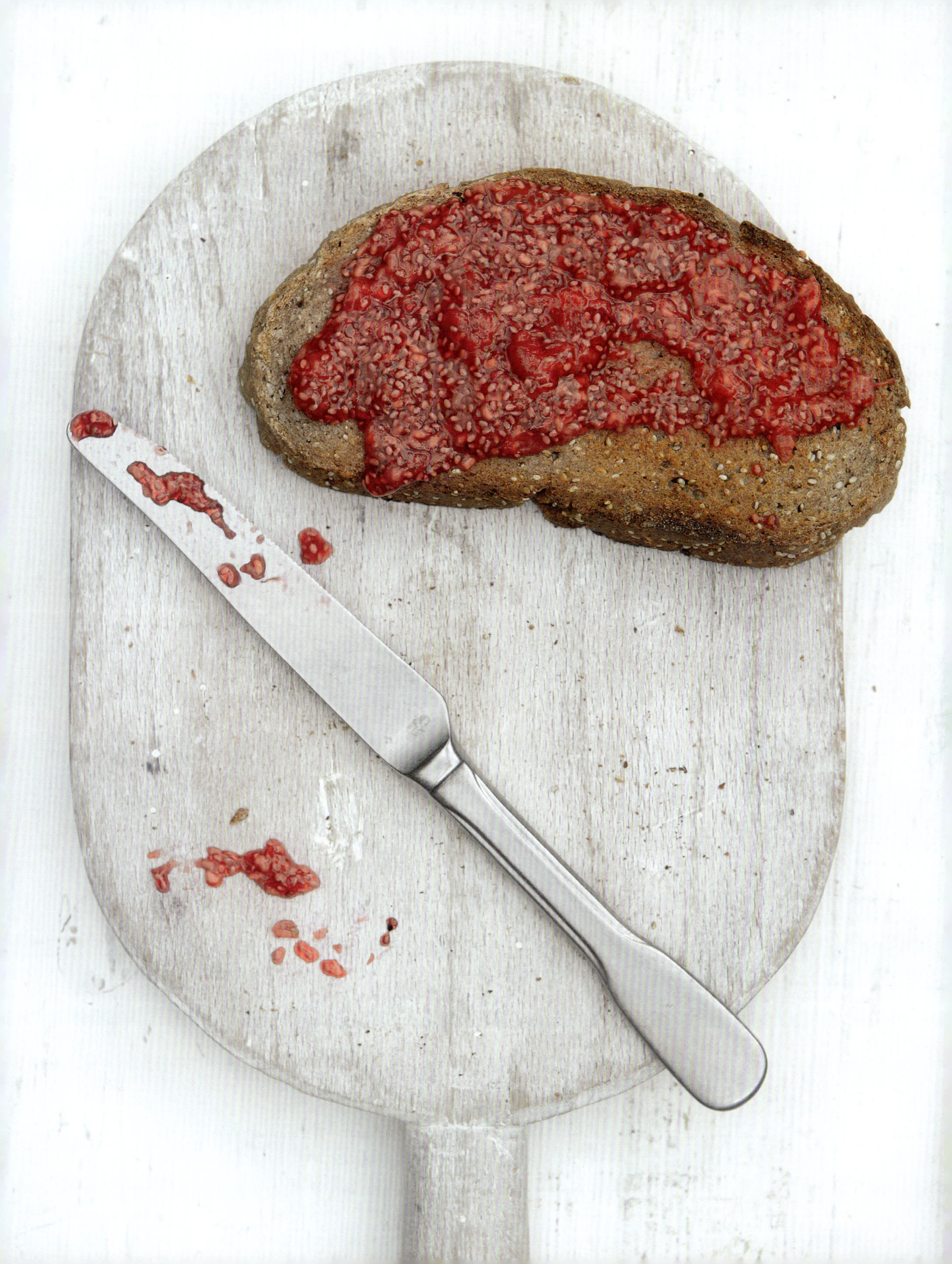

Puffed breakfast crispies

I used to love Rice Krispies, as a kid, so after discovering these puffed grains I thought I had gone to healthy heaven. Make up a big batch and store them in an airtight container, so you have a healthy start to the day at your fingertips. I love to eat the crispies with a dairy-free coconut milk yogurt and grapefruit segments for a zingy start to the day.

Preheat the oven to 325°F/170°C/gas mark 3.

Put the puffed grains into a bowl, add the chia seed oil, grapefruit zest, 2 tablespoons of the syrup, the nutmeg, and vanilla extract and mix well until everything's well coated. Spread onto a baking tray and bake in a preheated oven for 5 minutes.

Meanwhile, mix together the sunflower seeds, pumpkin seeds, and the remaining ½ teablespoon syrup and, after 5 minutes of baking time, open the oven door and sprinkle this over the mixture in the baking tray. Close the oven door and continue to bake for another 5 minutes, stirring every minute or so, so they don't get too brown but get an even, golden brown color.

Remove the crispies from the oven and let them cool on the baking tray. When they're completely cool, transfer them to an airtight container, where they'll keep for a couple of weeks.

makes 2½ cups (180g)

2 cups (35g) puffed millet

2 cups (35g) puffed rice

2 tbsp chia seed oil or sunflower oil

finely grated zest of ½ grapefruit

2½ tbsp agave nectar or coconut blossom syrup

¼ tsp nutmeg

½ tbsp vanilla extract

¼ cup (30g) sunflower seeds

¼ cup (30g) pumpkin seeds

Nutmeg matcha latte

Matcha latte is all the fashion now, so here is how to make your very own at home, with a nutty twist. You can use a milk frother rather than a high-speed blender, if you like. Matcha has more antioxidants than green tea, and will give you the morning or afternoon pick-me-up you need. It also has thermogenic properties, which means it boosts your metabolism, so it's raised all the time, even when sitting down, enjoying a matcha latte!

Heat the milk in a small saucepan until hot, not boiling. Transfer to a blender. Add the remaining ingredients and blend until completely mixed. Serve hot in a mug and grate a little more nutmeg over the top.

serves 1

1 cup (250ml) almond milk

1 tsp matcha powder

4 good grinds of nutmeg, plus extra to garnish

1 tsp coconut oil

1 tsp coconut blossom syrup or agave nectar

Matcha has a vibrant green color to it. This is because of the abundance of natural chlorophyll in the leaves.

Baked eggs in avocado

I love to eat avocado and eggs for breakfast but I thought it would be good to mix it up a little. This breakfast dish uses the same ingredients, but in a slightly unusual way. Give it a go and see for yourself. To transform this dish into something more substantial for lunch or dinner, serve with a velvety miso dressing (see below) and some salad.

Preheat the oven to 350°F/180°C/gas mark 4.

Halve the avocado and carefully remove the pit. Slightly enlarge the hole, left by the pit, by scooping out some of the avocado flesh with a spoon – eat this while the egg is baking.

Turn the avocado over and take a small slice off the bottom to keep it from wobbling in the oven. Place each avocado half on a baking tray and then crack an egg into each hole. Season and bake in a preheated oven for 12–15 minutes, or until the eggs are cooked.

Remove the avocado halves from the oven, transfer to 2 plates, and sprinkle over the lemon zest and a drizzle of oil. These are best eaten hot.

serves 2

1 avocado

2 eggs

finely grated zest of ½ lemon

a pinch of Himalayan pink salt

cracked black pepper

olive oil

For a velvety miso dressing, just mix 1 tablespoon of miso with 1 teaspoon of water and a pinch of salt.

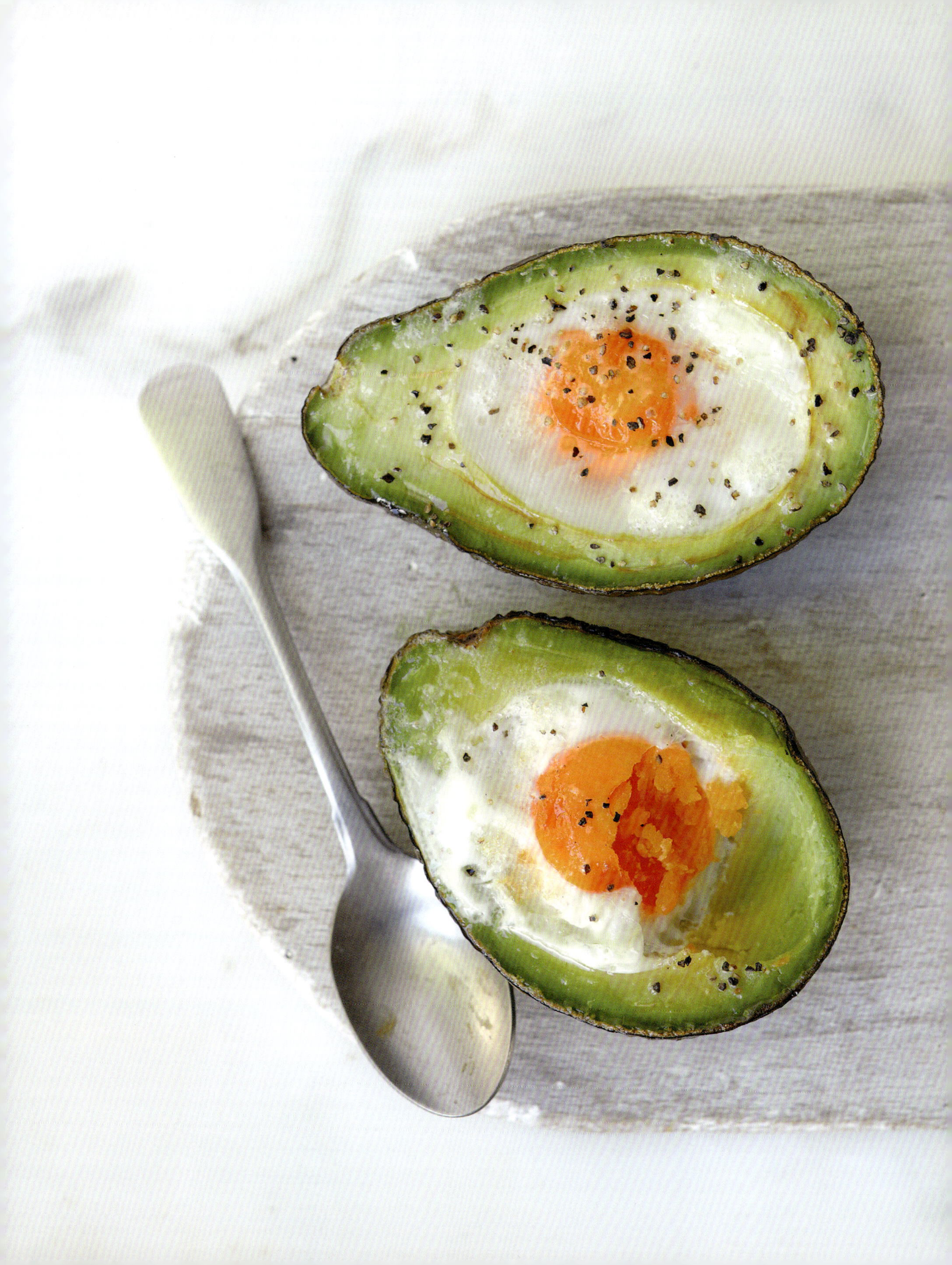

#meals

Kale salad

I sometimes think I should start a kale fan club – it is one of my all-time favorite ingredients and I miss it terribly when it is out of season. As well as being fat-free and rich in iron, kale is a fantastic source of calcium, folate, and lutein (an antioxidant that keeps eyes healthy), as well as vitamins A, C, and K. I try to pack it into as many of my dishes as possible, but it's utterly delicious with just a little garlic and lemon.

Heat the coconut oil in a very large saucepan, add the garlic, and sauté for 1 minute until it softens. Add the chopped kale – it's important to use a big pan, as you want there to be enough space around the kale for it to get crispy. Cook for 2–3 minutes until it starts to wilt and crisp up around the edges. Transfer the contents of the pan to a serving platter or bowl and set aside.

Return the pan to the heat, add the tamari, followed by the artichokes, and cook for 1 minute, just so they are warmed through and have absorbed the flavors from the pan.

Next, make the dressing. Blend together the miso, water, and lime juice until smooth. Drizzle over the salad and garnish with the zest, sprouts, and shoots.

serves 2

2 tbsp coconut oil

1 clove garlic, sliced

⅔ cup (40g) chopped kale

1 tbsp tamari

18–20 (150g) grilled artichokes

for the dressing:

2 tbsp miso paste

2 tbsp water

juice of 1 lime

to garnish:

finely grated zest of 1 lime

broccoli sprouts

radish sprouts

pea shoots

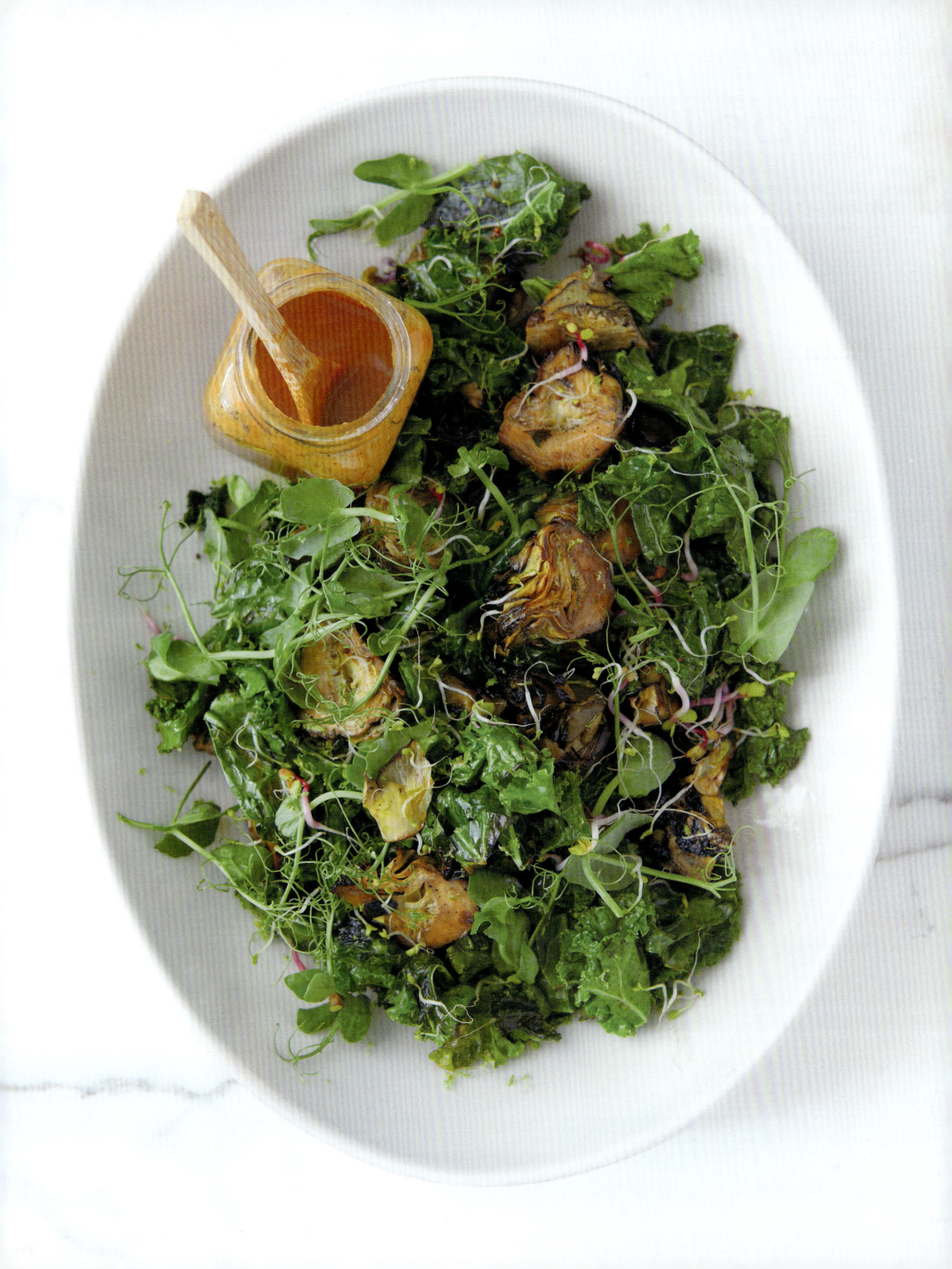

Winter Greek salad in a bag

As much as I love a Greek salad, I wanted to create a more warming version. When I went to the local farmers' market, I was inspired by all the colors and so filled my basket with the vibrant produce and incorporated them in the recipe below. If you are a vegan, simply omit the feta and you're still left with an utterly delicious and fuss-free dish.

Preheat the oven to 350°F/180°C/gas mark 4. Line a baking tray with enough parchment paper to cover the surface and to wrap around the veggies that will go in the bag.

Place the sweet potato, beets, carrots, red onion, garlic, and rosemary on the parchment paper. Sprinkle with the oil and salt, then fold the paper over the mixture to make an airtight bag.

Bake in a preheated oven for 30 minutes. Take the tray out of the oven, carefully open up the bag, and add the olives and mushrooms on top of the other vegetables, allowing the oil from the olives to drip onto the mushrooms. Return the tray to the oven with the bag open for another 15 minutes.

Remove the bag from the oven, scatter over the feta, and serve immediately.

serves 3-4

1½ cups (200g) sweet potatoes, cut into ⅓in (1cm) cubes

¾ cup (100g) raw candy beets, cut in ¼in (5mm) slices and then into quarters

1⅓ cups (160g) rainbow carrots, cut at an angle into ¾in (2cm) slices

½ red onion, thinly sliced

3 cloves garlic, unpeeled

3 sprigs rosemary

2 tbsp sunflower oil

a pinch of Himalayan pink salt

1¼ cups (100g) button or shiitake mushrooms, sliced

¾ cup (100g) pitted green olives in oil

¾ cup (100g) feta cheese, cubed

Chickpea dumplings

If you're in need of something filling and spicy, then this quick-to-make recipe is your go-to dish. I've suggested using soy yogurt, as I like to make it dairy-free, but you could use goat, sheep, or coconut milk yogurt instead, if you like. For a more substantial meal, serve on a bed of wilted spinach.

Put the flour, ginger, salt, garlic, cilantro, water, and chili pepper into a bowl and mix together to form a sticky dough

To make the dumplings, take ping-pong sized pieces of the dough and roll them into balls (you should get about eight balls), then squash them gently to flatten them.

In a frying pan, heat the sesame oil and, when hot, sauté the dumplings for about 30–60 seconds on each side to sear and give them a little color. Transfer the dumplings to a plate and set aside.

To make the sauce, heat the sesame oil in the empty pan. When hot, sauté the onion, garlic, cumin, fennel seeds, turmeric, smoked paprika, and chili powder for 2 minutes and then add the water. Continue to cook for 2 minutes more and then add the soy yogurt, followed by the lime zest. Mix together well.

Next, transfer the dumplings to the sauce and bring to a boil. Stir the cilantro into the sauce just before you serve.

serves 2, makes 8

1⅓ cups (130g) chickpea flour

1in (2.5cm) piece of ginger, grated

¼ tsp Himalayan pink salt

1 clove garlic, grated

⅔ cup (10g) cilantro leaves, chopped

3 tbsp water

2in (5cm) red chili pepper, diced

2 tbsp sesame oil

for the sauce:

1 tbsp sesame oil

½ red onion, diced

1 clove garlic, grated

½ tsp ground cumin

½ tsp fennel seeds

¼ tsp ground turmeric

¼ tsp smoked paprika

¼ tsp chili powder, or to taste

4 tbsp water

1¼ cups (300g) soy yogurt

finely grated zest of 1 lime

1¼ cups (20g) cilantro leaves

Portobello burgers

I love the idea of using Portobello mushrooms as the buns for a burger – they are melt-in-the-mouth delicious, as well. I like to sandwich them with fresh greens plus some Broccoli pesto and Cashew cheese, and serve them with special fries.

serves 2

4 Portobello mushrooms
a pinch of Himalayan pink salt
Broccoli pesto (see page 142)
1 cup (20g) arugula
1 large vine-ripened tomato, sliced
1 scallion, sliced
⅛ cup (10g) flat leaf parsley, leaves picked
Cashew cheese (see recipe on the right)
1 tbsp raw sesame seeds
1 tbsp sunflower oil
almond-crusted zucchini fries (see page 187)

Preheat the oven to 325°F/170°C/gas mark 3.

Carefully cut the stalks off the mushrooms and massage the oil into the caps. Place them on a baking tray, with the gills facing up, and sprinkle with salt. Bake for 10 minutes, then turn them over and bake for 5 minutes more.

To serve, put a mushroom cap on a plate, add a dollop of broccoli pesto, then some arugula and a slice of tomato, along with some scallion and parsley. Place another mushroom cap on the plate and spread some cashew cheese on it, then sit it on top of the vegetables to form the top half of the "bun." Sprinkle with sesame seeds to make it look like a real hamburger bun.

Serve with the zucchini fries and sprinkle with apple cider vinegar and salt.

Cashew cheese

Here's a fantastic cheese replacement that's dairy-free. As well as being perfect with the Portobello burgers, you can spread it on toast or crackers as a snack, add it to salads, or stir it through pasta to give it that creamy texture.

fills a small ⅓ cup (70ml) canning jar

2⅛ cups (250g) raw cashews
⅔ cup (150ml) water
¼ cup (15g) nutritional yeast
juice of ½ lemon
1 clove garlic

Soak the cashews in the water for 30 minutes, if using a high-speed blender. If using a standard blender, soak them for at least 2 hours: they need to be extra soft.

Put all the ingredients, including the cashews' soaking water, into the blender and process until velvety smooth. Pour into a clean jar and pop into the fridge to cool and set.

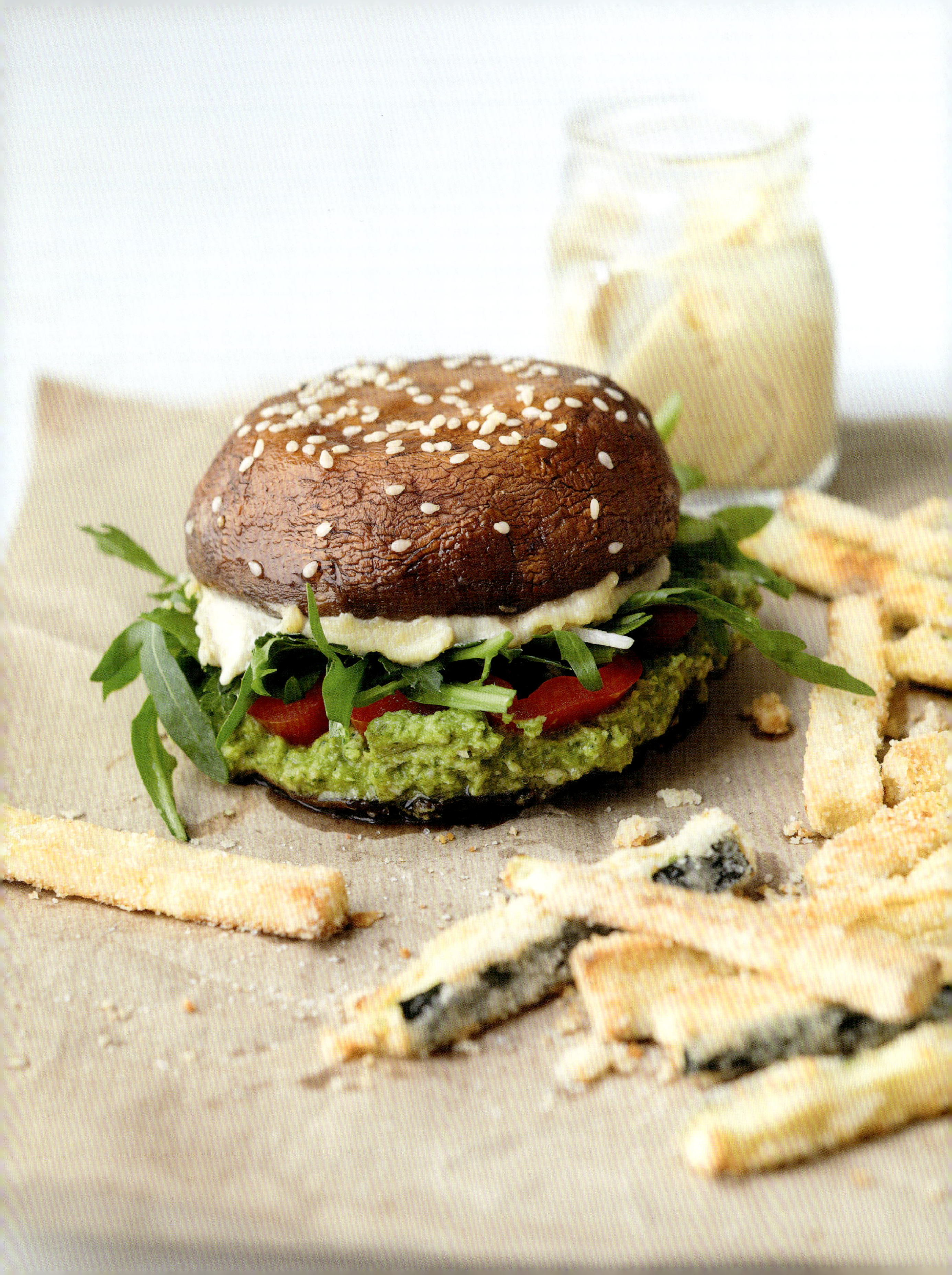

Almond-crusted zucchini fries

If, like me, you get cravings for traditional fries, but they make you feel groggy afterwards, try out these tasty and healthy alternatives. As well as adding a coating of protein, the ground almonds crisp up the fries – perfect! Enjoy them with the Portobello burger (see page 184), or even as a great garnish for a salad.

Preheat the oven to 325°F/170°C/gas mark 3.

Slice the zucchini into long, French fry-like shapes – the thinner they are, the crunchier they will become.

Combine the salt and almonds in a wide shallow bowl.

Massage the zucchini "fries" with the oil, then roll them into the almond mixture. Place on a baking sheet and bake for 15-20 minutes until they start to brown. Remove from the oven and serve immediately.

serves 2

2 zucchini

a pinch of Himalayan pink salt

1 cup (100g) ground almonds

2 tbsp sunflower oil

You might find it a little tricky to get the ground almonds to stick to the zucchini. Just gently press them on and they will turn out perfectly.

Watercress, bean, and hazelnut salad

Another green leafy vegetable I'm a great fan of is watercress. Not only is it very alkaline, but it is also packed with many other nutrients (calcium, Vitamins C and E, and iron) – it's another superfood in my book. I love the hot, peppery taste of watercress, but if it's out of season, you could use spinach instead. You can be flexible with the beans, too; lima beans also work well for adding texture to this salad.

In a pan, sauté the leeks in the sunflower oil for about 3 minutes until soft and starting to turn brown at the edges. Transfer to a plate and set aside.

Put the beans and tamari in the empty pan and return to the heat. Add the lemon juice and warm through, about 1–2 minutes, then add the hazelnuts.

To serve, arrange the salad greens on 2 plates and spoon the bean mixture over them. Place the leeks on top.

Drizzle with the pumpkin oil and garnish with the lemon zest, sprouts, and flaxseeds.

serves 2

1 tbsp sunflower oil

1⅛ cups (100g) leeks, halved lengthwise, then cut across the width

1⅓ cups (240g) cooked kidney or cannellini beans, drained

1 tsp tamari

juice of ½ lemon

⅓ cup (50g) raw hazelnuts

1⅛ cups (40g) mixed watercress and salad greens

a pinch of Himalayan pink salt

to garnish:

1 tbsp pumpkin oil

finely grated zest of ½ lemon

broccoli or alfalfa sprouts

a pinch of golden flaxseeds

Vermicelli stir-fry

I love the Far East, and on my last trip to Vietnam I ate stir-fries almost daily. When I came back to England I found that I really missed these dishes, so I've created a supertasty and healthy version that I can rustle up when I arrive home hungry after a long day. This dish tastes just like ones I used to have when I was on holiday.

Heat the sesame oil in a wok and stir-fry in the onion, garlic, and ginger for 1 minute. Add 4 tablespoons of the water plus the rice vinegar and cook for another minute.

Add the carrots, cook for 1 minute and, when the liquid has been absorbed, add another 4 tablespoons of water along with the broccoli. Cook for another minute, then add another 4 tablespoons of water followed by the tamari, tomatoes, and leeks and cook for another minute.

Next, throw in the mushrooms, zucchini ribbons and bell pepper slices and cook for another minute. Add the last of the measured water along with the lime juice and cook for 2 minutes, after which add the kale.

Cook the noodles according to the instructions on the package; I cook mine for about 3 minutes in boiling water. Drain the noodles and add them to the wok and mix well.

Transfer the wok's contents to a platter or serving bowl and garnish with mint, chili, if using, and the lime zest.

serves 2

1 tbsp sesame oil

½ red onion, sliced

1 clove garlic, finely chopped

2in (5cm) piece ginger, grated

1 cup (240ml) water

1 tsp brown rice vinegar

1 carrot, thinly sliced

1½ cups 2in (2cm) pieces (75g) broccoli

2 tbsp tamari

¾ cup (80g) cherry tomatoes, quartered

½ cup (40g) leeks, sliced at an angle

¾ cup (50g) Portobello mushrooms, sliced

¾ cup (40g) wild mushrooms (I like chanterelles), sliced if necessary

1 zucchini, sliced into ribbons

1 red bell pepper, sliced

juice of 2 limes

1 cup chopped (60g) kale

1⅓oz (40g) vermicelli noodles

to garnish:

⅓ cup (5g) mint leaves

1 red chili pepper, chopped (optional)

finely grated zest of 2 limes

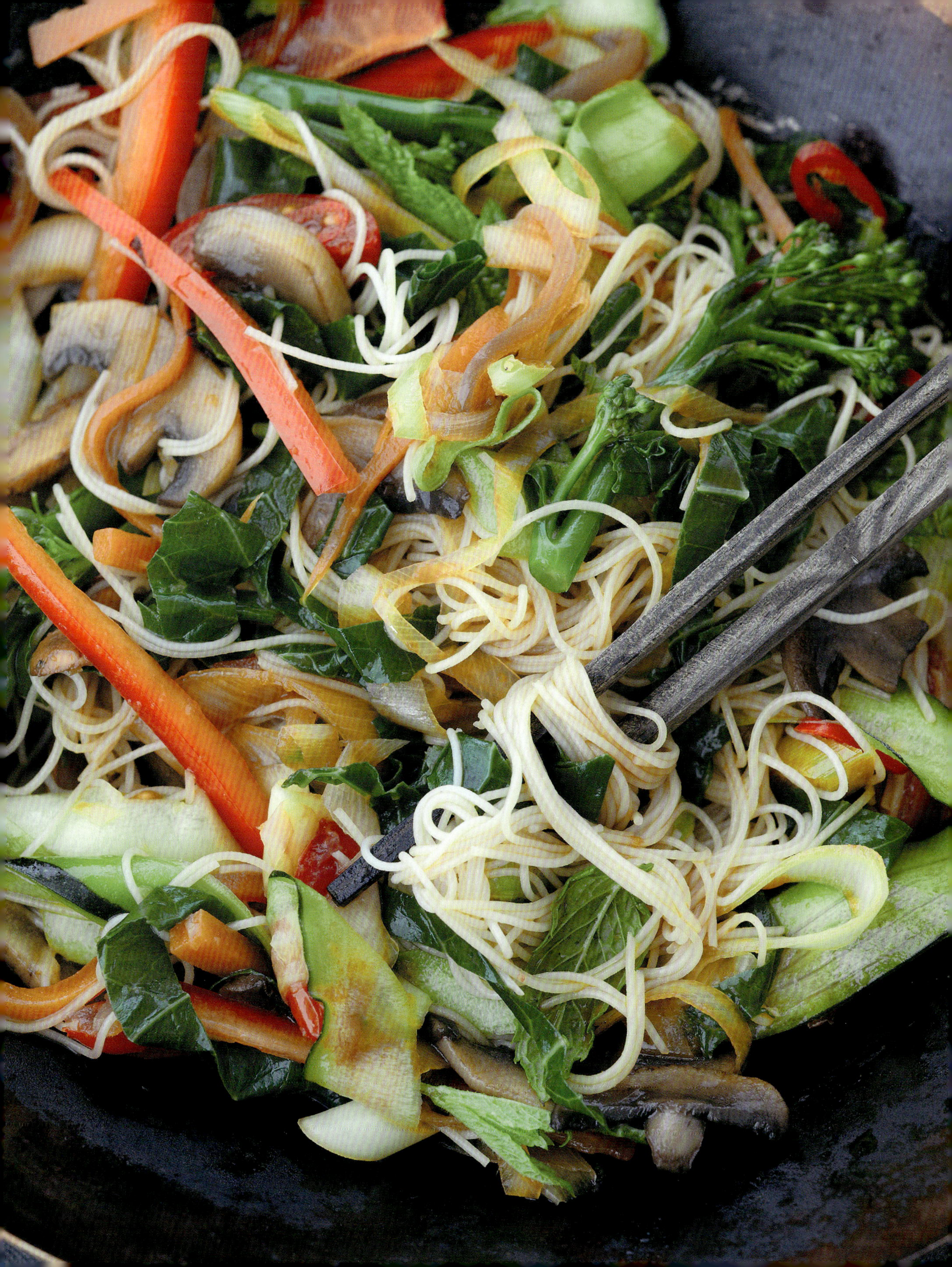

Zesty pear and fennel salad

I have always loved the combination of pear and fennel since I wrote my first book and created a pear and fennel soup for it. If you liked that soup, you'll love this salad, which contains the same – and my favorite – toxin-reducing ingredients. The taste is super-zesty and refreshing, which is just perfect when you're cleansing.

Peel the pear and immediately squeeze half the lemon over it to keep it from oxidizing and turning brown.

Finely slice the fennel, preferably with a mandoline, and squeeze the other half of the lemon over it.

Place the pomegranate cut side down in your palm and bang the back of a wooden spoon on the rounded side. This releases the seeds into your palm, and you can then just let them fall between your fingers into a bowl. (This clever trick means you don't get any of the white pith.)

In a pan, put the tamari and allspice over low heat and stir in the pumpkin seeds; the delicious spices attach themselves to the seeds while they're warmed. After 2 minutes, remove the pan from the heat and set aside to cool.

Meanwhile, make the dressing. Put all the ingredients (except the zest) into a blender and process until smooth.

Put the arugula, diced pear, sliced fennel, and cubed cucumber into a bowl. Pour over the dressing and toss well.

Top with a sprinkle of lime zest, the toasted pumpkin seeds, fennel fronds, and pomegranate seeds.

serves 2

1 pear, cored and sliced

juice of 1 lemon

1 fennel bulb, fronds reserved for garnish

seeds from ½ pomegranate

1 tbsp tamari

¼ tsp ground allspice

⅛ cup (20g) pumpkin seeds

4⅓ cups (180g) arugula

1 small cucumber, 1¾ cups sliced (about 220g)

for the dressing:

4 tbsp olive oil

juice and zest finely grated of 1 lime

1⅛ cups (10g) sprigs of dill

Himalayan pink salt

Quinoa-stuffed acorn squash

This dish makes a great alternative to a traditional Sunday lunch – the stuffing really tastes like the stuffing I had when I was a kid, but this one is healthy! If you can't get hold of acorn squash, use slices of butternut squash instead.

Preheat the oven to 325°F/170°C/gas mark 3.

Chop the squash in half and remove the seeds (save them for another recipe). Place the squash on a baking tray and drizzle with 1 tablespoon of the sunflower oil. Bake in a preheated oven for around 30 minutes or until the flesh softens and you can easily pierce it with a knife.

Meanwhile, add the bouillon powder to the boiling water, stirring until dissolved. Use this stock to cook the quinoa over a medium heat.

While the quinoa is cooking, heat the remaining oil in another pan and sauté the onion and garlic for around 2 minutes until translucent, adding a splash of water if the pan gets too hot.

Once the quinoa is cooked and its "tails" have sprouted, add the onions and garlic along with the chestnuts, salt, parsley, apricots, lemon juice, and zest and mix through. If the mixture is looking a little dry, add a splash of water to loosen it.

If you want to prepare the crust, gently dry-toast the sunflower seeds and chestnuts (see page 74). Transfer them to a food processor or blender and pulse to a rough consistency. Alternatively, pound using a pestle and mortar. Put them into a bowl and mix through the remaining crust ingredients.

Once the squash is cooked, stuff the center with the quinoa mixture, pressing down so it is well compacted and flat. Top with the crust mixture, making it about 5mm thick.

(If using a butternut squash, scrape out some of the flesh so that you have a bigger area in which to stuff the quinoa. Use a fork to do this and then mix the extra flesh through the quinoa stuffing.)

Return the stuffed squash to the oven for 15 minutes more or until the crust begins to crisp up.

Remove from the oven and serve immediately.

serves 4

1 large acorn squash

2 tbsp sunflower oil

1 tsp bouillon powder

1 cup (240ml) boiling water

⅓ cup (60g) quinoa

1 red onion, finely chopped

1 large clove garlic, finely chopped

5–6 whole (50g) ready-cooked chestnuts, chopped

¼ tsp Himalayan pink salt

2 tbsp finely chopped flat leaf parsley

5–6 unsulphured dried apricots, chopped

finely grated zest and juice ¼ lemon

for the seeded crust (optional):

½ cup (70g) raw sunflower seeds

5–6 whole (50g) ready-cooked chestnuts, chopped

1 tbsp sunflower oil

¼ tsp Himalayan pink salt

freshly ground black pepper

3 tbsp finely chopped flat leaf parsley

a squeeze of lemon

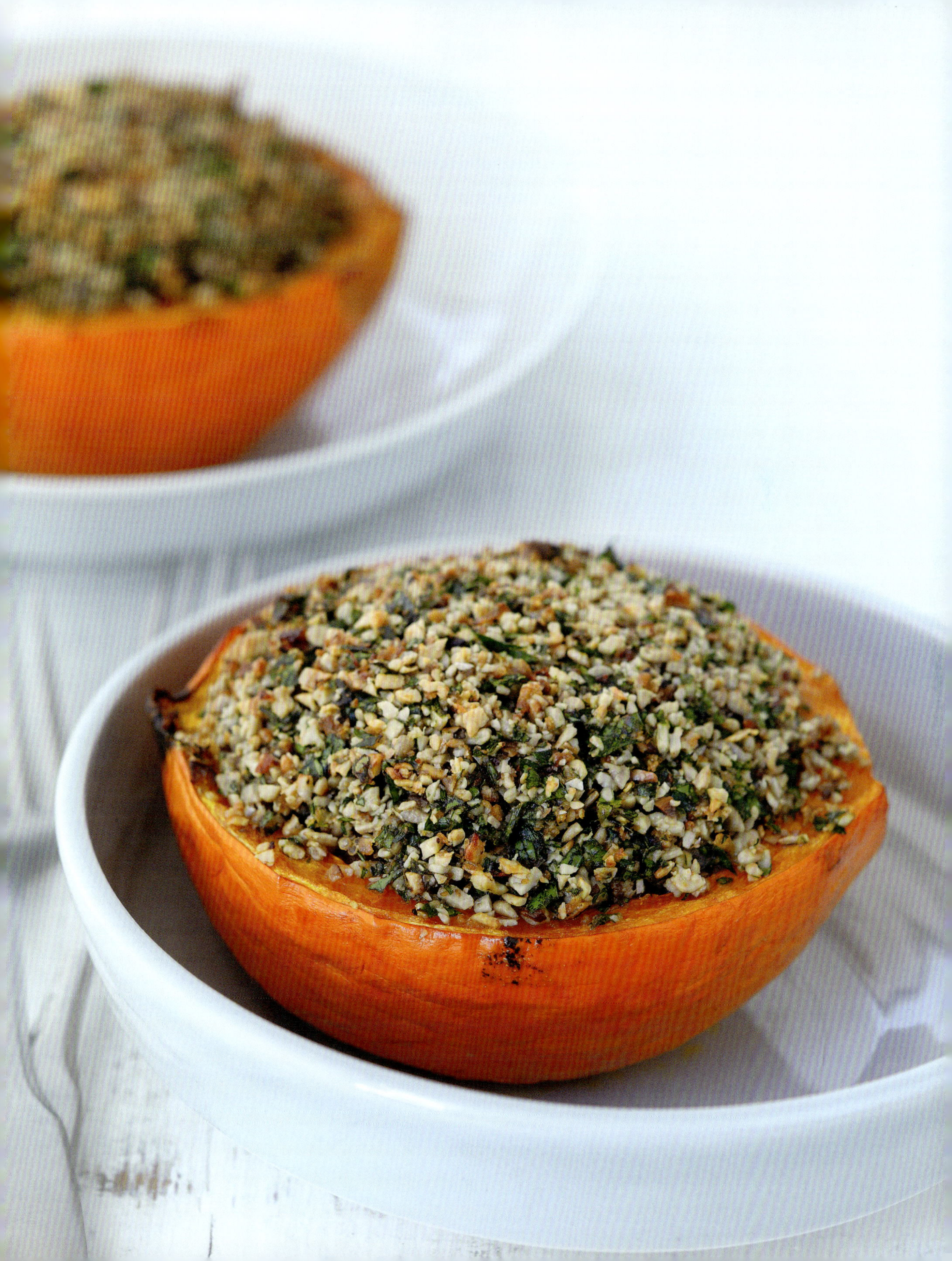

Baked and stuffed eggplant

This dish is not only delicious for dinner, but also makes a great cold lunch the next day. If you are planning to exercise hard you can make it more substantial by adding some cooked quinoa or brown rice to the basic tomato filling.

Preheat the oven to 350°F/180°C/gas mark 4.

Score the flesh of each eggplant half with a sharp knife. Place on a baking tray, drizzle with 2 tablespoons of sunflower oil and sprinkle over the onion seeds. Bake in a preheated oven for 40–45 minutes until the flesh is soft.

Meanwhile, make the filling. Heat the remaining oil in a large pan and sauté the garlic, onion, cumin, turmeric, and coriander seeds for 1 minute. Once the oil is absorbed, add the tomatoes and one-third of the water. Simmer over medium/high heat for 15 minutes until the mixture has reduced and the tomatoes are soft and saucy.

Take the eggplants out of the oven and carefully scoop out the flesh, leaving the skin intact. Roughly chop the flesh and add this to the tomato mixture. Cook for 5 minutes more and then add the cilantro.

Spoon the filling into the eggplant skins and either serve as they are or finely grate some pecorino over the top and return to the oven until melted. Sprinkle over some sprigs of cilantro and serve with a salad, if you like, but the eggplants are delicious on their own.

serves 4

2 eggplants, halved lengthwise

3 tbsp sunflower oil

¼ tsp black onion seeds

for the filling:

1 clove garlic, grated

1 red onion, diced

¼ tsp ground cumin

¼ tsp ground turmeric

1 tsp coriander seeds

3–4 (1⅓lbs/600g) vine-ripened tomatoes, quartered

1 cup (240ml) water

2 tbsp chopped cilantro, plus sprigs to garnish

¼ cup grated (20g) pecorino cheese (optional)

Broccoli-crust pizza

Sometimes you want a pizza, but just don't want to start getting flour out and making a dough. So I've found a rather quick and delicious alternative to a grain-based pizza crust. It's green as well, which makes me smile from the inside out!

Preheat the oven to 325°F/170°C/gas mark 3. Line a baking sheet with parchment paper and spread the oil over it – just enough to keep the crust from sticking.

Put the ground chia seeds and water in a small bowl and set aside for 10 minutes until the mixture becomes wonderfully gloopy.

Meanwhile, put the broccoli florets into a food processor or blender and process until they are finely chopped, but not yet a paste. Transfer to another bowl.

Next, add the ground almonds, rosemary, seasoning, and soaked chia. Mix all these ingredients together with your hands into a "dough" ready to roll out.

Put the ball of dough in the middle of the prepared baking sheet and flatten it into a circle about ¼in (5mm) thick.

Bake in a preheated oven for 30 minutes until the surface starts to color.

Meanwhile, make the sauce. Put the coconut oil and garlic in a pan over medium heat. After 30 seconds add 3 tablespoons of the water to cool down the pan, and then add the mustard seeds and leave for 1 minute. Add the chopped tomatoes and stir for a minute. Once the liquid starts to reduce, add 4 tablespoons of water and simmer for 20 minutes until it becomes a thick sauce. When ready, add the basil, remove from the heat and set aside.

Take the crust out of the oven but keep it on the baking tray. Spoon the sauce over the crust, leaving a ⅓in (1cm) border around the edge.

Now add your favorite crust toppings. Here are a few I love:

pan-fried wild field mushrooms with goat cheese

arugula and mozzarella

artichoke and black olives with basil

makes 1 large pizza crust, enough for 2; the sauce is enough for 2 pizzas

1 tbsp sunflower oil

2½ tbsp (15g) ground chia seeds

¼ cup (60ml) water

2½ cups (180g) broccoli florets

1 cup (100g) ground almonds

1 sprig rosemary, chopped

a pinch of Himalayan pink salt

freshly ground black pepper

for the pizza sauce:

1 tbsp coconut oil

1 clove garlic, finely chopped

7 tbsp water

¼ tsp yellow mustard seeds

1 cup (200g) vine-ripened tomatoes, chopped

⅔ cup (4g) basil leaves, chopped

juice of ½ lemon

Red beet wraps

The great thing about these wraps is that they are easy to transport – to work, on a car trip or to a picnic in the park. If you don't have beet juice powder don't worry, you can leave it out, but it's a great antioxidant and adds the vibrant color. Try wrapping up some roasted vegetables or grilled broccoli with fresh herbs and a gorgeous dressing for a nutritious lunch.

Combine the flour and xanthan gum in a largish bowl. Make a well in the middle, pour in the warm water, and mix together until a dough forms. (I find the various brands of gluten-free flour work slightly differently, so you might need to add a little more flour if the dough still feels gluey.)

Sprinkle in the beet juice powder and knead it into the dough on a floured surface – don't mix too thoroughly if you want to achieve a marbled effect when it's rolled out.

Dust the work surface with some more flour and cut the dough into 4 equal pieces. Roll each one into a circle about ⅟₁₆in (2mm) thick – the thinner the better.

Put a non-stick frying pan over high heat. When the pan is very hot, wipe it with oil (just for a coating, and make sure there are no blobs anywhere), then fry each circle of dough for about 1 minute on each side – it will start to develop little bubbles and turn brown. Transfer to a plate and fry the other circles in the same way.

serves 4

⅓ cup (50g) gluten-free all-purpose flour

¾ tsp xanthan gum

½ cup (120ml) warm water

2 tbsp beet juice powder

sunflower oil, for frying

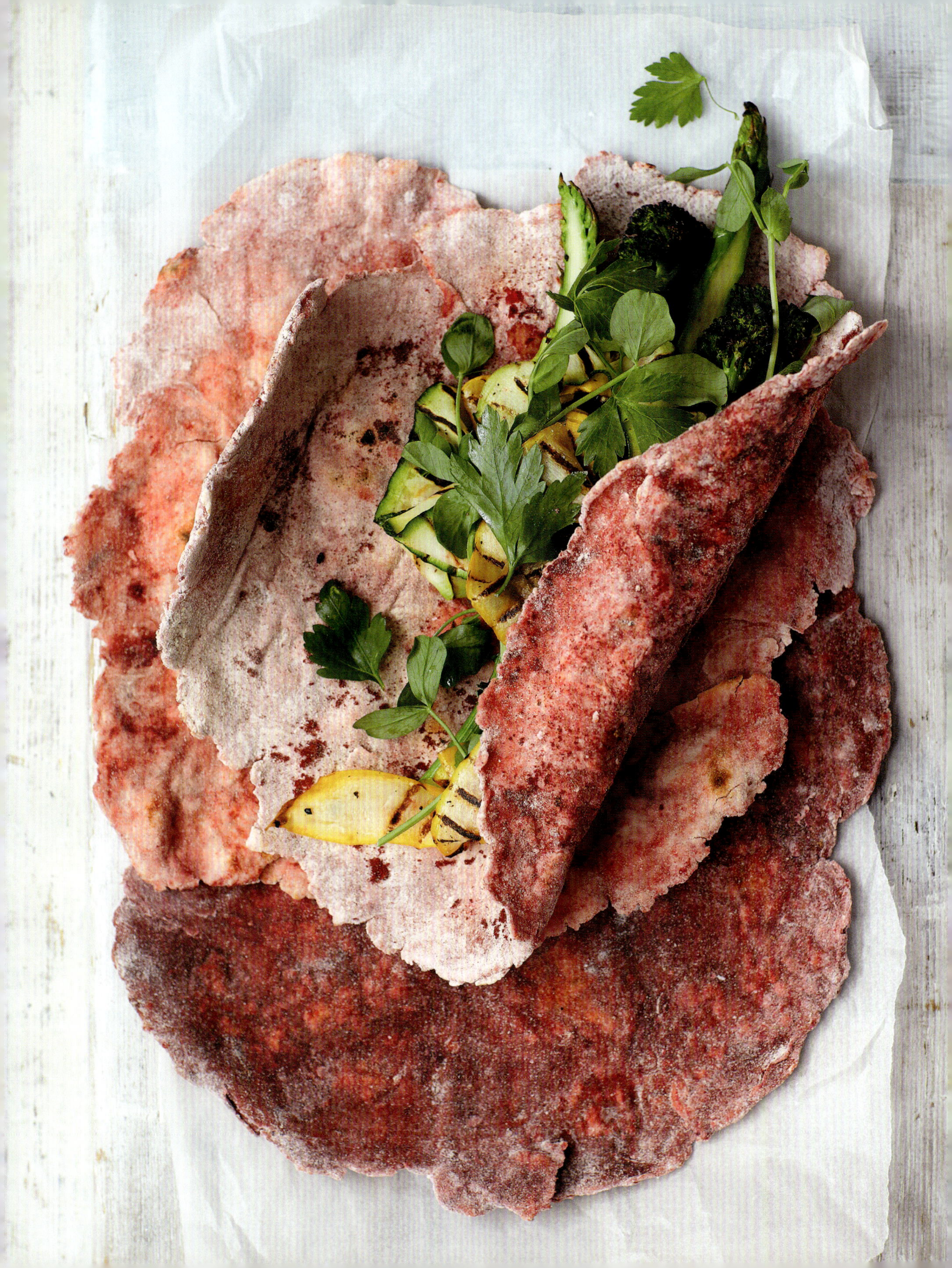

Chanterelle mushroom pot

Mushrooms are among nature's great medicinal plants. The Reishi mushroom is said to be the king of them, boosting the immune system to help ward off disease. They are also high in vitamin D, which is what people in unsunny climes often lack, and which is vital for healthy bones. This warming and comforting dish allows the mushroom to take center stage and you to benefit from its properties.

Soak the porcini mushrooms in a small bowl with the warm water.

Heat the oil in a pan and sauté the onions and garlic for about 3–5 minutes until translucent. Next, add the celery and lemon zest and continue to cook until softened.

Strain the porcini, being careful to keep the soaking water. If the mushrooms are big, chop them into pieces about ⅝in (1.5cm) long, then add to the pan and continue to sauté for 3 more minutes.

Gently stir in the zucchini and chanterelles, then add the porcini water and simmer for about 3–4 minutes, until all of the vegetables have softened.

Remove the pan from the heat and stir through the lemon juice, parsley and seasoning.

Serve in a bowl with a topping of finely grated sheep's milk cheese, such as Manchego or pecorino.

serves 2–3

½ cup (10g) dried porcini mushrooms

2⅛ cups (500ml) warm water

1 tbsp sunflower oil

1 onion, sliced

2 cloves garlic, chopped

1½ × 8in pieces (70g) celery, cut into ⅓in (1cm) pieces

finely grated zest and juice of 1 lemon

1 cup (225g) zucchini, cut into 1in (2.5cm) cubes

3⅔ cups (200g) chanterelle mushrooms, halved if large

2⅓ cups (75g) spinach

4 tbsp finely chopped flat leaf parsley

¼ tsp Himalayan pink salt

freshly ground black pepper

hard sheep's milk cheese, grated, to garnish

Braised fennel and grapefruit salad

This beautiful salad is super-cleansing and makes a showstopper dish for a dinner party: just scale the recipe up to match the number of guests. Fennel is a wonderful vegetable for drawing toxins from the body, as well as being diuretic and helping your body get rid of excess fluid. And you might not know that although a grapefruit tastes acidic, its effect on the body is actually alkaline when digested.

Preheat the oven to 325°F/170°C/gas mark 3, and line a baking tray with foil.

Cut the whole fennel bulb into 6 lengthwise pieces, and cut the half bulb into 3. Put the oil in a frying pan over medium heat and cook the fennel for 2 minutes on each side until it starts to color. Transfer to the baking tray.

Whisk the bouillon powder into the water and pour over the fennel, along with the apple cider vinegar.

Cover the fennel with foil and braise in the oven for 20–25 minutes until you can easily pierce it with a sharp knife.

Meanwhile, cook the fava beans in boiling water until soft, then cool quickly in a sieve under cold running water. Combine with the rest of the salad ingredients on a platter or in a bowl.

Whisk together all of the ingredients for the dressing.

Arrange the braised fennel over the top of the salad and drizzle with the dressing. Chop the fennel fronds and sprinkle them over the top before serving.

serves 2

1½ bulbs fennel, fronds reserved

1 tbsp sunflower oil

1 tsp bouillon powder

½ cup (125ml) hot water

1 tbsp apple cider vinegar

1⅓ cups (210g) fava beans

1 large handful mâche (or watercress)

1 large handful arugula leaves

1 handful iceberg lettuce, very finely sliced

2 scallions, finely chopped at an angle

½ pink grapefruit and ½ white grapefruit, peeled and segmented

for the dressing:

¼ cup (50ml) freshly squeezed grapefruit juice

⅛ cup (25ml) extra virgin olive oil

1½ tsp apple cider vinegar

1 tsp agave nectar

2 tbsp finely chopped cilantro

Roasted artichoke with coconut and lemon dressing

Artichokes are one of my favorite vegetables. People often shy away from these beautiful globes, as they're unsure of how to prepare them, but they are simple to clean up and roast, so give this recipe a go. These artichokes would also be amazing on a bed of arugula or other fresh salad greens, and once you've tasted this coconut dressing, you'll be making it every week.

Preheat the oven to 325°F/170°C/gas mark 3, and line a baking tray with parchment paper.

Get a large bowl of cold water and squeeze in the juice of 3 lemon quarters.

Clean the artichokes by cutting the tops off. Remove the outer leaves until you get to the softer leaves. Chop the artichokes in half and rub the lemon quarters over the outside right away to keep them from turning brown. Transfer to the lemony water until you are ready to put them into the oven.

Drain the artichokes and put them into the prepared tray, along with the unsqueezed lemon quarter, sunflower oil, salt, and smoked paprika. Roast for 15–20 minutes in a preheated oven until the leaves start to crisp up at the edges.

Make the dressing by mixing together all the dressing ingredients with the juice from the roasted lemon.

Mix together the artichokes and edamame, drizzle over the dressing and serve.

serves 2

1 lemon, quartered

5 baby artichokes

1 tbsp sunflower oil

a pinch of Himalayan pink salt

¼ tsp smoked paprika

½ cup (120g) shelled edamame beans, defrosted if frozen

for the dressing:

2 tbsp desiccated coconut

3–4 tbsp olive oil

a pinch of Himalayan pink salt

⅓ cup (3g) dill, chopped

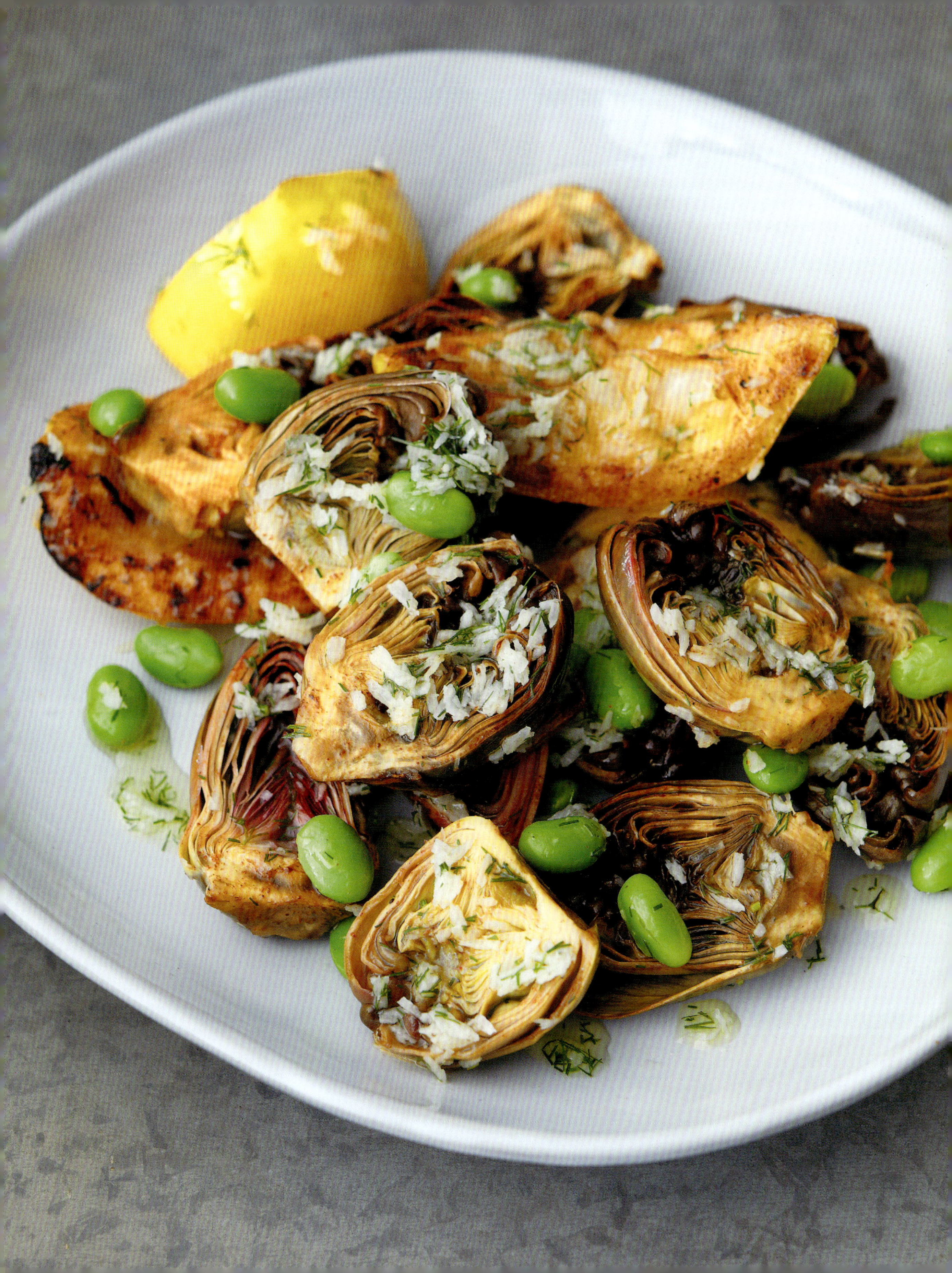

Butternut squash and spinach tagine

This is a dish I love to serve at a dinner party; what's more, it's simple to make and you can do all the prep and cooking the night before, leaving you more time with your guests. Butternut squash is an alkaline food, and the cinnamon included here gives it an antiviral boost, something we all benefit from during the winter months.

Heat the oil in a frying pan and sauté the onion for 2 minutes until it starts to soften. Add all the spices, chili, ginger, and raw honey/agave. Stir well and continue to cook for 5 minutes more.

Add the butternut squash and continue to sauté for another 5 minutes, adding a tablespoon of water if the pan gets too hot.

Add the bouillon powder to the boiling water to make a vegetable stock and stir until the powder has dissolved. Set aside.

Preheat the oven to 325°F/170°C/gas mark 3.

Add the apricots, lemon zest, and the bouillon to the squash mix and simmer over medium heat until the squash is soft, but not quite mashable.

If using the almonds, toast them on a baking sheet in the oven for about 5 minutes, until they start to release a delicious aroma. Remove them from the oven, chop them finely, and set aside.

If serving the millet couscous with the tagine, cook the millet according to the instructions on the package. While the millet is cooking, caramelize the onions in a pan with the sunflower oil. Once they begin to develop a good color, add the cumin and garlic, and continue to sauté for a further 2 minutes. Remove from the heat and set aside.

Roughly chop the herbs. Add the onions to the cooked millet and stir through with the chopped herbs and salt. If the mixture is looking too thick, stir through some water to loosen it. Finally, stir through the lemon juice, check the seasoning, and set aside until the tagine is ready.

The sauce will have reduced a little during cooking. Five minutes before serving, stir through the spinach until it has all wilted. Finally, stir through the chopped cilantro and sprinkle over the almonds (if using) before serving.

serves 6

1 tbsp sunflower oil

1 large red onion, finely chopped

4 cardamom pods

¼ tsp ground nutmeg

½ tsp ground cumin

1 tsp ground coriander

½ tsp ground cinnamon

1 tsp chopped red chili

1 tsp chopped ginger

1 tsp agave nectar

5 cups (700g) butternut squash, cut into ¾in (2cm) cubes

1 tsp bouillon powder

1⅔ cups (400ml) boiling water

¾ cup (150g) unsulphured dried apricots, chopped

finely grated zest of ½ lemon

1 cup (140g) almonds (optional)

6⅔ cups (200g) spinach

4 tbsp roughly chopped cilantro leaves

for the millet couscous (optional)

1 cup (200g) millet

1 onion, sliced

1 tsp sunflower oil

1 garlic clove, chopped

1 tsp ground cumin

2 tbsp each mint, parsley and cilantro

Juice of ½ a lemon

Almond-crust pizza

If you have a hankering for the broccoli-crust pizza on page 198, but don't have any broccoli on hand, you could make this version instead. I use ground chia seeds to help set the crust, but if you can't get hold of these, use ground flaxseeds (or flaxseed meal) instead.

Preheat the oven to 325°F/170°C/gas mark 3. Line a baking tray with parchment paper and brush lightly with oil.

Put the chia seeds in a small bowl, add the water, and set aside to soak for 10 minutes until wonderfully gloppy.

Meanwhile, mix the ground almonds, cumin, and seasoning in a bowl and add the soaked chia. Mix all these ingredients together with your hands until a dough forms.

Place the ball of dough in the middle of the prepared baking tray and flatten it with your hands until it is an even circle, about ¼in (5mm) thick.

Bake the dough in a preheated oven for 30 minutes until its surface starts to color.

Take the crust out of the oven but keep it on the baking tray. Spoon the sauce over the crust, leaving about ⅓in (1cm) uncovered around the edge.

Now add your favorite toppings. Here are a few I love:

pan-fried wild field mushrooms with goat cheese

arugula and mozzarella

artichoke and black olives with basil

makes 1 large pizza crust, enough for 2 servings

1 tbsp sunflower oil

1½ tbsp (15g) ground chia seeds

¼ cup (60ml) water

1 cup (100g) ground almonds

¼ tsp ground cumin

a pinch of Himalayan pink salt

freshly ground black pepper

1 quantity pizza sauce (see page 198)

Roasted butternut squash with balsamic onions

This vibrant side dish can be transformed into a complete meal when served with a salad or grain. It's become one of my staple dishes; I make up a batch on a Sunday night, so that I have plenty in my fridge for the week ahead – it's especially good for a lunch at work.

Preheat the oven to 350°F/180°C/gas mark 4.

Put the squash on a baking tray, drizzle with the sunflower oil, and sprinkle over the pink salt. Roast in a preheated oven for 15 minutes.

Take the tray out of the oven. Sprinkle over the onion slices and drizzle with the balsamic vinegar. Return to the oven for another 15 minutes

Meanwhile, make the dressing. Whisk all the ingredients together in a cup or small bowl; it will begin to curdle, but don't worry – just keep whisking. If it looks too watery, add a touch more tahini; if it's too thick, add a little water (a tablespoon at a time) to loosen it up.

Take the roasted vegetables out of the oven, transfer them to a serving dish, drizzle over the dressing, and serve immediately.

serves 2 as a side dish

2½ cups (310g) butternut squash, sliced into half-moons ¼in (5mm) thick

1 tbsp sunflower oil

a pinch of Himalayan pink salt

½ red onion, sliced into thin wedges

1 tbsp balsamic vinegar

for the dressing:

1 tbsp tahini

3 tbsp water

juice of ½ lemon

a pinch of Himalayan pink salt

Watermelon, tomato, ginger, and pomegranate molasses salad

This salad is a taste of Asia on a plate. The dressing here also works well as a marinade for flavoring and cooking tofu, or drizzling over noodles. Aside from lemon and lime, watermelon is one of the most alkaline fruits, so enjoy this salad while doing your body good at the same time.

Slice or dice the tomatoes (whichever you prefer) and cube the watermelon. Put both into a bowl.

To make the dressing, put the sesame oil, pomegranate molasses, salt, and ginger into a pan and warm over medium heat, adding the water gradually. Reduce the mixture for 3–4 minutes, then pour into a cup and set aside.

Put the sesame oil into the empty pan with the pomegranate molasses, ginger, and scallions, and cook for 30 seconds. Add the oyster mushrooms and the water, and cook over medium heat for 3 minutes.

To serve, arrange the arugula on serving plates. Pour the dressing over the watermelon and tomatoes in their bowl and toss gently. Spoon on top of the arugula, then add the mushrooms. Garnish with the mint and cilantro leaves.

serves 2

1–3 (6oz/170g) heirloom or unusually colored tomatoes

1½ cups cubed (245g) watermelon

2 tbsp sesame oil

1 tbsp pomegranate molasses

¾in (2cm) piece of ginger, diced

2 scallions, thinly sliced at an angle

⅔ cup sliced (60g) oyster mushrooms

2 tbsp water

1⅓ cups (60g) arugula

¼ cup (4g) mint leaves

¼ cup (4g) cilantro leaves

for the dressing:

2 tbsp sesame oil

2¼ tsp pomegranate molasses

¼ tsp Himalayan pink salt

1⅛in (3cm) piece of ginger, diced

4 tbsp water

Daikon "noodles" and grilled ribbon salad with turmeric dressing

I love making noodles out of vegetables – it's a great way to fill up and get amazing raw nutrients straight into the body. Turmeric has not only a beautiful color but also immune-boosting properties, making it the perfect topping for any healthy meal.

Spiralize the daikon (see page 66) and put into a bowl.

Using a potato peeler, make ribbons from the zucchini, butternut squash, and carrots.

Very thinly slice the fennel and squeeze over the lemon juice to keep it from turning brown.

Wipe the sunflower oil over a grill pan and place over the heat. When hot, add the vegetable ribbons. Cook until they start to get the characteristic lines from the grill pan. Transfer to a plate and set aside.

Slice the cucumber in half lengthwise and season with salt. Put it cut side down on the grill pan and, as before, grill until charred lines appear – about 5 minutes – then turn over and grill the other side.

Next, make the dressing by blending all the dressing ingredients together until smooth.

To serve, put the pieces of cucumber on a plate. Mix half the dill with half of the ribboned vegetables and stir through the daikon "noodles." Pile this mixture on top of the cucumber. Put the remaining vegetables on top and then drizzle the dressing over the whole salad.

serves 1

2in (5cm) piece (80g) daikon radish

½ small (50g) zucchini

¼ cup chopped (30g) butternut squash

½ 2in (5cm) (30g) carrot

¼ cup sliced (25g) fennel

juice of ½ lemon

1 tbsp sunflower oil

1 medium (200g) cucumber

a pinch of Himalayan pink salt

⅔ cup (6g) sprigs of dill

for the dressing:

3 tbsp olive oil

¼ tsp turmeric

juice of ¼ lemon

1 tsp date syrup

1 tbsp coconut oil, melted

Pea, fava bean, and pine nut salad

When you need a lunch or dinner in a flash, rustle up this super-cleansing summery salad. If you can't get fava beans, add the same weight in extra peas – it will be just as delicious and just as good for you.

If you're using fresh, shelled peas and fava beans, just wash and put them into a bowl. If using frozen, defrost them in a bowl of boiling water until soft, then strain and put into a bowl.

Slice the savoy cabbage thinly and put into a separate bowl.

Mix together the mirin, rice vinegar, olive oil, and half the lemon juice, pour over the cabbage and massage into the leaves until they become soft.

Finely slice the fennel and squeeze the rest of the lemon over the top, so it doesn't turn brown. Add this to the bowl of beans and peas, then stir in the cabbage, sumac, and mint.

Lastly, dry-toast the pine nuts (see page 74).

Line 2 salad bowls with 2 outer leaves of the cabbage (I like to use these as they're so beautiful). Divide the salad between the bowls and sprinkle over the warm pine nuts. Serve straight away.

serves 2

½ cup (80g) peas, preferably freshly shelled, but frozen peas work too

½ cup (70g) fava beans, preferably freshly shelled, but frozen beans work too

1⅓ cups (90g) Savoy cabbage, plus 4 outer leaves to serve

1 tsp mirin

1 tsp rice vinegar

1 tbsp olive oil

juice of 1 lemon

½ cup (60g) fennel

1 tbsp sumac

1⅓ cups (20g) mint leaves, chopped

¼ cup (30g) pine nuts

Sumac is a beautifully bright red powder made from ground sumac berries. It has all kinds of health benefits: it's a great antioxidant; it lowers blood sugar levels and helps in their regulation; it is a diuretic, so can help to rid your body of retained water; it soothes the digestive system; and it is packed full of vitamin C and omega-3 fatty acids. Soon you'll be adding it to all your food!

Vegan Caesar salad

Close your eyes when you taste the dressing for this salad and you'd never guess there's no cheese in it! I love making this vegan sauce, and the flavor comes from the nutritional yeast. I buy the version with added vitamin B12, which is especially important for vegetarians and vegans, who aren't able to get it from animal products.

First make the dressing. Soak the cashews in the water for 1 hour. If you don't have a high-speed blender, soak the cashews for an extra hour so that they break down more easily in a standard blender.

Put the soaked cashews, water, nutritional yeast, and a pinch of salt into a blender and blend until completely smooth. Set aside.

Melt the coconut oil in a frying pan, add the scallion, desiccated coconut, and salt, and sauté until golden – this should take about 1 minute. Take off the heat and transfer the pan's contents to a bowl, as the mixture will continue to cook, and you don't want it to burn.

Put the salad greens into a bowl and pour the dressing over them. Garnish with the coconut mixture and the cubed toast, if using.

serves 1

1 tbsp coconut oil

1 scallion

2 tbsp desiccated coconut

a pinch of Himalayan pink salt

3 cups (130g) salad greens

2 slices gluten-free bread, toasted and cubed (optional)

for the dressing:

¾ cup (100g) cashews

½ cup (120ml) water, plus 2 tbsp

2 tbsp nutritional yeast

pinch of Himalayan pink salt

#bites

Ginger-tamari-dressed edamame

These beans make a tangy and perfect snack, with a salty edge. If you've not met tamari before, it is wheat-free soy sauce and is readily available. When buying edamame, choose ones that are organic and non-genetically modified. At any time it's important not to put chemicals into your body – I buy organic produce whenever possible – but it's especially important when you're cleansing, as these toxins are acid-forming and stress your body at a time when you want to be supporting the natural detoxification process.

Put the edamame beans, in their shells, into a pan of boiling water and cook until they're piping hot throughout. Drain well.

Meanwhile, make the dressing by blending the rest of the ingredients until smooth.

Pour this dressing over the hot beans and serve immediately.

serves 2–3

1¼ cups (150g) frozen edamame beans in their shells

3½ tbsp tamari

1 clove garlic

1in (2.5cm) piece of ginger

1½ tbsp sesame oil

2 tsp water

Pea and mint pesto

Sometimes all you want is a light and fresh pesto to serve with pasta, to stir into quinoa, or maybe drizzle over a vibrant salad. This pesto is definitely one for your repertoire, and literally sings of summer sunshine.

Put the mint leaves in a high-speed blender with all of the other ingredients and process until you get a coarse texture. Taste a tiny bit and add a little more lime juice and seasoning to taste.

serves 2

½ cup (15g) mint leaves

½ cup (75g) peas, defrosted if frozen

3 tbsp olive oil

2 tbsp water

a pinch of Himalayan pink salt

juice of ½ lime, or to taste

If you don't have any peas on hand, you could use fava beans or edamame for an equally delicious result.

Raw chia and hemp bars

These deliciously crumbly and tasty bars make a perfect snack, if you're trying to cut down on your grains, as quinoa is actually a seed. Not only will these seed bars super-charge your energy levels, they'll also make your skin glow, radiating health from the inside out.

Put the dates and boiling water into a high-speed blender and blend into a smooth paste. If you don't have a high-speed blender, then soak the dates in boiling water first, to soften them, so the paste will be smoother.

Put the date paste, along with the rest of the ingredients, in a bowl and mix together until the quinoa flakes are completely coated.

Line a baking sheet with parchment paper, put the quinoa mixture on it, and press into a rectangle, about ¾in (2cm) thick.

Put the mixture into the fridge for 1–2 hours until set, then cut it into bars and store in an airtight container in the fridge for up to a week.

makes 8

14 (100g) deglet noor dates, pitted

4 tbsp boiling water

½ cup (160g) quinoa flakes

⅓ cup (40g) raw hemp seeds

3½ tbsp (35g) chia seeds

3 tbsp melted coconut oil

2 tbsp cacao powder

2 tbsp rice syrup

¼ tsp orange-flower water

Ginger coconut loaf

Two words describe this loaf – delicious and healthy! I am not one to remove sweet foods from my diet – I love them too much – so this loaf-cake is great to call on when I'm in need of a sweet fix, or when I want to bake for someone's birthday to share the love. The cinnamon, nutmeg, and ginger in this loaf provide important immune-boosting chemicals.

Preheat the oven to 350°F/180°C/gas mark 4, and line an 8 × 4in loaf pan (bottom and sides) with parchment paper.

Put all the dry ingredients into a bowl.

In a separate bowl, beat the eggs until frothy, then add the vanilla extract, date syrup, and melted coconut oil (make sure this is not too hot or you'll end up with scrambled eggs).

Stir the dry ingredients into the wet mixture, then pour the batter into the loaf pan and bake in a preheated oven for 25–30 minutes. It is ready when a knife inserted into the center comes out clean; if not, return it to the oven for another 5 minutes.

Remove the pan from the oven, let the loaf cool in the pan for 10–15 minutes and transfer it to a wire rack to cool completely.

serves 12

1½ cups (150g) ground almonds

½ tsp baking powder

½ tsp Himalayan pink salt

1 tbsp ground ginger

½ tsp freshly grated nutmeg

½ tsp ground cinnamon

3 eggs

½ tsp vanilla extract

¼ cup (70g) date syrup

½ cup (120ml) melted coconut oil

Gooey vegan brownies

Brownies on a cleanse? You're kidding! No, I'm not. These are one exceptional treat – perhaps the healthiest brownie recipe I have ever created and, I have to say, it's utterly delicious. You might be surprised to see tahini in the ingredients list, but this high-protein paste has a wonderfully nutty taste. Give it a try.

Put the dates in a bowl, cover with hot water, and soak for 20 minutes.

Meanwhile, preheat the oven to 325°F/170°C/gas mark 3, and line a shallow baking pan with parchment paper.

Put the chia seeds and measured water in a small bowl and leave to soak until the mixture is thick and gloppy.

Drain the dates, discarding the soaking water, and put them into a blender, along with the melted coconut oil, tahini, rice milk, agave nectar, and vanilla extract, and blend until fairly smooth (a few small lumps of date are fine, as they add to the brownies' texture).

Put the salt, baking powder, coconut flour, and cacao powder in a bowl.

Pour the mixture from the blender into the bowl of dry ingredients, mix, and then add the soaked chia seeds. You'll end up with a really thick batter.

Pour the mixture into the prepared pan (it should sit about 1in/2.5cm deep all around) and bake in a preheated oven for 25–30 minutes.

Take the pan out of the oven and let the brownie cool on a rack before cutting it into bars. Enjoy the wonderfully gooey interior of this chocolate delight.

makes 4

14 (100g) deglet noor dates

2 tbsp chia seeds

6 tbsp water

¼ cup (45g) coconut oil, melted

⅓ cup (85g) tahini

¼ cup (50ml) rice milk

¼ cup (80g) agave nectar

1 tsp vanilla extract

a generous pinch of Himalayan pink salt

½ tsp baking powder

¼ cup (30g) coconut flour

½ cup (50g) cacao powder

Acai coconut bites

Acai is the jungle's superfood – a bitter fruit that is full of antioxidants and has amazing weight-loss properties. You can buy it in powdered form, which is easily added to smoothies, as well as these delicious frozen bites.

Line a small dish (or lipped plate), about 4½in (12cm) in diameter, with plastic wrap.

Melt the coconut manna, as much as you can, in a heatproof bowl set over a pan of simmering water (it won't melt fully like coconut oil).

Place in a blender with the melted coconut oil, desiccated coconut, acai powder, and rice syrup, and blend until smooth.

Pour the mixture into the prepared dish and put it in the freezer for about 2 hours.

Remove from the freezer, turn the mixture out of the dish onto a board and cut into little bites. Store in the freezer for up to 4 weeks.

makes 12 bites

3 tbsp (40g) coconut manna

2 tbsp coconut oil, melted

3 tbsp desiccated coconut

3 tbsp acai powder

3 tbsp brown rice syrup

Because these bites are made with coconut oil, try not to handle them too much, as they will get soft. When cool they are very fudge-like.

#sweet

Raw avocado super-cake

I fed this cake to the fashion designer Julien Macdonald, during an interview for my column in *Harper's Bazaar*, and he couldn't believe he was eating something so tasty that was healthy, too! This cake is packed full of vitamin E and essential fatty acids, which help keep the skin looking young and feeling soft, because of the high avocado content.

Line an 8in (21cm) round springform cake pan with parchment paper.

To make the crust, put the almonds, dates, Brazil nuts, and pecans in a bowl, cover with water, and soak for 1 hour.

Drain the water and put the soaked nuts and fruit into a food processor, along with the melted coconut oil and desiccated coconut. Process until you get a crumb-like texture that sticks together when you squeeze it between your fingers.

Put the crumbs into the prepared pan and press evenly over the bottom. Pop into the freezer for 20 minutes.

Meanwhile, make the filling. Peel and pit the avocados and squeeze the juice from both lemons over them immediately; this will keep them from turning brown. Transfer the contents of the bowl to a high-speed blender, along with the agave nectar, melted coconut oil, vanilla extract, and rosewater. Blend until you get an extremely smooth texture.

Take the crust out of the freezer and pour the filling over it. Pop it back into the freezer for another 30 minutes, then transfer to the fridge for another hour. Keep chilled until ready to serve.

Carefully remove the cake from the pan, put it on a plate, and garnish with lemon and lime zests.

serves 12

5 very ripe avocados

2 lemons

½ cup (150g) agave nectar

⅔ cup (150g) coconut oil, melted

¼ tsp vanilla extract

½ tbsp rosewater

finely grated zest of ½ lemon and 1 lime, to garnish

for the crust:

⅓ cup (45g) raw almonds

21 (150g) deglet noor dates

½ cup (65g) raw Brazil nuts

½ cup (35g) raw pecans

2 tbsp coconut oil, melted

⅔ cup (53g) desiccated coconut

Crimson crumble

Here's a fantastic crumble based on a fruit compote that is thickened with kuzu. A bit like arrowroot, kuzu root starch is made from the root of a Japanese plant. As well as being a fabulous thickening agent, it has amazing healing properties (from its flavonoids), and is both soothing and easy to digest.

Preheat the oven to 325°F/170°C/gas mark 3.

Mix the kuzu root starch with the cold water until there are no lumps.

Put the apple, blackberries, water, star anise, and cinnamon in a pan over medium-high heat for 5–6 minutes until the apple softens and the liquid becomes a beautiful crimson color.

Take the pan off the heat and stir in the kuzu root mixture until the compote thickens.

Make the crumble by mixing all the topping ingredients together in a bowl until they form a sticky crumb texture.

Spoon the crimson berry mixture into the bottom of the ovenproof dish and sprinkle the crumble over the top.

Bake in a preheated oven for 10 minutes or until it starts to bubble over and the crumble turns golden brown.

Serve the crumble by itself or with yogurt or dairy-free vanilla ice cream.

serves 2-4

1½ tbsp kuzu root starch

3 tbsp cold water

1 apple, cored and thinly sliced

1¾ cups (250g) blackberries

¾ cup (180ml) water

1 star anise

¼ tsp ground cinnamon

For the crumble topping:

1 cup (100g) rolled oats

2 tbsp rice syrup

¼ cup (50g) coconut palm sugar

2 tbsp coconut oil

2 tbsp coconut flour

The compote and the crumble mixture can be made in advance and stored separately in the fridge until needed. Simply reheat the fruit, then put the dish together as described above.

Salted coconut ice-cream popsicles

Move over salted caramel – salted coconut is the new must-eat dessert, and it's healthy, too. It's oh so easy to make and you can leave the salt out, if you're serving it to kids. You can also play around with the coulis flavor and color as well: raspberries and strawberries both work well. When sourcing coconut milk, be sure to buy organic, because some brands are full of chemicals.

Put the coconut milk, desiccated coconut, lucuma, xylitol, and salt into a blender and process until smooth.

Make the coulis by putting the blueberries and 6 tablespoons of the water into a pan and simmering for 10 minutes over medium heat. Add the remaining 2 tablespoons of water and set aside.

To make the popsicles, I like to put a dollop of coulis in the bottom of each mold, then leave it in the freezer for 20 minutes. Fill the molds with the coconut ice-cream and figs, if using (you could do some the other way around if you like: put the ice cream in first and then the coulis).

Finish with popsicle sticks and freeze for 20 minutes.

makes 4–6 popsicles

1⅔ cups (400ml) coconut milk

⅓ cup (30g) desiccated coconut

1 tbsp lucuma powder (optional)

1 tbsp xylitol

¼ tsp Himalayan pink salt

slices of figs, to put down the sides of the popsicle molds (optional)

for the coulis:

1 cup (150g) blueberries

8 tbsp water

Pear and juniper tart

I use the tart crust here for all sorts of desserts. It's a great basic for your repertoire, and, what's more, it's quick and easy to make. Freeze-dried plum powder is exactly that: made from dehydrated plums and their kernels, it adds a wonderful sweet saltiness to whatever you make with it. Your guests will never guess that their delicious dessert is healthy, too!

First make the cashew cream, if including. Soak the cashews in the water for 1 hour. Transfer to a blender and process until smooth. Set aside.

Preheat the oven to 325°F/170°C/gas mark 3. Line an 8in (20cm) loose-bottomed tart pan with parchment paper, or grease it with coconut oil or vegan butter.

To make the crust, mix all the ingredients together to form a dough. Place it in the middle of the prepared pan. Spread it out and press it down well, making sure that the dough is even all the way around and up the sides of the pan, as well.

Bake in a preheated oven for 8–10 minutes until golden brown. Remove from the oven and set aside.

To make the filling, put the hot water into a pan with the juniper berries, agave nectar, and plum powder. Place the pan over medium heat and simmer for a minute.

Add the pears to the pan, coating them with the gorgeous red liquid, and simmer for 8–10 minutes, depending on how ripe the pears are; the riper they are, the less time they will need to poach. You want them to be soft, but still have a little bit of a bite. Take the pears out of the pan and place them in a fan shape in the center of the tart crust.

Mix the arrowroot or cornstarch with the water in a cup until you have a thick white liquid. Add the mixture to the red sauce in the pan and stir for a minute to thicken. Once thick, pour over the pears sitting in the crust.

This tart is delicious served warm or cold, and I like to add a dollop of cashew cream or coconut yogurt on the side.

serves 6

1 cup (250ml) hot water

2 tbsp juniper berries

2 tbsp agave nectar

1¼ tbsp freeze-dried plum powder (optional)

2 ripe pears, peeled, cored and quartered

½ tbsp arrowroot or cornstarch

2 tbsp cold water

for the cashew cream (optional):

½ cup (50g) raw cashews

⅔ cup (160ml) water

for the crust:

coconut oil or vegan butter, for greasing

2⅛ cups (200g) ground almonds

1 beaten egg, or 3 tbsp ground chia seeds soaked in 6 tbsp water if you want the tart to be vegan

1 tbsp agave nectar

Lemon yogurt cake

Sometimes only a sweet zesty hit will do. This cake tastes just like a lemon drizzle cake, but is a healthier alternative, so you can sit back and enjoy a slice, when on the #lifechanging plan. If you can't get your hands on coconut milk yogurt, you can get the same taste and texture using the same amount of the "cream" from the top of a can of coconut milk.

Preheat the oven to 350°F/180°C/gas mark 4 and line an 8in (20cm) round baking pan with parchment paper.

Mix together all the dry ingredients in a bowl.

In a separate bowl, mix together the eggs, coconut yogurt, lemon zest, and juice, butter, and vanilla extract until completely smooth.

Add the wet mixture to the dry ingredients and mix until thoroughly combined, then pour into the prepared cake pan.

Bake in a preheated oven for 45 minutes or until the cake is golden and a knife inserted into the center comes out clean.

Remove from the oven and cool in the pan for 15 minutes, then transfer the cake to a wire rack to cool completely.

Slice and serve with a drizzle of your chosen syrup.

serves 8

1½ cups (140g) ground almonds

⅔ cup (70g) rice flour

⅔ cup (130g) rapadura sugar (or turbinado or other unrefined sugar)

1 tsp baking powder

1 tsp baking soda

5 eggs

½ cup (130g) coconut milk yogurt

finely grated zest and juice of 1 lemon

½ cup (100g) vegan non-hydrogenated butter, softened

1 tsp vanilla extract

sugar syrup (agave, coconut blossom, or date), to serve

Gooey chocolate pots

If you think a gooey chocolate dessert can't be healthy, then think again! These wonderfully indulgent pots are sugar-, gluten-, wheat- and dairy-free, but no one would guess that from the taste. Pop them in the oven and then when they come out, simply sink your spoon in and watch the goo run out… Enjoy this dessert safe in the knowledge that there are powerful antioxidants in the raw cacao, while the xylitol adds sweetness and helps create the gooey texture.

Preheat the oven to 400°F/200°C/gas mark 6.

Melt the coconut oil and let it cool. Meanwhile, whisk the eggs, milk, and xylitol together, then add the cooled, melted coconut oil.

Next, mix in the raw cacao powder, almonds, and flour until well combined.

Place 4 ramekins inside a baking tray and fill them with the batter. Pour enough boiling water into the baking tray to come about halfway up the ramekins.

Carefully transfer the baking tray to a preheated oven and bake for 12–15 minutes.

Remove from the oven, carefully pick up each ramekin and serve warm, while the chocolate center is still soft and runny.

serves 4

4 tbsp coconut oil

2 eggs

½ cup (120ml) almond milk

3 tbsp xylitol

½ cup (50g) raw cacao powder

1 tbsp ground almonds

1 tbsp coconut flour

Autumn stewed fruit in coconut milk and lime

Visually, this is a beautiful and vibrant dish. Having an abundance of colors is really important to me – and it helps to encourage even the biggest cynics to see that healthy food is not boring! Not only are limes really alkaline fruits, they also help your body rid itself of toxins, neutralize free radicals in the body, boost immunity, and provide a great source of vitamin C.

Squeeze the lime juice over the pear, then put all the ingredients in a large pan and simmer for 5 minutes, stirring occasionally. Serve attactively arranged on serving plates, and garnish with the lime zest.

serves 2–3

juice of 1 lime

1 pear, cored and quartered

3 figs, halved

1 plum, pitted and halved

¾ cup (200ml) coconut milk

3 star anise

finely grated zest of 1 lime, to garnish

Make up a batch for dinner and you can also have it for breakfast with granola sprinkled over the top.

#index

About the author

Since changing her diet to follow alkaline eating principles, Natasha Corrett has transformed her own health and launched her hugely popular Honestly Healthy website. Already a bestselling author of two Honestly Healthy books, *Eating the Alkaline Way* and *Honestly Healthy For Life*, with nutritionist Vicki Edgson, Natasha has been at the vanguard of the healthy eating revolution with her mouth-watering recipes that are all about taste and flavor.

STERLING EPICURE
New York

An Imprint of Sterling Publishing
1166 Avenue of the Americas
New York, NY 10036

STERLING EPICURE is a trademark of Sterling Publishing Co., Inc.
The distinctive Sterling logo is a registered trademark of Sterling
Publishing Co., Inc.

This Sterling Epicure edition published in 2016 by Sterling
Publishing

First published in Great Britain in 2015 by Hodder & Stoughton
An Hachette UK company

ISBN 978-1-4549-1951-3

Distributed in Canada by Sterling Publishing
c/o Canadian Manda Group, 664 Annette Street
Toronto, Ontario, Canada M6S 2C8

For information about custom editions, special sales, and premium
and corporate purchases, please contact Sterling Special Sales at
800-805-5489 or specialsales@sterlingpublishing.com.

Manufactured in China

10 9 8 7 6 5 4 3 2 1

www.sterlingpublishing.com